D0722108

Why America Failed

Books by Morris Berman

Social Change and Scientific Organization

Trilogy on human consciousness:
The Reenchantment of the World
Coming to Our Senses
Wandering God: A Study in Nomadic Sprituality

Trilogy on America:
The Twilight of American Culture
Dark Ages America: The Final Phase of Empire
Why America Failed: The Roots of Imperial Decline

A Question of Values (essays)
Counting Blessings (poetry)
Destiny (fiction)

Why America Failed

The Roots of Imperial Decline

Morris Berman

WILEY

John Wiley & Sons, Inc.

Published by John Wiley & Sons, Inc., Hoboken, New Jersey
Published simultaneously in Canada

For general information about our other products and services, please contact our Customer Care Department within the United States at (800) 762–2974, outside the United States at (317) 572–3993 or fax (317) 572–4002.

Wiley also publishes its books in a variety of electronic formats. Some content that appears in print may not be available in electronic books. For more information about Wiley products, visit our web site at www.wiley.com.

Library of Congress Cataloging-in-Publication Data

Berman, Morris, date.
    Why America failed: the roots of imperial decline/Morris Berman.
    p. cm.
    "Published simultaneously in Canada"—T.p. verso.
    Includes bibliographical references and index.
    ISBN 978-1-118-06181-7 (hardback); ISBN 978-1-118-08794-7 (ebk);
    ISBN 978-1-118-08795-4 (ebk); ISBN 978-1-118-08796-1 (ebk)
    1. United States—Civilization. 2. Regression (Civilization) 3. National charateristics, America. 4. United States—Politics and government.
5. Imperialism—History. 6. United States—Social conditions. 7. Social change—United States—History. 8. United States—Economic conditions.
  I. Title.
  E169.1.B48 2011
  973.9—dc23

                                             2011026140

Printed in the United States of America

10 9 8 7 6 5 4 3 2 1

For Ferenc M. Szasz (1940–2010)

A good deal of modern American culture is an extended experiment in the effects of depriving people of what they crave most.
—Thomas Lewis et al., *A General Theory of Love*

The whole modern system seems to me to be grounded on a false view of man. . . . There is a spirit of self-confidence in it, which, left to its natural tendencies, will inevitably bring a deeper and wider woe upon man than earth has ever yet known.
—Richard Henry Dana, *1853*

Any history of capitalism must contain the shadow history of anticapitalism.
—Joyce Appleby, *The Relentless Revolution*

Contents

PREFACE

When the dust finally settles on the American empire, and our history is rewritten from the vantage point of the post-American era, what will American civilization look like, in retrospect? "The creation of the United States of America," writes the historian Walter McDougall, "is the central event of the past four hundred years." No doubt. The question is, What was America ultimately about? What, in the fullness of time, did it really stand for? In fact, if we look in the right places, we really don't have to wait for 2040 or 2050 for an answer. As McDougall tells us, along with historians David Potter, William Appleman Williams, and a few others of note, America was from the outset a business civilization. Richard Hakluyt's *Discourse of Western Planting* (1584), which McDougall calls a "masterpiece of promotional literature," explained the strategic advantages England would gain by colonizing North America, including timber, fish, furs, and burgeoning markets for the woolen trade. "Even in the sixteenth century," adds historian Leo Marx, "the American countryside was the object of something like a calculated real estate promotion." This commercial orientation effectively became our trademark. The principal goal of North American civilization, and of its inhabitants, is and always has been an ever-expanding economy—affluence—and endless technological innovation—"progress." A nation of hustlers, writes McDougall; a people relentlessly on the make.[1]

Of course, a case can be made for the existence of an alternative tradition, essentially moral or "spiritual" in nature, that saw the pursuit of affluence as a shallow goal, devoid of any real meaning and a threat to any spiritual purpose the nation might hope to have. As I shall show in the pages that follow, this country has never lacked for spokesmen for that tradition, from Captain John Smith to President Jimmy Carter. Overlapping with this was a classical "republican" tradition that was opposed to luxury, and that defined virtue in terms of public service rather than naked self-interest ("corruption"). Indeed, a number of historians have argued that this tradition was central to the ideology of the American Revolution. The problem is that in terms of actual behavior, as opposed to rhetoric, things such as Puritanism and republicanism proved to be no match for the dominant tradition. Especially after the War of Independence, the alternative critics were not able to change the "vector," the general direction of America, in any substantive way. We can see the overwhelming power or momentum of this "vector," for example, in the responses to the two great "wake-up calls" for laissez-faire economics during the past hundred years, namely the crashes of 1929 and 2008.

To take the aftermath of 1929, for example: what characterized the New Deal was not a serious reassessment and restructuring of the U.S. economy, but a few concessions to the poor and the working class. The historical role of Franklin Roosevelt, as most historians will tell you, was not to abolish capitalism but to preserve it; which is what he did. Similarly, the decision of President Obama to appoint neoliberal economic advisers (such as Timothy Geithner and Lawrence Summers) with close ties to the very banking industries they subsequently bailed out (to the tune of $12 trillion, and eventually much more) was an attempt to carry on with business as usual and hope for the best—a move that didn't change anything for the millions of unemployed, and that lined the pockets of the rich. Branding these presidents as "socialists" is little more than the demented ravings of the political right.[2]

I am not, in any case, going to be talking about organized socialist opposition to the dominant tradition in this book, although I will talk about social concern and social safety nets. That organized, political socialism never had a chance in the United States is a theme well-explored by sociologists from Werner Sombart to Seymour Martin Lipset. The general consensus is that unlike Europe, where the working class resented social inequality and formed viable left-wing (including Communist) parties, in the United States the lower classes could always be bought off by Horatio Alger stories and the myth of the self-made man. In fact, the statistical evidence clearly shows that the vast majority of Americans die in the same social class into which they are born. No matter; Bill Gates is a hero to most Americans because they nurture the misguided belief ("hallucination" would be closer to the mark) that they too may someday have $50 billion in the bank, enjoy celebrity status, and entertain on a lavish scale. That there might be something perverse about a system that allows a single individual to accumulate that sort of wealth never crosses their minds. Thus despite the fact that America does not really provide its citizens with the basic needs for a happy, fulfilling life, in the United States the rich sleep easily in their beds.[3]

It also can be argued that in terms of substantive critique of the dominant culture, socialism falls quite short. As Jackson Lears correctly notes (in *No Place of Grace*), "the acids of modernity are often as corrosive under socialist as under capitalist regimes." For socialism is inherently "progressive" in its outlook; it was never opposed to wealth, or modernization, or technological innovation—it just wanted the benefits of the system to be distributed more evenly. Nor did it make any real distinction between moral and material progress—a distinction I regard as absolutely crucial, if we are talking about genuine alternatives. This is why, as Lears concludes, "the most power-ful critics of capitalism have often looked backward rather than forward," and why conservatism, in the sense of preserving things such as family, craft, and community, is the real radical-ism, the real alternative to what we now have. But to my mind it also must include—and as already noted, often did include—a deep moral or spiritual opposition to the pursuit of wealth. The fact that it was a lost cause may be unfortunate, but that makes little difference for the critique itself.[4]

There is, of course, a positive side to hustling, or opportun-ism, as McDougall is quick to point out. Ambition, innovation, hard work, organization, and the Yankee "can-do" mentality resulted in the United States turning out a third of the world's manufactured goods within a century after its founding. No mean achievement, as I'm sure we can all agree. But finally, what was it all for? In the century following that, the dominant tradition began to turn against us, and in that sense the George W. Bush years, for example, don't really seem all that discon-tinuous from what came before. Our ill-starred involvement in Iraq was surely part of the can-do, expansionist mentality, and the gross profiteering of Halliburton, Blackwater, CACI, and Titan in that imperial adventure is by now well documented. It should come as no surprise that the fraud that prevailed at Enron is, to one degree or another, endemic to many American corporations, and that the habits of ruthlessness, deception, and unlimited self-indulgence are common to almost all. Indeed, business survival in the United States depends on such behav-ior, as any corporate executive can tell you (off the record, of course). This occurs at the level of municipal government as well. Thus we find that the Democratic mayor of Baltimore, Sheila Dixon, was stealing money earmarked for needy families so she could buy herself electronic toys. What in the world could she have been thinking? In this regard, it is noteworthy that Ms. Dixon was not repentant after her conviction, never apologized to the city of Baltimore, and began drawing a pension of $83,000 upon her resignation. The Maryland state prosecutor was indignant, asserting that Dixon apparently believed corruption was not that big a deal, and that she had "lost touch with reality." But which reality are we talking about here? One might reasonably argue that what she did was only a slightly distorted reflection of how the American economy works in general. This too was hustling, after all.[5]

Technology and "progress"—defined in a strictly material sense—have, of course, played a key role in the pursuit of affluence. The Austrian economist, Joseph Schumpeter, saw endless technological innovation as the key to economic expansion; "creative destruction," he called it. The problem is that we are now in a situation in which the destruction far outweighs the creation, a situation facilitated by "progress" being defined strictly in terms of what is tangible. What we lose, however, is intangible, and thus it is difficult for most people to understand what they are actually losing. Is it progress to have forty-seven (or whatever) different types of razor blades available on the market? Is it progress to have dinner with a group of friends while half of them spend the evening talking on their cell phones (usually right at the dinner table) rather than to each other? Or when a group of Wal-Mart shoppers literally trample someone to death to get their hands on discounted DVD players, and then refuse to get out of the way when the medics arrive?[6] If this is progress, I'm not sure we can endure much more of it. But we won't renounce it, any more than we shall renounce hustling; that's simply not in the cards. Modern technology is nothing if not addictive, and it meshes extremely well with the hustling mentality. "Creative destruction" is an ironically apt description of how it operates.

Which brings up an interesting point. With the collapse of the Soviet Union, bourgeois liberal civilization defeated its old socialist enemy. Yet as many scholars have pointed out, we had a lot in common with that enemy. Our own system is a socialist one—not for the average citizen, of course, but for the corporations, for the extremely wealthy. It is they whom the government does most of its business with, and whom it protects in times of crisis: corporate welfare capitalism, as Ralph Nader (or Joseph Stiglitz) might put it. If we turn to Islamic societies, on the other hand, we find something that truly is different, for they are predominantly traditional in nature. Whatever one might think of Allah, in Islamic societies religion comes first, and it gives those societies a meaningful communal foundation. Contrary to already faltering theories about "soft power," the only way to force our notion of progress onto these cultures is war—which is precisely what the North did to the South starting in 1861 (see chapter 4). True, these societies are repressive, they treat women badly, and they tend to be intellectually static. But they also have gracious codes of hospitality, and put great emphasis on family, community, and loyalty. And while the global economy has handed them extremes of wealth and poverty, hustling is not part of the Islamic ethos, and neither is technological innovation. In the long run, and despite our best efforts, we shall not be able to dominate or defeat these traditional societies, such as in Iraq or Iran or Afghanistan; and as for the purported "war on terror," it is nothing more than a fool's errand, as anyone with half a brain knows. In a word, we shall not be able to do to Islam what the North did to the South in the Civil War, either culturally or militarily. This raises the question as to how this dialectic will play out. If I had to guess, I would say that they probably will adapt, learn a lot from us (for the most part, what they need to beat us at our own game); while we, being obtuse and xenophobic, probably will ignore any positive part of their culture worth emulating, so convinced are we of the primacy of our lifestyle.[7]

All that aside, we finally come to the issue of the future of the alternative tradition in the United States. In terms of political impact, of course, it has no future, since the percentage of Americans not interested in hustling, or dedicated to public service in a noncareerist way, is probably quite small. If a commitment to craft, community, the public good, the natural environment, spiritual practice, and the "simple life"—"plain living and high thinking," as Wordsworth put it—has had its adherents over the years, this commitment, with the exception of marginal utopian communities such as the Shakers or the Amish, was easily co-opted by the dominant culture, and/or transmuted into popular fads and trends. (Martha Stewart's media empire, to take a contemporary example, is built on the commercialization of domesticity, simplicity, and the benefits of working with one's hands.) Even republicanism managed to get pressed into the service of the hustling life, ironically enough; Benjamin Franklin is a good example of this.[8] As already noted, the slow, traditional life never acquired a political form, except in the South. I can imagine, however, one scenario in which such a development might be possible, namely the complete breakdown of the dominant culture. Of course, if the day should come when water doesn't come out of the tap, there is no food in the stores, hospitals and airports are closed, and the electrical grid shuts down, we can be sure that the army will be patrolling the streets. But what if military discipline also breaks down? After all, the government can't patrol every street of every city, and in any case soldiers are people too; they could well regard the whole exercise as pointless, and desert in droves. In such a context, technological gadgets and large bank accounts won't be of much use, and conspicuous consumption will be impossible, not to say ridiculous. The emptiness of this way of life might, at that point, be too obvious to deny, and the values of the alternative tradition might come to the fore—in a serious way, not merely as a short-term trend or type of radical chic. We may see secessionist movements arise as well, with the Union powerless to do anything about it this time around.[9]

All of this may seem far-fetched, but 2008 is hardly the last or the severest economic meltdown we are going to live through. We're at the fag-end of our civilization, my friends; things are going to look very different in 2040—perhaps even in 2025— than they do today.[10]

The sad (or incredibly frustrating) thing is that true meaning, true value in life, has been there all along in American history; it always was there for the taking. Or at least, it was a possibility. Given the fact that hustling and technological innovation do have an upside, the real issue is one of balance: where these things fit in the overall purpose, or "moral ecology," of human life. If they become the purpose of life, then by definition life has no purpose, because "more" is not a purpose. This is what one of Jimmy Carter's advisers was referring to when he characterized the United States as "a goal-oriented society without goals." For what, finally, was the "City on a Hill" that John Winthrop had in mind in 1630, in that famous sermon he preached on the *Arabella* as it was making its way from England to America? What you must be vigilant about, he told his flock, is that the "good of the public oversway all private interests." Not hustling, not goods, but *the good*—the commonweal. We chose not to follow that path, and now we are paying the price.[11]

M.B.
Mexico
2011

THE PURSUIT OF
AFFLUENCE

As one digs deeper into the national character of the Americans, one sees that they have sought the value of everything in this world only in the answer to this single question: how much money will it bring in?

—Alexis de Tocqueville,
letter to Ernest de Chabrol, June 9, 1831

L ET US THEN TAKE A closer look at the argument of Walter McDougall, that at the center of the American character lies a "penchant for hustling." Indeed, he says, American English contains more than two hundred nouns and verbs referring to a swindle. Whereas Joseph Schumpeter saw the cycles of capitalism as being driven by "creative destruction," McDougall believes that American history is characterized by "creative corruption." We have, he maintains, always been scramblers and speculators, and nearly everyone in early America was concerned not with what might be good for the colonies or the nation but with "What's in it for me?" Americans take it for granted, he writes, that "everyone's got an angle," and ours is a society "devoted by general consensus to fleeing as quickly as possible into the future." A hustler, after all, is always in a hurry; to what end is not clear. We can (and McDougall does) put a positive spin on much of this (it's ambition, it's "energy," etc.); but in the end it contains a sordid reality, a "ubiquitous sleaze" that won't go away. This is a way of life with very high costs.[1]

Self-interest and the pursuit of wealth, however, did not constitute the only ideological strain in the colonial outlook. Ideals of enlightened material restraint and public service were certainly present in the hearts and minds of our Puritan forefathers, and the colonists were attracted to the New World for both idealistic and materialistic reasons. New England Puritanism was opposed to avarice, not to prosperity per se.

In the 1630s, for example, the Reverend John Cotton of Massachusetts emphasized that a Christian was honor-bound to work for the public good—hardly a radical notion at the time. For much of the seventeenth century, in fact, some type of balance did exist between economic pursuit and the communal order, and Puritans saw no necessary conflict between the two.[2]

The origins of this way of thinking go back to classical civilization, and feudal Europe was imbued with it as well. In both, virtue was defined as the ability to put the public good above your own private interest. On the classical view, this is what made republics possible: free men realized their human potential in service to the commonwealth.[3] It was an ideal central to organic, hierarchical society, the tradition of noblesse oblige. Born out of social inequality, it was nevertheless seen by Christian civilization in general as the cornerstone of both human fulfillment and good government alike.

That there is something higher than individual achievement is, of course, a notion central to all traditional societies. Their way of life is characterized by stability rather than progress, and by nonlinear time. It is unhurried. Communication is face-to-face; labor, leisure, religion, family, and community are all woven together, and there is very little aspiration toward "improvement." The public welfare comes first. This includes feudal societies, as already noted; and in postclassical times feudalism was the template upon which a communitarian ethos rested. This ethos, including the classical republican notion of virtue, was handed down to American colonists via their British ancestry. Prior to the Puritan Revolution, for example (1642–49), which marks the beginning of the bourgeois era in political terms, English Puritans believed that individual calling was subordinate to the general welfare and that poverty was not a personal sin but a function of the economic system (and hence the responsibility of the state). Needless to say, this was a very different sort of world than the one that was to follow.[4]

Of course, one of the great ironies of the American Revolution was that the colonists took the ideals of republicanism and used them against the mother country, which they viewed as corrupt, tyrannical, and in violation of its own ideals. But what *was* republicanism, really? Oddly enough, nobody seemed to know—a curious situation that persists down to the present day. Let's look at this a bit more closely.

The one characteristic of republicanism that everyone did seem to agree on was its opposition to inherited political power—in particular, monarchy—in favor of a government that is "by and for the people." The Constitution refers to a republican form of government, but leaves the exact meaning of this up in the air. John Adams famously referred to the word as meaning "anything, everything, or nothing," adding (in 1807), "There is not a more unintelligible word in the English language." The key terms associated with it, such as "virtue," "republic," and "commonweal," were quite slippery; their meanings changed over time.[5]

Virtue was probably the crux of the matter. As already noted, the classical definition meant subordination of private interest to the public good. Historian Gordon Wood sees it as a near-utopian force in the 1770s, an ideology that made the Revolution possible. The "sacrifice of individual interests to the greater good of the whole," he writes, "formed the essence of republicanism and comprehended for Americans the idealistic goal of their Revolution." Conversely, corruption—identified strongly with Great Britain during this time—was not simply venality or fraud; it also was the absence of civic virtue. In the classical tradition, a corrupt man was preoccupied with his own career and oblivious to the public good. And this way of life, framed by the industrial "takeoff" of about 1760, was ubiquitous in England during the latter part of the eighteenth century, and seemingly sanctioned by the writings of John Locke. In *An Essay Concerning Human Understanding*, Locke specifically linked commercial activity to "uneasiness," which he regarded as its motivating factor. Once motivated, he wrote, men had a never-ending "itch after honour, power, and riches," which then triggered further uneasiness, and so on. If that wasn't bad enough, Locke actually saw this pattern as virtuous. The new notion of virtue not only rejected the classic republican defini-tion; it also turned it on its head. "The moral and virtuous man was no longer defined by his civic activity but by his economic activity," says historian Isaac Kramnick. Anticipating Adam Smith and the concept of the "invisible hand" of the market, the idea here was that you contributed to the public good by means of your own individual economic activity, which was actually aimed at private gain. This outlook came to be known as liberalism.[6]

Meanwhile, what was happening on the other side of the Atlantic? To historians such as Wood, who choose to empha-size the (republican) ideological fervor of the Revolution, Joyce Appleby poses an obvious dilemma:

> If the Revolution was fought in a frenzy over cor-ruption, out of fear of tyranny, and with hopes for redemption through civic virtue, where and when are scholars to find the sources for the aggressive individ-ualism, the optimistic materialism, and the pragmatic interest-group politics that became so salient so early in the life of the new nation?

The point is that these "unvirtuous" qualities were there all along, as William McDougall tells us, and as Louis Hartz (*The Liberal Tradition in America*) argued decades ago. American society, said Hartz, was essentially Lockean: individualistic, ambitious, and protocapitalistic ("liberal"). Put succinctly, mate-rialistic values ruled. Appleby has argued that the 1790s saw the definition of virtue change from the republican conception to the liberal one, undergoing a complete inversion (following the British pattern) by the time of Jefferson's election in 1800. A corrupt system, for Jefferson, was one not based on merit, and an unvirtuous person was a lazy one. For Thomas Cooper, a British industrialist who eventually settled in America, only those with "insatiable ambition" could be virtuous. In his pamphlet *Political Arithmetic*, Cooper baldly declared that "The consumers form the nation," and Jefferson wasted no time distributing this text as election campaign material.[7]

Hartz's book, published in 1955, was followed two years later by another classic work, *The American Political Tradition*, by Richard Hofstadter. Hofstadter argued that all major American statesmen from Jefferson to Herbert Hoover were committed to an ideology of economic individualism and competitive capitalism; and that the absence of a hereditary aristocracy to reject or disdain these values had rendered the American mentality one-dimensional. America, he said, was a "democracy of cupidity," not one of fraternity or community.

In fact, a good case (à la McDougall) can be made for rapidly shifting sensibilities occurring much earlier than the late eighteenth century. In 1616, for example, Captain John Smith expressed the concern that most of his countrymen were motivated to colonize the New World purely for material gain. "I am not so simple to think," he wrote, "that ever any other motive than wealth will erect there a Commonweal." As historian Eric Foner tells us, "during the whole of the colonial era promotional literature that sought to lure settlers to America publicized the image of the New World as a place of exceptional opportunity for social mobility and the acquisition of property." And as David Shi notes in *The Simple Life*, the number of settlers who fell into this category increased as the years went by. Boston merchants and artisans began to prioritize hard work and individual success over the communal ideal. Popular resentment led to the repeal of wage and price regulations in

1635, and an increased interest in luxury goods was visible by 1637. By midcentury it was reported that throughout the Massachusetts Bay Colony, "men were generally failing in their duty to the community, seeking their own aggrandizement in the rich opportunities afforded by land, commerce, crafts, and speculators, to the detriment of the community." Preachers railed against this, legislation was passed to curb or arrest it, but all of this, observes Shi, "did little to stem the tide of social upheaval and personal ambition." Indeed, he goes on, the "pristine vision of the colony's founders continued to be dashed upon the rock of selfish individualism." Already by 1700, he concludes, medieval communalism had given way to Lockean individualism.[8]

A detailed map of the process for the period 1690 to 1765 in Connecticut has been provided by Richard Bushman in his aptly titled book *From Puritan to Yankee*. Town settlements, he writes, were fairly stable and traditional for most of the seventeenth century. Land grants bound inhabitants to the towns, and the farmer depended on the town to buy his surplus. In other words, the town sold land, roads, pasture, and common fencing, and an owner was thereby part of the community. After 1690, however, this began to change. "Outlivers" began to migrate from town settlements to stake out new ones; their focus was property and independence from community life. They "make the Gains of the World their main Aim, End, and Design," complained a pamphlet of 1739. A speculative spirit thus began to undermine the communal order; transactions were increasingly about cash value, nothing more. By 1765, Lockean theories were very much in vogue: men formed the state in pursuit of naked self-interest. Indeed, that was just about the only glue left to the social order, says Bushman—if naked self-interest can indeed be regarded as any type of social glue.[9]

Many preachers by then also had changed their tune, again anticipating the ideas of Adam Smith. Self-interest, they argued, would work to promote the common good, and should be made the foundation of civil society. By the 1760s it became popular to insist that government existed to serve private interests. Throughout New England hard work, more specifically the gains thereby derived, became its own ethic, devoid of any spiritual content. The pursuit of wealth, according to Bushman, was so avid in the eighteenth century that it managed to rupture traditional bonds and boundaries. In the process, transcendent values were left behind in the dust.[10]

How idealistic was the American Revolution, really? In many ways, it only served to push things further in a liberal direction. "Time is Money," Benjamin Franklin had written in 1748; by 1776, colonial society had become a great deal speedier. The American iron industry, by that date, was producing a seventh of the world's total output of crude iron. The care and leisure of the craft tradition began to have less appeal, as machines were now built for rapid use rather than durability. The new was what counted now, and mass-produced goods, especially guns, clocks, and textiles, soon would be in great demand. Another popular phrase of the time was "the pursuit of happiness," by which was really meant the pursuit of property; in particular, of land. The Revolution shined a light on the possibility of upward mobility, individual financial success. It served as a catalyst for a new dynamism—a quantum leap in the level of hustling, one might say. At about this time Samuel Adams observed that the "Rage for Profit and Commerce" had become the American norm. George Washington himself, during the war years, referred to the "insatiable thirst for riches" that had seized American society, adding that he had never seen such a "dearth of public spirit and want of virtue." By 1820 the country had more banks (307, to be exact) and insurance companies than any other country in the world, and by the 1830s, more than 2,000 banks nationwide—statistics that give us some idea of how dramatically the nation was transforming itself.[11]

Republicanism or liberalism, then? Perhaps the real question is, Rhetoric or reality? It has been said of the French, in the nineteenth and twentieth centuries, that they voted with their hearts on the left and their wallets on the right; and something similar might be said of Americans from about 1770 to 1840. How to classify Thomas Paine, for example, an obvious proponent of the republican ideal, and yet a man keen on the attractions of laissez-faire economics? In *The Elusive Republic*, Drew McCoy describes a "hybrid republican vision," quite visible by the 1770s, in which the moral dimensions of classical republicanism were adapted to modern commercial ends. Thus the maxims of Poor Richard, as given to us by Benjamin Franklin, were an obvious effort to blend the classical notion of virtue with its opposite, the new "virtue" of commerce and self-aggrandizement. As historian Lance Banning points out, while it is true that liberalism and republicanism are logically derived from irreconcilable philosophies, in practice many colonists subscribed to both.[12]

Three things need to be kept in mind in trying to sort this question out. The first is that for the most part, the Founding Fathers were quite unusual men, very different from the average citizen. They constituted a galaxy of talent, as brilliant and idealistic a group as has ever existed. There is no doubt that they were serious about their republican convictions, at least initially. Second—as the cases of Paine and Franklin make clear, and which was common enough among the gentry—they often had conflicts of interest regarding their commitment to that ideology (although they themselves may not have seen it that way). And third, the idealism of the Revolution was a brief moment in time. Yet even during the Revolution, as we have seen, the liberal tradition was the basic American outlook—as Hartz and Hofstadter convincingly argued. Americans may have occasionally or frequently used the language of republicanism, says historian John Diggins in *The Lost Soul of American Politics*, but it was never a doctrine on which they based their real lives.[13]

In a word, once the dust settled on the Revolution, it began to look as though the Founding Fathers had had one type of society in mind, and the general citizenry another. The latter was interested in profit, competition, and new consumer goods, whereas the former believed that these things were important, but by themselves could not constitute the stuff of commonwealth. John Adams and James Madison even began to wonder if monarchy was all that bad, for at least it organized a nation around a higher purpose than getting and spending, as Wordsworth would put it just a few years later. Adams claimed that the United States had proven to be "more Avaricious than any other Nation that ever existed." "Bedollared," Benjamin Rush called the place, adding that without a civilizing influence, this not-so-enlightened citizenry would start "devouring each other like beasts of prey." (One wonders what these men, if they were alive today, would think of Goldman Sachs and AIG.) Forrest McDonald, in *Novus Ordo Seclorum*, says of the passing of this generation: "After that, the *Populares* took over, and a race of pygmies came to infest the public councils."[14]

As for conflicts of interest: these were philosophical as well as material. Diggins argues that republicanism was in large part language and symbol for the Founding Fathers, and that while Madison, Hamilton, and Adams did believe in the classical ideal, they nevertheless

> created a government with no need for men committed to civic humanism. The constitution they created represented the eclipse of political and moral authority and the legitimation of pluralism, individualism, and materialism, the very forces the humanist tradition identified with corruption and loss of virtue. The Founders created a weak government whose center had no compelling moral ballast.

"Virtue" had been useful as a protest against (British) corruption, but it could not serve as a source of authority for a population largely engaged in a commercial free-for-all. The problem, says Diggins, was that "the [classical] idea of virtue had no determinative content, no transcendent quality that stood over and against the objective world of power and interests, no moral vision that inspired the individual to identify with values higher than his own interests." It couldn't compel anything, when all was said and done.[15]

Thus republicanism never really took hold in America, despite its persistent allure. It survived as rhetoric through the Jackson presidency, began to fade thereafter, and was pretty much killed off by the Civil War. Historian Robert Shalhope writes:

> There simply is no doubt that the majority of Americans did, indeed, behave in a materialistic, individualistic manner. At the same time, though, it is equally clear that most of those same Americans continued to perceive themselves and their society in republican terms. That is, republicanism—a familiar ideology permeating all walks of life—shaped Americans' minds; it offered them a self-image that provided meaning and identity to their lives. Thus, while rapidly transforming their society in an open, competitive, modern direction, Americans idealized communal harmony and virtuous social order. In this sense, then, republicanism formalized or ritualized a mode of thought that ran counter to the flow of history; it idealized the traditional values of a world rapidly fading, rather than the market conditions and liberal capitalistic mentality swiftly emerging in the late eighteenth century.

When John Kennedy posed the republican vs. liberal choice in his inaugural address ("Ask not what your country can do for you ...."), Americans may have felt a vague kind of idealistic stir-ring; but it is also very likely that the vast majority heard it as a kind of poetry. The Peace Corps notwithstanding, it is unlikely that more than a handful acted on the call, gave up the life of get-ting and spending, and dedicated themselves to public service.[16]

As many observers of the American scene have pointed out over the centuries, there is a tragic side to all of this. To take just the Jacksonian period (1830s): In *Democracy in America*, Alexis de Tocqueville repeatedly describes the anxious, driven quality of American life. It is a worried life, he writes, in which people pursue a success that forever eludes them. Their goal is an undefined material success, to be provided by the larg-est returns in the shortest amount of time. These are unquiet souls, he adds; their way of life is unrelenting. James Fenimore Cooper portrayed this in his novels, seeing the country drifting toward "a world without moral foundations." Author Francis Grund, who immigrated to the United States in 1826, wrote that "Business is the very soul of an American: he pursues it, not as a means of procuring for himself and his family the nec-essary comforts of life, but as the fountain of all human felic-ity." One English traveler similarly noted that he had never "overheard Americans conversing without the word DOLLAR being pronounced," and added that it didn't matter whether the conversation took place "in the street, on the road, or in the field, at the theatre, the coffee-house or at home." One of his compatriots, Charles Dickens, also saw us as a nation of grubs, endlessly chasing the "almighty dollar" (a phrase actually coined by Washington Irving a few years earlier), while jour-nalist Thomas Low Nichols, in *Forty Years of American Life*, observed that "In no country are the faces of the people fur-rowed with harder lines of care. . . . Everyone is tugging, trying, scheming to advance." The German-American jurist Francis (Franz) Lieber commented on the "diseased anxiety to be equal to the wealthiest," which resulted in an "appalling frequency of alienation of mind." "There is little of what is called *fun* in

America," he added, and the American publisher Freeman Hunt agreed: "Youth robbed of its sunshine." And this is only a partial list, and from a relatively short period. Emerson and Thoreau and Melville and Poe and later Henry Adams all were to write brilliantly about a society that had no sacred center, no soul, and the toll that that was taking on the nation; but this was just "literature," after all—nothing really changed as a result.[17]

Facilitating the pursuit of economic expansion, writes William Appleman Williams (*The Contours of American History*), was the factor of geographic expansion—the frontier. It began domestically, as Manifest Destiny (which included swallowing up half of Mexico in 1848); by the end of the nineteenth century it had turned into imperialism. Adams and Madison were strong advocates of it; so were workers, farmers, and members of the middle class. The idea behind it, says Williams, was that it would act as a safety valve, reconciling the scramble for private property with the ideal of a Christian commonwealth. Empire, he wrote, "was the only way to honor [both] avarice and morality." But ultimately, depending on your point of view, it failed, because unlimited expansion proved to be a poor substitute for actually having a commonwealth, or even having a vision of one. Basically it amounted to more hustling, a "gate of escape" (in the words of Frederick Jackson Turner) that enabled Americans to put off the question of the public good indefinitely. Problems at home? Just pull up stakes and go West. It thus weakened the sense of community, for it made it difficult to impose any restraints on private interests that undercut the general welfare. Tocqueville wrote, "Focused on the single goal of making his fortune, the settler ends up creating a completely individual existence. . . . He holds that man comes into the world only to become well-off and to enjoy the conveniences of life." And, of course, once the frontier was officially declared closed in 1890, there was always the technological frontier, the next "new thing" for Americans to chase.

Williams points out that the dependence of the United States on this mechanism became so fierce that anything or anybody that stood in the way of expansion—Native Americans, the Confederacy, the Soviet Union, and finally the Third World—was regarded as unalloyed evil, beyond redemption. We hardly wound up in Iraq by accident.[18]

But this is to get ahead of ourselves. If the early to mid-nineteenth century saw an avid pursuit of affluence, it also witnessed a spiritual rejection of this way of life as well, as the writings of Emerson and others would indicate. Yet this rejection, which put great emphasis on economic self-restraint, often had a particularly American twist to it: it conceived of the non-hustling life in purely individual terms. It was *self*-reliance, not the commonweal, that the romantics and Transcendentalists were interested in—the quality of the individual soul. As one might expect, this narrow type of focus undercut the possibility of having any widespread impact, and it left the movement open to co-optation, to being pressed into the service of the dominant culture. Leaving the period of the Civil War aside for the moment (I shall address that at length in chapter 4), this dynamic of spiritual resistance and eventual assimilation was a familiar one during the Progressive Era and the Gilded Age, as Jackson Lears documents in painstaking detail. His conclusions are two: first, that the various expressions of "antimodernism" were quite genuine, being rooted in a religious longing for meaning that the hustling life was not able to provide; and second, that the ultimately aesthetic and individualistic nature of these attempts at changing the culture actually wound up facilitating the transition from entrepreneurial to corporate capitalism. Given the legacy of these two aspects of this period in American history, it might be worth our while to sketch these events in greater detail.[19]

The first thing that stands out for 1890–1930 is that these years witnessed the most accelerated commercialization of American life up to that point. Not that the previous era had been slow. During 1800–50 the GNP increased sevenfold, and by 1860 the basic outlines of the modern American economy were already visible: mass consumption, mass production, and capital-intensive agriculture. By the mid-1880s the United States had the world's largest economy—25 percent of the whole. In the few short decades following that, corporations, banks, department stores, chain stores, mail-order houses, hotels, and amusement parks literally swept across the American landscape. Advertising, brokering, and mass production reconfigured the country in a dramatic way so that it became, in the words of William Leach in *Land of Desire*, "the world's most powerful culture of consumption." This was the age of Du Pont, U.S. Steel, Standard Oil, and of Marshall Field and Macy's. Between 1897 and 1903 more than three hundred corporate consolidations took place in the United States, and the greed and ruthlessness of the robber barons are legendary. Speaking of John D. Rockefeller Sr., Lears writes: "Anyone who blocked his implacable will to profit was overwhelmed through secrecy, deception, and the brutal exercise of market power." Thorstein Veblen coined the phrase "conspicuous consumption" in 1899, and as he pointed out, it was hardly restricted to the leisure class. Status-seeking was in full swing long before Vance Packard ever arrived on the scene; upward mobility was the theme of the hour. A race for success alternated with periodic nervous breakdowns, and by 1907 Henry James, in *The American Scene*, was telling his readers that the so-called liberty of the laissez-faire economy was a sham. It produced an inability to face solitude, he wrote, and was unable to create a society based on a sense of community. What it did provide, he concluded, was the "freedom to grow up blighted." In the context of the contemporary financial hurricane, however, not too many Americans were listening. Solitude? Community? What are *they*? Andrew Carnegie's dicta that we must always be changing and improving, and that life was a race to be won by the swiftest, were much more attuned to the spirit of the age, and they were accepted by labor leaders, socialists, and farmers alike.[20]

But the period saw numerous critiques of this Darwinian struggle for existence, in addition to those of Henry James and Thorstein Veblen. Mental illness was so rife during this era that George Miller Beard, a New York neurologist, was moved to document it in *American Nervousness* (1880). America, he asserted, was the most nervous country in the world because it was at the cutting edge of modernization. Other doctors and writers joined Beard in attesting to epidemics of depression and anxiety that were engulfing the nation, pointing to factors such as time pressure and work compulsion. By the early twentieth century, nervous exhaustion was a popular topic of conversation in the daily newspapers.[21]

"The truth," said Woodrow Wilson in 1912, "is [that] we are all caught in a great economic system which is heartless." Ten years later, Sinclair Lewis attacked that system in *Babbitt*, but of course to little effect. William James decried the American worship of success, stating, "That—with the squalid cash interpretation put on the word success—is our national disease." A host of writers and intellectuals recoiled against the culture of unrelenting commerce and argued for a life of greater depth (or simply depth)—Charles Eliot Norton, Henry Adams, and Henry Demarest Lloyd, to name but a few—but it was like swimming upstream in molasses. In one form or another, their argument was that you could not have any sort of commonwealth in a situation where human survival was based on competitive success. But obviously, three hundred years of hustling were not going to be reversed by a few books, and in any case most Americans were more likely to be reading tales of self-made millionaires than something like Lloyd's *Wealth Versus Commonwealth* or Lewis' *Babbitt*. Frazzled or not, the typical

American wanted not to smirk at George Babbitt but to *be* him, and to swim in an ocean of consumer goods.[22]

As Lears shows, the antimodernist pitch for authenticity and simplicity was easily commodified, made to serve the dominant culture—much as what happened to the counterculture of the sixties a few decades later. His best example is probably that of the Arts and Crafts movement, originally inspired by the writings of John Ruskin and William Morris in England. Both of these men saw the Middle Ages as a period of craft integrity, in contrast to the tawdry products of subsequent mass production. Medieval artisanry, they held, was not alienated labor, not a job one simply endured for the sake of a paycheck, or so that one could relax on Sunday after six days of mind-numbing work. Morris extolled the guild tradition; factories, on his view, were degrading to labor and to human life. He was a socialist, but his major point was that work had to be enjoyable, above all.[23]

The writings of Ruskin and Morris had a great impact on certain circles in the United States, notably the educated and the well-off. The figure of the premodern artisan seemed to shine with authentic selfhood. His or her work was real, physical, and rooted in the community—a model of wholeness. The crafts movement in the United States emphasized the simple life, and leaders such as Charles Eliot Norton (a professor at Harvard and a friend of Ruskin's) believed that obsession with private gain had led to the destruction of community in the post–Civil War era. The crafts revival sponsored manual training in public schools, and founded Arts and Crafts societies in various cities. The Boston society published a magazine, *Handicraft*, which lasted for many years. Crafts colonies sprang up in Pennsylvania and Massachusetts; Gustav Stickley opened a United Crafts furniture workshop in Syracuse in 1898, and published the *Craftsman* between 1901 and 1916. The movement was quite broad and attracted a large following.

In terms of social change, however, the Arts and Crafts movement proved to be a failure. For one thing, the leaders, not wanting to alienate potential recruits, emphasized the moral and aesthetic qualities of handicrafts and dropped all references to William Morris' socialism or hatred of the factory system in their writings. The focus was on good taste, not on the downside of the affluent life. In fact, handicrafts clients tended to be rich; Veblen saw the whole thing as chic. As for the working class, its interest was in a higher hourly wage, not in good taste and the supposed pleasures of labor. In addition, as Lears indicates, American crafts leaders were ultimately not interested in community renewal, but in individual wholeness; not in social justice, but in feeling good. They also believed in the inevitability of technological "progress," which couldn't have been more opposite to the ideas of Ruskin and Morris, and which basically undercut their own ideology. As a result, they "transformed what might have been an alternative to alienated labor into a revivifying hobby for the affluent."

Yet it wasn't a total waste. The American crafts movement did, according to Lears, contain a genuine protest against the commercial life. It was part of a tradition that stretched backward to antebellum utopians and forward to the agrarian communities of the New Deal and the 1960s. The movement also had an influence on intellectuals who would subsequently emphasize the importance of small-scale decentralized institutions for genuine democracy—Paul Goodman, Lewis Mumford, and E. F. Schumacher, to name the most illustrious of the group. Indeed, if we take the antimodernist tradition as a whole, says Lears, the central, powerful insight that it hammered home, despite the unwillingness of most Americans to hear the message, is that when all is said and done, "the modern secular utopia was . . . a fraud."

The pattern of great expectations and subsequent deflation, in any case, got repeated during the years of the Great

Depression. As in the past, this period didn't lack for critics
of the hustling life. Uppermost in their minds was the question of national purpose, especially in the wake of the Roaring
Twenties and a decade of I-own-therefore-I-am psychology.
What they hoped for was that necessity might become a virtue; that Americans would embrace the simple life—"permanently curtailed consumption," in the words of historian
Daniel Horowitz—because they had no other choice. Typical
of this chastened outlook was Robert Lynd, co-author, with his
wife, Helen, of the classic study *Middletown* (1929). Writing
in *Parents' Magazine* in 1934, Lynd predicted that the lives of
the next generation would "probably be [defined] less in terms
of whopping accumulations of material things and more in
terms of more inconspicuous, hard-won personal satisfactions."
This new generation, he went on, would be "relieved from a
part of our irrelevant strain of endless competitive acquisition
for its own sake" and from the pressure of "trying to excel and
get ahead." Of course, it was precisely this generation that spent
its eyeballs out as soon as World War II ended and that took
hustling to new and unprecedented heights.[24]

The most formidable critic of the acquisitive life during this
time and the decades following was Lewis Mumford, one of the
greatest writers and thinkers America has ever produced. His
active career spans nearly sixty years, from the 1920s to the early
eighties. Since the major focus of his criticism was technology and misguided notions of "progress," I shall leave part of
my discussion of his ideas for chapter 3. But so committed was
Mumford to the notion that hustling was deeply destructive of
America, and of human life in general, that we need to take just
a moment to look at his general role as the nation's conscience,
as some writers have labeled him.

In the 1920s, the work that most influenced Mumford was
Oswald Spengler's *The Decline of the West*. Spengler believed
that every civilization was defined by an essential Idea, in the

Platonic sense, which expressed itself in every aspect of its culture. In addition, each civilization went through the phases of birth, efflorescence, and decay, during which time there was a shift from the organic and the creative to the mechanical and the bureaucratic. The "Faustian" culture of northern Europe, according to Spengler, had become embodied in world cities, which displaced older, regionally based centers that were rooted in traditional ways of life. This northern urban culture was characterized by bigness and rationality; in its final phase, it was dominated by the soldier, the engineer, and the businessman (sound familiar?). All that is left to it now, he concluded, was fossilization and death.[25]

Mumford repeated this schema in his book *The Golden Day* (1926), but with a twist: he was optimistic. He envisioned a post-Faustian world, one based on a revival of regional and organic life. Regionalism, Mumford argued, could shorten the period of "fossilization" and move the West toward renewal and rebirth. With this in mind, Mumford helped found the Regional Planning Association of America in New York in 1923. Its explicit goal was to promote regional culture. Central to this was the "garden city" concept, which emphasized limited-scale development in the form of communities that would combine home and work in one locale. These were not suburbs in any sense of the word, then; no commuting would be involved. They would be surrounded by a "greenbelt" of farmland and forests, and be owned by the community in general. The goal, in Mumford's mind, was to institutionalize the good life, which for him had nothing to do with consumer acquisition and economic competition. By the good life, said Mumford, "One means the birth and nurture of children, the preservation of human health and well-being, the culture of the human personality, and the perfection of the natural and civic environment as the theater of all of these activities." Life in these communities, adds David Shi, was to be "a richly integrated and cooperative social experience in which people, regardless of their economic circumstances, would enjoy a sense of belonging with each other, with nature, and with their work."

For the most part, the garden city concept never got off the ground. For one thing, once the Depression struck there was no money available for projects of this nature. But prior to the crash of 1929, one such community was built, namely Sunnyside Gardens in Queens, designed for workers and the lower middle class. The houses are small, and many of them front inward, toward a common green area. Public courtyards and service roads also serve to give it a village atmosphere, down to the present time. It was a real break with the model of commercial real estate development; a humane, planned community. Today, it is privately owned and quite upscale, but it retains a very different ambience from that of your typical corporate-constructed "community."[26]

Mumford believed that a real change in America could only come about through a radical change in values. The problem with Marxism, he argued, was that it wasn't all that revolutionary. The country needed to slow down the pace of industrialization and "turn society from its feverish preoccupation with money-making inventions, goods, profits, salesmanship . . . to the deliberate promotion of the more human functions of life." Not a Red Republic, wrote Mumford, but a Green one. His vision, that of a morally disciplined, nonacquisitive life, is about as un-American as one could imagine.[27]

If Mumford was heir to Spengler, he also was in the lineage of Thoreau, and he pushed for this radical revisioning of mainstream American ideology during the years of the Depression and beyond. In *Technics and Civilization* (1934), notes Daniel Horowitz, Mumford "envisioned the replacement of an age overcommitted to technology, capitalism, materialism, and growth by the emergence of a humane, life-affirming economy based on the values of regionalism, community, and restraint."

One has to wonder what country Mumford thought he was living in; his writing is occasionally so out of touch with American
reality that he sometimes sounds deranged (if wonderfully
so). Thus in an article he did for the *New Republic* in 1939, he
claimed that America was beginning to shift from an emphasis
on individual consumer demands to a commitment to public
well-being. Public services and facilities, he told his readers,
would eventually displace capitalist ideology. The following
year, he declared that democracy could only be reinvigorated
by substituting spiritual pleasures for material ones, and that
the true birthright of the American people was not "a life of
material abundance" but one of "comradeship, art and love."
(Clearly, the man had not spent a lot of time studying American
history.) We must have an "economy of sacrifice," he went on,
not an "economy of comfort." Mumford encouraged his fellow citizens to turn away from the American Dream, that of
a "deceptive orgy of economic expansion." We must, he wrote,
become creative individuals, committed to "human co-opera-
tion and communion." It's not entirely clear why he didn't also
call for a reversal of the earth's gravitational field.[28]

Mumford did, however, strike a semirealistic note in *The
Condition of Man* (1944), which was partly influenced by his
study of the late Roman Empire. It didn't help Rome, he
observed, that its rulers during this period refused to believe
that the empire was falling apart. It was precisely the unwillingness of the Roman people to look at their way of life, one
founded on "pillage and pilfer," and to revamp it, that led to the
fall of Rome.[29] But Mumford apparently believed that sounding
the alarm would wake his countrymen up from the American
Dream, and, of course, nothing of the sort happened. As with
the Romans, the last thing Americans have been interested in is
serious introspection and national redirection. Mumford began
to understand this as the years wore on. His writing became
increasingly pessimistic, and with good reason: literally no one

was paying any attention to his prescriptions for health. The doctor counseled diet and exercise, but the couch potato chose to glut himself on pie and cake. Mumford was able to stop Robert Moses, New York City's controversial urban planner, from destroying Greenwich Village in the sixties, but beyond that, his calls for an end to hustling and for a redefinition of the idea of "progress" (see chapter 3) went completely unheeded. He never really grasped the addictive nature of material acquisition and technological innovation, it seems to me; he didn't understand that these things were druglike substitutes for a commonwealth, a truly human way of life, that Americans had largely rejected from very early on. Today his writings come off as both inspiring and wistful: they are finally about a different country, not the United States.

(Just by way of comparison, a contemporary of Mumford's who *was* writing about and for the United States was Dale Carnegie, who probably outsold Mumford at a ratio of ten thousand to one, if not more. *How to Win Friends and Influence People* is possibly the ultimate guide to hustling, a manual for "how to make more money by false geniality," as one historian characterized it. Indeed, it was an instant best seller since its first appearance in 1936, and it remains popular today. The peak achievement described in the book, says Barbara Ehrenreich, "is to learn how to fake sincerity" so as to get ahead in your career.[30])

Where was the New Deal during all of this? It started off well enough, I suppose: in his first inaugural, FDR said that the true mission of the United States was to embody social values that were "more noble than mere monetary profit." To put this into effect, Roosevelt hoped to create a nationwide back-to-the-land movement, which he believed would encourage a simpler life. Thus the Civilian Conservation Corps, launched in 1933, had half a million young Americans enrolled by 1935, planting trees and carrying out soil reclamation projects. The Tennessee

Valley Authority, also started in 1933, built dams and under-took programs for soil conservation and reforestation. Arthur Morgan, the TVA's first director, believed that work of this nature would generate a community ethic capable of displacing laissez-faire capitalism, and a "spirit of cooperation" that would overshadow the "aberration" of rugged individualism. Under his tutelage, for example, the TVA organized handicrafts industries and other cooperatives.[31]

Very little of this withstood the test of time. Rugged individ-ualism is no "aberration" in the United States; rather, the "spirit of cooperation" is. Morgan, in short, was as out of touch with the mainstream American ethos as Lewis Mumford was. His own project for a garden city, Norris, Tennessee, which was designed for TVA employees, was to exemplify the ideology of public good over private interest. But it didn't take long for the residents of Norris to reject this notion, to label it "socialism," and thus to recoil from it. In addition, other New Dealers didn't share Morgan's vision; they saw the TVA strictly in economic terms, not as a vehicle for the ethical redirection of American life. FDR finally fired Morgan in 1938.

The same fate befell the homestead program, also designed to create a new community life that would eschew competitive materialism. About a hundred New Deal communities were set up along these lines, but the residents, says David Shi, "found it impossible to shed their ingrained individualism." They were not the least bit interest in the communal ideal. Instead, they viewed the homestead communities as little more than housing projects; they spent very little time in the community centers, for example. Roosevelt himself, as the years went by, seemed to think that happiness would come not through a revaluation of values, but through increased industrial production and more jobs. Thus his administration made rural regions profitable for massive corporate investment, and it was through such regional development that corporate America expanded dramatically after the Depression. New Deal thinking increasingly saw consumption as central to the nation's economy.[32] By moving in this direction, Roosevelt was only being realistic: no amount of legislation, or uplifting speeches, were going to remake the American psyche, as it were. For it was the American people who killed the New Deal; that seems clear enough. Social experiments of a cooperative nature could make no headway in a "society" of individual atoms, each of which had been raised to believe that "getting mine" was what life was all about. With the end of World War II, the American population, notes Shi, "exploded in a frenzy of indiscriminate buying." So much for the alternative tradition.

And yet, although the alternative tradition never manages to make a substantive difference for business as usual in the United States, it nevertheless seems to have an odd habit of refusing to go away, and of enlisting the best minds of each generation in its support. If the period 1945–65 witnessed an orgy of suburbanization and consumer spending, it also produced a number of devastating critiques of the acquisitive way of life (in addition to that of Lewis Mumford, who was still hard at it): Erich Fromm, C. Wright Mills, Vance Packard, John Kenneth Galbraith, Paul Goodman, David Riesman—America hardly lacked for sophisticated "alternative" talent during these years. All of these writers wanted Americans to have loftier goals, to have real meaning in their lives beyond the latest toaster or electric lawn mower. All of them wrote best-selling books; Packard's work was literally off the charts. Americans read, nodded in agreement, and then went out and bought a second car and a truckload of appliances.[33]

As a cultural phenomenon, Vance Packard remains a fascinating study. His three books of 1957–60 alone, which skewered the emptiness and destructiveness of American consumerism, sold five million copies. As a writer doing a kind of pop sociology, Packard's influence was enormous; and despite the fact that professional sociologists dismissed the work as simplistic or sloppy, the truth is that he got the questions right: he intuitively understood that the core of America's problem was the hustling life. Subsequent social critics, such as Oscar Lewis or Michael Harrington, argued that the real issue was not suburban affluence but urban poverty, and of course they had a point.[34] But I believe that what Packard was pointing to (and Galbraith as well, in *The Affluent Society*), namely the basic worldview of the American people, is finally the crucial factor here. After all, capitalism by its very nature divides people into winners and losers. If a society is going to be governed by the pursuit of affluence as its highest value rather than the public good ("wealth is the chief end of man," said Calvin Coolidge), a large gap between rich and poor will be the inevitable result. Urban poverty, in other words, is not a separate issue from suburban wealth; they are a matched set, so to speak. And once we grasp how pervasive that worldview or value system is, it becomes obvious that the only difference between rich and poor is that the former have lots of money and the latter do not. Capitalism is above all a culture, a mind-set, as Joyce Appleby points out in her recent book *The Relentless Revolution*. With rare exceptions, as the labor leader Samuel Gompers once made perfectly clear, the poor in America have never wanted a fundamentally different type of society; they just wanted a larger cut of the pie. But a poor hustler is still a hustler; the social vision (if so it can be called) remains the same. As indicated earlier, Americans do not find George Babbitt pathetic, or see Bill Gates as an entrepreneurial vampire; far from it. Rather, they wish to *be* these people, and believe that what America fundamentally is and should be about is the encouragement and opportunity to do so. The hustling life is finally a type of cancer at the very center of the nation's soul, and it is this that Packard rightly denounced.

Packard took all this on in his "affluence trilogy"—*The Hidden Persuaders*, *The Status Seekers*, and *The Waste Makers*. He showed how advertisers manipulated Americans into chasing ever-higher levels of consumption by means of "motivational research," which played on their fears of sexual inadequacy and low social status. These techniques, he said, had turned his fellow citizens "into voracious, wasteful, compulsive consumers." It also turned adults into emotionally needy children, and was fundamentally disrespectful of human beings, in his view. But neither did he regard these consumers as innocent victims; after all, he said, "we can choose not to be persuaded." For Packard, it came down to what type of society we wanted to have and what type of people we wanted to be. The "morality of a society that was built on happiness derived primarily from consumer goods," remarks Daniel Horowitz, was for Packard no morality at all. Packard argued that there was no real difference between the Roman masses going to the circuses and the American masses going to shopping malls or department stores. Instead of "the all-pervading smog of commercialism," wrote Packard, we could have a "mature citizenry" interested in "self-respect, serenity, and individual fulfillment." Americans, he went on, must come "to see that cherished values and integrity of the soul have more to do with a well-spent life than self-indulgence." As in the case of Mumford, we have to wonder what planet he was living on; but clearly, his heart was in the right place.[35]

Packard's solution to our national disease was thus voluntaristic. A "modern Isaiah crying out in the wilderness of tail fins" (as one minister in Pittsburgh called him), he appealed to individual effort, and possibly to the activity of nonprofit organizations, to precipitate a major shift in our fundamental sensibilities and way of life. He sought to reverse the American formula of private opulence/public poverty, and attacked the idea that an expanding GDP (or GNP, as it was then called) was the mark of national success. He was a bit ahead of his time in calling for limits on population growth, an end to planned obsolescence, and plans for recycling used materials. But he conceded that all of this might not work; that there might be no alternative, in the United States, to a life of wasteful consumption. Packard was, in other words, a realist as well as a prophet.

And speaking of reality, what was the result of this life-long jeremiad? One reviewer notes that although readers were enthusiastic about his work, they "seemed astoundingly resistant to its critical message." They actually wrote in to ask Packard how they might use motivational psychology to get ahead! Fans of *The Status Seekers* were extremely eager to learn how they might improve their social status. Apparently the book provided them with useful material in this regard, as it identified the most lucrative occupations and the cars/houses/colleges that were the best markers of elevated social status. Packard's writings also led to a demand for more motivational research by corporations and manufacturers, and advertisements for goods that Packard personally despised subsequently played on themes he introduced in his work. I very much doubt that the irony of these sorts of things was lost on him.

We get some idea, then, of the fate of all this. Horowitz notes that Packard's vision was that of "a better world, one characterized by honest work, simple living, and community cohesion. . . . Packard stood for a virtuous life based on civic responsibility. . . . He remained skeptical about the benefits of material progress, which he believed threatened to undermine a moral economy." This is, of course, quite admirable, but the responses of companies seeking to hone their advertising techniques, and of readers in search of "insider info" on how to better move up the social ladder, do tend to put a damper on the ultimate effectiveness of this modern Isaiah. And if we look at where the United States eventually wound up in the wake of all this—at ever more grotesque levels of conspicuous consumption, and an ever greater commitment to Reaganomics and the pursuit of wealth—it is hard to see Packard as anything more than a brilliant comet that momentarily streaked across the night sky and then was gone. In the context of what America is, this may well be the best we can expect from the alternative tradition in general. And yet the members of this generation, including Mumford, Galbraith, Rachel Carson, Paul Goodman, and the beatniks of the fifties, did set the stage for an unusual period in American history, roughly that of 1965–80, when the alternative tradition did enlist relatively large numbers of people in its cause. It culminated in the "spiritual malaise" speech of President Carter in 1979, which I regard as the alternative tradition's last stand. After that, hustling and Reaganism took over in earnest, with a force that even the economic crash of 2008 has not been able to derail.[36] Over and over again, the message is clear: what we were in the late sixteenth century, we continue to be today. The alternative tradition, republicanism included, is finally nothing more than a gadfly in American history, or a kind of parenthesis, if you will.

The sixties, of course, were about a lot of things, most notably the opposition to the war in Vietnam. For our purposes— the critique of affluence and the rejection of the hustling life—this period did have great significance, at least for a time, in terms of ideology, symbolism, and values. If it, along with the seventies, can be called a parenthesis within the dominant tradition, it was nevertheless a dramatic one. Works such as *Life Against Death* (1959), by Norman O. Brown, *One-Dimensional Man* (1964), by Herbert Marcuse, and *The Pursuit of Loneliness* (1970), by Philip Slater, were milestones in psychology, political theory, and sociology. They shined a harsh and unsparing light on the destructive nature of the techno-commercial society, and the enormous human costs it extracts. Best-selling works such as *The Greening of America* (1970), by Charles Reich, and *The Making of a Counter Culture* (1969), by Theodore Roszak, said similar things, but in a much more popular (and often misguided and superficial) way. *The Graduate*, released in 1967, was memorable for its depiction of the vapidity of affluence, and included the famous word of advice to Dustin Hoffman's character—"plastics"—that was as much a reference to the older generation's way of life as it was to new career and investment opportunities. The rejection of that way of life was everywhere in evidence, as huge numbers of young people had sex, took drugs, dropped out of "the system," formed or joined communes, read Eastern philosophy, and wound up at Woodstock. Shortly after that, they had a good laugh at Janis Joplin's ridicule of the middle-class prayer for a Mercedes-Benz. From the viewpoint of the dominant culture, it was as though American society had gone completely loco; but since the alternative tradition, now unexpectedly "overground," regarded the dominant culture as the insane one, it was largely a matter of which end of the telescope one was looking through.

The movement, as it turned out, had several huge drawbacks. For one thing, it wasn't a movement. It was generally unfocused, a scattershot kind of protest aimed at "the establishment." Its politics were largely that of an alternate lifestyle, emphasizing things such as music and dress, and heavily based on the idea of a change in consciousness as the crucial factor. Protesters tended to come from middle-class and well-off families, and their focus was (in typical American style) primarily on individual rather than social change, especially as the sixties mutated into the seventies. As has been said many times, the whole thing was easily co-opted by Madison Avenue, as the alternative lifestyle became chic and lent itself to a vast array of trendy products and advertising. The superficiality and self-centeredness of this era, ironically enough, eventually transitioned into Thatcherism and Reaganism; and the "me" decade of the seventies saw a plethora of aggressive, hustling-type books such as the Ayn Randish texts of Robert J. Ringer (*Winning Through Intimidation*, *Looking Out for Number One*, and *Restoring the American Dream*). As someone famously observed, the "summer of love" lasted about two months. Woodstock and Wall Street were never really that far apart anyway.[37]

That being said, I confess I am not as cynical about this era as are many other writers and historians, although the channeling of countercultural energy into big business was real enough. But it seems to me that the sixties served as an important bridge between the social analysis mounted by thinkers such as Galbraith and Packard in the fifties, and the subsequent concern about the environment. It also sent shock waves around the world: no matter how superficial much of it was, it provided a clear demonstration that potentially millions of people did not want mindless nine-to-five jobs, bigger tail fins on their cars, and a life of unending competition and acquisition. The period was not all frivolity and co-optation, in short; it was also characterized by a major search for meaning, an asking of fundamental philosophical questions, publicly debated: What is a human being? What are we doing on this earth? What can we, and should we, hope for? What is the good society? The decade generated some very admirable leaders, such as Mario Savio and Tom Hayden, who stuck to their ideals after the bubble burst, as well as activists who later took up careers in pollution and poverty law, for example. Not everyone went the way of Jerry Rubin.

By and large it did, of course, morph into the "me" decade, as Tom Wolfe called it; but as noted, the 1970s also saw the rise of a serious environmental movement that was clearly connected to a critique of affluence and conspicuous consumption. The connection between automobiles and pollution was the most obvious example, but it went far beyond this, for it was becoming obvious that the earth did not have the carrying capacity to tolerate a population increase of several billion more people (*The Population Bomb*, by Paul Ehrlich in 1968, was a runaway best seller), nor the endlessly expanding economic growth model epitomized by the United States. The first Earth

Day celebration took place on April 22, 1970; the remainder of the decade saw the publication of *The Closing Circle* (1971), by Barry Commoner; *The Limits to Growth* (1972), by the Club of Rome; *Small Is Beautiful* (1973), by E. F. Schumacher; *Turtle Island* (1975), by Gary Snyder (which won him a Pulitzer, and which contained his famous 1969 ecological essay "Four Changes"); Laurance Rockefeller's 1976 *Reader's Digest* article "The Case for the Simple Life-Style"; and James Lovelock's *Gaia: A New Look at Life on Earth* (1979), which argued that the earth was a single living organism. Environmental activists and readers were additionally inundated by the work of William Ophuls, Herman Daly, Amory Lovins, and Wendell Berry, as well as publications such as *The Whole Earth Catalog* and *Mother Earth News*.[38]

There were many components to the environmental message, but at the top of the list was the notion that the earth was running out of resources and that only the practice of a simpler lifestyle and chastened consumption could save us and it. "Plain living and high thinking," along with "voluntary simplicity," were definitely de rigueur in those days, along with the idea of a steady-state economy. Growth for growth's sake was regarded as gross; organic gardening, recycling, "appropriate (or soft) technology," and "human scale" were the new buzzwords and activities. Much of this was fueled (no pun intended) by the Arab oil embargo of 1973–74, which also led to bicycle riding and car pooling. Various polls taken during the decade revealed that a substantial fraction of the American population was attracted to simple living and to a lifestyle of self-restraint. Indeed, the value of an economic crunch for austerity and asceticism (now seen as positive) was a popular theme during this era. *New York Times* editor James Reston thought shortages a good thing in this regard, leading him to encourage his fellow Americans "to cut down, slow up, stay at home, run around the block, eat vegetable soup, call up old friends and read a book once in a while." And meditate, of course: Buddhism was very much in vogue during this time as well.

Considering how virtually all of this blew away like dandelion spores in the wind in the wake of Reagan's inauguration and the reassertion of the dominant tradition, it is interesting to peer back into that decade and recapture the sense of permanence with which many of its participants viewed all these changes. In 1979, for example, the historian Ray Allen Billington wrote that we had reached the limits of the acquisitive lifestyle and that future historians would regard the seventies as the turning point in American civilization. Another historian, Richard Brown, argued that modernization was not the same thing as improvement and that the direction in which it pointed—illustrated by *1984* and *Brave New World*—was hardly better than the traditional societies of premodern peoples (shades of Claude Lévi-Strauss). The epilogue to Brown's book on the subject (published in 1976) made it clear that he believed the new change in outlook was here to stay. In this, Brown was merely echoing a belief held by many at the time, that the American way of life was finally at an end and that the world of "small is beautiful" and "limits to growth" was, in effect, America's new social and economic regime. Confidence in modernization is waning, he wrote; once it was a bright hope, now a source of anxiety. Americans have come to see it as destructive of their personal lives, their society, and the natural environment. Progress and the rational economic order have been called into question; we now realize that we have been on the wrong path. We no longer believe in unlimited economic expansion, he concluded, for we finally recognize that "dignity and human scale are essential if life is to have any meaning." Lewis Mumford couldn't have said it better.[39]

It was in this cultural climate—or so he thought—that Jimmy Carter was led to deliver his "spiritual malaise" speech of July 15, 1979. It was quite remarkable: to my knowledge, no other president ever gave an address that rejected the hustling tradition in extended detail, and in no uncertain terms. But as I argue in *Dark Ages America*, Carter was an anomaly: given the history of America down to 1973, he never should have been nominated, let alone elected. The period of 1974–76, however, was an unusual one, and it enabled him to land in the White House almost by accident. There was the defeat in Vietnam, a venture that had the taint, by the early seventies, of appearing shabby and immoral. The year 1974 saw the disgraceful resignation of a Republican president who came off looking like a hood, a vulgar mafioso; and then came the Senate hearings of 1975–76 (the Church Committee) on the dirty tricks of the CIA, including its role in engineering the violent overthrow of the democratically elected president of Chile. The Arab oil embargo had pointedly demonstrated our dependence on foreign energy and hence the vulnerability of our economy, which in turn threw the ideology of unlimited economic expansion into question. That the country had seriously gone astray was a rather glaring fact of American political life. We not only looked weak, we actually looked squalid, even in our own eyes. And then along comes a dark horse, a relative political unknown, who says all of this up front and who insists (using Christian rhetoric) that the nation needed to do some serious soul-searching, put its *own* house in order, and stop blaming everybody else (notably the Soviet Union) for all its problems. Selling weapons systems to developing countries and propping up dictators and torture regimes, said Mr. Carter, are not what America is supposed to be about. Decency, dignity, human rights, self-determination—*these* are the things with which America should concern itself. For a brief moment in time, lasting about two years or so into his presidency, the message struck a resonant chord.[40]

In his inaugural address, Mr. Carter threw down the gauntlet: more was not necessarily better; and this, along with the closely related question of energy consumption, became a major theme of his administration. Like one of his heroes, E. F. Schumacher, whom he invited to the White House in 1977, the new president deliberately cultivated a "plain style." After his inauguration, he walked from the Capitol to the White House. He sold off the presidential yacht, eliminated other official trappings of wealth, and subsequently installed solar panels (removed by Ronald Reagan in 1986) on top of the presidential residence. The message he was sending to the American people was clear; and given the temper of the times, and the apparently widespread appetite for a whole new way of life, it seemed like the right moment to try to turn the nation around.[41]

Americans, however, have a very short memory, and this did not work in Jimmy's favor. By 1979, they had managed to recover from the shame of Watergate and Vietnam, and wanted to return to a more muscular and military foreign policy. Increasingly, Carter was branded a "liberal" (in the American political sense), as if that were somehow a badge of shame. There was, by this time, a strong desire to get back to business as usual in every sphere of American life, and it was in this context that he addressed the nation on what he felt was ailing it. Whether the president understood it or not, by 1979 he was definitely swimming against the tide. Given his conviction that the root of the problem was a major error in value systems, it was hard to avoid coming off like an Old Testament prophet. Mr. Carter never actually used the world "malaise" in his speech, but that was what he was talking about. "In a nation that was proud of hard work, strong families, close-knit communities, and our faith in God," he told his listeners,

> too many of us now tend to worship self-indulgence and consumption. Human identity is no longer defined by what one does, but by what one owns. But we've discovered that owning things and consuming

things does not satisfy our longing for meaning. We've learned that piling up material goods cannot fill the emptiness of lives which have no confidence or purpose.

We can, he went on, choose "the path that leads to fragmentation and self-interest. Down that road lies a mistaken idea of freedom, the right to grasp for ourselves some advantage over others." The other path, the one we should be on, is that of "common purpose and the restoration of American values"—republicanism, in a word.[42]

Where was the president coming from? One thing that stands out is his roots in the American South. The speech sounded like something the South might have said to the North, or about the North (and in fact did say, in so many words) on the eve of the Civil War. As will be seen in chapter 4, the South saw itself as the traditional representative of American values, of virtue in the classical sense of the term, and regarded the North as hustling, greedy, and acquisitive. Like a white southerner, Carter emphasized integrity and simplicity. But in addition, he had recently taken three prominent intellectuals as his advisers—Daniel Bell, Christopher Lasch, and Robert Bellah—all of whom had written with concern and even anger about the hedonism and self-indulgence of the American way of life. Bell, in *The Cultural Contradictions of Capitalism* (1976), castigated "the temptation of private enrichment at the expense of the public weal," and declared that America was essentially nihilistic in its orientation. Bellah, in *The Broken Covenant* (1975), wrote that "this society is a cruel and bitter one" and that there was little motive in the United States to do anything beyond the self. Hence, he predicted, what lay ahead for the nation was not revival but decline. Lasch, in his best-selling *The Culture of Narcissism* (1979), argued that the ethic of consumption and competitive individualism had led to a war of all against all and was finishing us off as a civilization. He subsequently described our way of life in incandescent phrases that captured the attitude of the Southern Agrarians of the 1930s (see chapter 4) perfectly: "rootless existence," "craving for novelty and contempt for the past," "'other-directed' round of life," etc.[43]

There were many problems with the speech, which was, of course, picked apart and debated in the press. But the major one was that it was out of touch with what the American people actually wanted. All that environmental activism to the contrary, most Americans wanted to go on consuming; they had no interest in changing their lives in any substantial way, and that was what the president was asking them to do. (This was not the "poetry" of JFK's inaugural address, in other words.) When Carter called for the "restoration of American values" as opposed to "the right to grasp for ourselves some advantage over others," he failed to understand that this latter mode of existence *was* the American value system, historically speaking, and not some recent kind of "deviant" behavior. Did Carter seriously think that America could pick up the republican thread of our Revolutionary days? What restoration did he possibly have in mind? Thoreau? Mumford? The antebellum South (minus the slavery)? As the saying goes, give me a break. It should not surprise us to learn that in the wake of that speech, some members of Congress took to the floor to question his mental health. And this probably wasn't rhetorical: in the United States, private interest *is* "virtue," and genuine dedication to the commonweal is, if not actually regarded as demented, then viewed as softheaded in the extreme. What Carter was attempting was nothing less than a reversal of nearly four hundred years of American history. It wasn't well received.[44]

The following year, during the presidential campaign, Ronald Reagan charged that Carter "mistook the malaise among his own advisers, and in the Washington liberal establishment in general, for a malady afflicting the nation as a whole." He had a point. As one critic has remarked, "best sellers do not constitute a political movement any more than they reveal much in depth about public opinion." If this was true of *The Status Seekers*, it was equally true of *The Whole Earth Catalog* and *Small Is Beautiful*. Much of the environmental movement had been froth; the ideas had not penetrated any deeper than the intellectual level, or that of cocktail-party chatter, and few of the changes that took place during the seventies were really widespread or enduring. What the movement amounted to, at least up to that point, was a kind of "ascetic chic." The notion of a purported shift in values from consumerism to the simple life had been very much overstated. The American public, it turned out, was not interested in some sermon or jeremiad about the limits to growth or the joys of solar power. Rather, they wanted to spend their eyeballs out once again, and it is no surprise that Mr. Reagan, who told them that they could and should do it, won by a landslide (489 to 49 electoral votes). No use blaming the Iran hostage crisis; given the dominant tradition in American history, Reagan's victory over Carter was like shooting fish in a barrel.[45]

After his inauguration, Mr. Carter walked down Pennsylvania Avenue. As for Mr. Reagan: bring on the limos, Jeeves; that man wasn't walking anywhere. The Reagan inauguration ran up a tab of $11 million. Nancy Reagan's wardrobe cost $25,000, and she subsequently bought a new set of china for the White House to the tune of $200,000. The lineup of private jets, jeweled boots, and fur coats led one columnist for the *Washington Post* to comment that "the absolutely appalling consumerism" made her sick. But it didn't make the American public sick, who had had it with Carter's cardigan sweaters and his boots from L. L. Bean, and who enjoyed participating in the new opulence—at least vicariously. This was what, in its mind, America was all about. A few months later, *U.S. News*

& *World Report* declared that a "flaunt-it-if-you-have-it lifestyle is rippling in concentric circles across the land." The president declared "America is back," by which he seemed to be saying, shop till you drop.[46]

Posing as the Marlboro Man (sans cigarettes) in his election campaign ads, Mr. Reagan knew what he was doing. America stood for the endless frontier, the world without limits, and as Reagan pursued that in government—tripling the national debt beyond the $3 trillion mark in very short order—so did he encourage the same among American citizens. He was, writes Andrew Bacevich, "the modern prophet of profligacy—the politician who gave moral sanction to the empire of consumption." His version of the American Dream included the belief that "credit has no limits, and the bills will never come due." The truth is that Reagan was a fiscal conservative in name only; he said one thing and did another. He didn't follow his own ideology, didn't once turn in a balanced budget to Congress. For Reagan "understood what made Americans tick: they wanted self-gratification, not self-denial." Personal savings, which had averaged 8 to 10 percent of disposable income during the post–World War II era, was almost down to zero by 1985.[47]

In retrospect, it is clear that Carter's "narrative" of American life—basically, that of the alternative tradition—could not possibly compete with Reagan's. Carter was calling for inner richness and outward simplicity; Reagan, for outward richness and inner vacuity, a combination that resonated extremely well with the American people. Indeed, the major appeal of the tried-and-true Reagan formula was that outward richness would serve as compensation for that vacuity; not much soul-searching was required. In so many ways, Reagan set the template for the next thirty years and beyond. The only Democratic president during that period was effectively a Republican, terminating the welfare system and subscribing to economic growth as the answer to America's ills. The dot-com crash of 2000 was but a hiccup in this trajectory; even the massive crash of 2008 made little difference for Reaganomics, or for the Reaganesque worldview. There was a bit of talk about resurrecting Keynes, but President Obama made sure to appoint neoliberal economic advisers who held the very ideology that led to the crash, and to bail out the banks and the wealthy, much as Reagan did with the savings and loan failures of the eighties. And by January 2010, Americans were back to spending, as the month saw a $5 billion increase in consumer credit. The lavishness and huge indebtedness of American life during the Reagan years were certainly repeated and amplified in the decades following, and there is every reason to believe that short of a complete and total breakdown of the system, they will endure, for they represent the deepest aspirations of the American people—their true religion. This was the sad fact of American history, and American life, that Mr. Carter never understood (or perhaps didn't want to face). To this day, in survey after survey, Americans consistently rank Ronald Reagan high on their list of presidents whom they admire. He offered them a fairy tale, and given the choice, Americans will always opt for the Disney version.[48]

But despite what most Americans believe, the Disney version is not real life; and a commitment to fantasy can only result in disaster. We saw this in 2008. Yet even then, Americans have a remarkable ability, as Garrison Keillor once pointed out, "to look reality right in the eye and deny it." The result is what any intelligent person might expect. Unfortunately for America, it doesn't seem to have too many such people among its population. Conventional wisdom to the contrary, Wall Street and Main Street are not that far apart.

THE REIGN OF
WALL STREET

That which seems to be wealth may in verity be only the gilded index of far-reaching ruin . . . the idea that directions can be given for the gaining of wealth, irrespectively of the consideration of its moral sources . . . is perhaps the most insolently futile of all that ever beguiled men through their vices.

—John Ruskin, *Unto This Last*

In the end, the triumph of economic growth is not a triumph of humanity over material wants; rather, it is the triumph of material wants over humanity.

—Richard Easterlin, *Growth Triumphant*

To look back at the eighties is to view a pretty familiar landscape. Newsstands were filled with *Money* magazines and other similar, glossy periodicals. Yuppie lifestyles were always in the news, and financial planning was all the rage. Steven Jobs, Donald Trump, and Bill Gates were the featured heroes; shows about millionaires, such as *Dynasty* and *Dallas*, were extremely popular. An article in *Business Week* in 1985 declared that "Consumers Are Spending the Economy to Health," as the yuppies had to have Cuisinarts and chic food products (Grey Poupon mustard, Dannon yogurt), car phones, Sony Walkmans, VCRs, home video game systems, and every other type of high-tech gadget imaginable. Between 1981 and 1985 alone, Americans purchased 62 million microwave ovens, 63 million VCRs, 57 million washers and dryers, 88 million cars and light trucks, 105 million color television sets, 31 million cordless phones, and 30 million telephone answering machines. They made 7 billion trips in and out of shopping centers, and eventually the home computer, along with TV channels such as the Home Shopping Network, added to the frenzy of buying, such that home shopping sales went from $1 million in 1982 to $1.4 billion in 1989. By the mideighties the average credit card holder carried no fewer than seven cards. Ads on television and in popular magazines showed attractive men and women dining in fashionable restaurants, driving BMWs, or sitting at gleaming computers in sleek corporate environments. Clearly, the "good life" was here to stay.[1]

The ideology that legitimized this way of life was a recycled New Age version of Norman Vincent Peale's "power of positive thinking." In one form or another—therapy, "recovery" groups, self-help books, Werner Erhard's "est," and the like—the notion that thought determined reality, and that individual effort joined to positive thinking was therefore the key to success, literally blanketed the United States during the Reagan-Clinton years. As Janice Peck shows in *The Age of Oprah*, it was the perfect philosophy (theology might be more accurate) for the neoliberal era, with Oprah Winfrey acting as its most visible spokesperson. If she never actually endorsed Mr. Reagan, the idea behind the "law of attraction" was that you made your own reality—a philosophy that puts the onus on the individual to think his or her way to success and fortune; the obvious corollary being that if you've failed to do this, it's due to a lack of will or "right thinking." "Freedom," in effect, was now defined as chic consumerism, hustling, and self-promotion with a pseudo-religious twist. Oprah presented herself as the ultimate rags-to-riches story, whereas in truth it was black political activism and the civil rights movement that made her career possible. The embarrassing facts of sociopolitical context, however, were systematically excluded from the "analysis" presented on *The Oprah Winfrey Show*, in which hard-core economic realities were inevitably dismissed or reduced to matters of individual psychology. Any discussion of a Marxist or sociological or sociocritical nature was repeatedly curtailed. Poverty as well as wealth, she stated repeatedly, came down to a personal decision, and this was a worldview that meshed extremely well with the laissez-faire ideology of Reaganomics and beyond. (Recall that Mr. Reagan once declared that homeless people were homeless because they wanted to be.) For one thing, it flattered the yuppie class, which was able to interpret its financial success in terms of its own individual efforts and personal (specifically, spiritual) qualities. By 2000, as Peck observes, Oprah's spiritual capitalism had acquired an "extraordinary consumer reach," having attracted the sponsorship of Ford, Microsoft, ABC/ Disney, and numerous other corporate sponsors (a sure sign, in my opinion, that something was seriously wrong with the whole thing). Her huge public acclaim reflects the fact that by and large, Americans regard capital accumulation as the purpose of life, and an abundance of consumer possessions as evidence of correct spiritual orientation (or even divine validation). Social context, let alone grassroots political organizing, doesn't figure very large in this vision, which is, like Reaganism, a species of fantasy.[2]

Meanwhile, what was Mr. Reagan up to, beyond engaging in an orgy of government spending that tripled the national debt? First, he made the rich much richer. During the eighties, most of the nation's income gains went to the top 1–2 percent of households. The program of lower taxes on high incomes, and deregulation of business, started a trajectory that saw to it that the income of the top .01 percent of Americans rose sevenfold over 1980–2007. The typical American family, however, saw no significant income gains during the Reagan administration. "Trickle-down" economics was basically a scam: very little trickled down. The real philosophy of the fortieth president, as William Greider notes, was "encourage the strong, forget the weak." The middle class was squeezed, the poverty rate increased, industrial wages stagnated, and there was an increasing loss of U.S. manufacturing, along with a massive assault on American labor. The country got a lot meaner; the general outlook was nakedly, as never before, every man for himself. The triumphalism of the Reagan era was false, an ever-expanding bubble. In *Day of Reckoning*, Benjamin Friedman branded Reaganomics a collective national folly, pointing out that the United States went from largest creditor nation in 1980 to largest debtor nation by 1986. "This sense of economic well-being was an illusion," he wrote; "America has thrown itself a party and billed the tab to the future."[3]

But it was even more pernicious than this. In *A Brief History of Neoliberalism*, David Harvey points out that what Reagan had in mind went beyond ordinary finance capital, as destructive as that was. Globalization and neoliberal economics, he says, constitute an ethic, a belief that all human action is to be governed by the market. The "neoliberal state" is what the United States became during the Reagan years, and what the country decided to export to the rest of the world—by force if necessary (hence the largest peacetime military buildup in American history during this time). In this vision, the basic purpose of the state apparatus is capital accumulation, such that "freedom" and "free enterprise" become one and the same. Across the nation, says Harvey, people welfare was replaced by corporate welfare. The result, he concludes, was increasing social incoherence. What you eventually got was more crime, sex trafficking, and even slavery (the return of sweatshops, even in New York). The mood became one of helplessness and anxiety, which has been pervasive in the United States for some time now, and which America has managed to export to the rest of the planet. On a world scale, this ethic leaves billions poorer while it creates a tiny, and immensely wealthy, elite. As for the middle class—what's left of it—life has been reduced to shopping, "a world of pseudo-satisfactions that is superficially exciting but hollow at its core."[4]

The nineties saw no letup from this pattern. Clinton's 1993 inauguration cost a whopping $33 million; his focus was the economy, and the unstated agenda of his presidency can be summarized as "Let's all make money!" These were the years of the dot-com bubble and its collapse, and the heyday of wealth as a virtue. The nation went into work overdrive. In 2000, the average

American couple worked a full seven weeks more than they did in 1990. People were constantly hustling, constantly scrambling to get ahead, always available via cell phone, beeper, fax, voice mail, e-mail, you name it. Parents spent less time with children, and spouses less time with each other. Friendship was practically a thing of the past, as Americans went "bowling alone." The market assumed the status of a divinity, and economists raved about the wealthy as the real winners in life. By 1995, 1 percent of the American population owned 47 percent of the nation's wealth, and during 1995–99, 86 percent of market advances went to the richest 10 percent of the population. Between 1998 and 2001 (the year the Enron scandal broke), one thousand corporate executives awarded themselves $66 billion in salaries and bonuses; Qwest transferred $2.3 billion from workers' pensions into the pockets of those running the company. The year 2002 saw a cascade of revelations regarding corporate fraud, including Qwest, WorldCom, AOL, and a host of others. Meanwhile, books with titles such as *God Wants You to Be Rich* and *Jesus, CEO*, filled the bookstore shelves, while *The Millionaire Next Door* (1996) sold more than two million copies and was on the best-seller list for more than three years. Its message: wealth is within reach of everybody. As in the case of Oprah, Suze Orman told her PBS viewing audience much the same thing, connecting cash flow to "spirituality." Meanwhile, real wages declined: workers were much worse off in the nineties than they had been in the sixties and seventies. Nonbusiness bankruptcy filings topped one million for the first time, in 1996. As for the poor, Mr. Clinton called on U.S. businesses to invest in depressed communities not because it was morally right, but because it would make them rich. (It never happened, in any case.)[5]

As might be expected, the George W. Bush years were among the worst. The 2001 inauguration cost $40 million, and the one in 2005 about the same, adjusting for inflation. At the

Alfred E. Smith memorial dinner in October 2000, Mr. Bush looked out over the $800-a-plate crowd and jokingly referred to them as "the haves and the have mores." "Some people call you the elite," he went on; "I call you my base." But Bush was not kidding; the remark was right on the money (so to speak). Bush reduced taxes on his "base" as the war in Iraq progressed, meaning that the cost of it would be borne by the rest of the population (which also traditionally does all the actual fighting and dying). During these years, the looting of the public sector for the benefit of private interests—what John Kenneth Galbraith's son would refer to as the "predator state"—was reaching unprecedented highs (or lows, might be more accurate). As for average Americans, in the wake of 9/11 the president suggested they visit Disney World, while other politicians urged them to go shopping ("market patriotism," Robert Reich called it). In general, writes Andrew Bacevich, "the Bush administration welcomed the average citizen's inclination to ignore the war and return to the mall." Personal savings continued to drop, with the total public debt exceeding $9 trillion in 2006 (nearly 70 percent of the GDP). The previous year, 2 million Americans filed for bankruptcy, or 1 in every 150 people.[6]

I have already suggested that very little changed with the 2008 presidential election. Mr. Obama praised Ronald Reagan during the election campaign for his "sense of dynamism and entrepreneurship that had been missing," thereby dismissing (and misunderstanding) what Jimmy Carter had been trying to do. The Obama inauguration was up there with the best of them—$45 million—and the general Reaganesque pattern of surface glitz and underlying human suffering, and of looting the public sector, continued apace. Writing in the *New York Times* in August 2009, economist Paul Krugman pointed out that "Washington . . . is still ruled by Reaganism." "I had actually hoped that the failure of Reaganism in practice would kill it," he continued. "It turns out, however, to be a zombie doctrine: even though it should be dead, it keeps on coming. . . . The astonishing thing about the current political scene is the extent to which nothing has changed." As already noted, Obama's economic advisers are neoliberals, and one of them, Lawrence Summers (a major proponent of deregulation), was apparently taking kickbacks (mostly lavish lecture fees) from the very banks he later helped to bail out—with not a whisper of reprimand from his boss (Summers left the job in November 2010). Ben Bernanke was reappointed chairman of the Federal Reserve in 2009, and the white paper published by the Treasury Department that year ("Financial Regulatory Reform") made no attempt to understand why the crash of 2008 even occurred. This suggests that the Obama administration does not know how to reform Wall Street, and probably doesn't wish to do so in any case. (Or oddly regards Wall Street's "innovations" as somehow up to the task. Once again, America put its faith in progress as the way to cure the ills brought on by progress.) As one observer points out, "much of Wall Street has already returned to the aggressive practices that were widespread before the crisis, including high levels of compensation and the creation and trading of risky derivative contracts." Joseph Stiglitz adds, "Instead of redesigning the system, the administration spent much of the money on reinforcing the existing, failed system." It started with a $700 billion bailout and quickly swelled to a commitment of $12 trillion, and finally wound up above $19 trillion. And while the Treasury Department could have required the recipients of this money to report on how they spent it, it chose not to; which means that there is a great likelihood of fraud and corruption. As the economist Dean Baker remarks, this is a way to subsidize banks without the public realizing that the government "gave money away to some of the richest people." The Obama strategy is basically What's good for Wall Street is good for the USA. Mr. Reagan would surely have agreed.[7]

The domination of America by Wall Street has been the subject of some pretty no-nonsense reporting during the past few years. Matt Taibbi, a journalist for *Rolling Stone*, and Nomi Prins, a former managing director of Goldman Sachs who left to devote her energies to the alternative tradition (if indeed it even exists anymore; she is now, in any case, a senior fellow at Demos, a progressive think tank), have both written about the incestuous relationship between the federal government and GS. Goldman Sachs has essentially packed the Treasury Department and the Federal Reserve with its alumni, such that we've now got Wall Street policing Wall Street—and the government. Taibbi calls it the "vampire squid"; "gangster elite" might be an equally apt description. Indeed, the whole process of the bailout becomes a lot clearer when you realize that the fox is guarding the henhouse. So Henry Paulson, GS CEO, becomes the Treasury secretary in 2004; Lloyd Blankfein succeeds him at GS, and gets praised by President Obama as a "savvy businessman" for awarding himself a bonus of $9 million. ("I, like most of the American people, don't begrudge people success or wealth. That is part of the free-market system.") Robert Rubin, a former GS CEO who served as Treasury secretary for Clinton, managed to get Mr. Obama to pick two of his protégés, Lawrence Summers and Timothy Geithner, as senior economic adviser and Treasury secretary, respectively. Geithner then selected Mark Patterson, a former GS lobbyist, as his chief of staff, and Gary Gensler, a former GS partner, was chosen by Mr. Obama to head the Commodities Futures Trading Commission. As Taibbi observes, nobody seems to notice this overlap or care very much, or else they argue that it makes sense to have experienced executives making major financial decisions for the federal government. He comments:

When Enron buys a seat at the table to conduct energy policy under the Bush administration, everyone knows what that is. When Reagan hires notorious union busters to run the National Labor Relations Board, everyone knows what that is. And when we hire investment bankers to run banking policy, and put investment bankers in charge of handing out bailout money to investment banks, we ought to know what that is. But for some reason we don't seem to see it the same way.[8]

In his notorious *Rolling Stone* exposé of Goldman Sachs of 2009, Taibbi again explicates the GS/federal government overlap and shows how GS promoted sham stocks in the 1990s (ones they knew would never make any money), which contributed to the dot-com crash, and how they subsequently created vehicles to package unreliable mortgages and sell them to insurance companies and pension funds, creating a mass market for toxic debt. It bothered them not at all that they were putting older people at risk, or potentially taking the American economy down the drain. He concludes:

After helping $5 trillion in wealth disappear from the NASDAQ, after pawning off thousands of toxic mortgages on pensioners and cities, after helping to drive the price of gas up to $4 a gallon and to push 100 million people around the world into hunger, after securing tens of billions of taxpayer dollars through a series of bailouts overseen by its former CEO, what did Goldman Sachs give back to the people of the United States in 2008?

Fourteen million dollars.

This is, he adds, an effective tax rate of 1 percent. It is not for nothing that the journalist Chris Hedges comments that "firms like Goldman Sachs are more dangerous to the nation than al-Qaida."[9]

As a former GS insider, Nomi Prins makes it abundantly clear that her ex-colleagues care absolutely nothing about the country, and everything about their own private wealth and power. The only good impression they hoped to make, in fact, was on each other; in this context, ethical considerations would have had the opposite effect. They believe, she writes, that their privileged position is their destiny, and regard themselves as being completely "above explaining their actions to the public or expressing anything that might look like contrition or humility." This proved to be true in April 2010, when the Senate finally dragged some of these executives to a hearing on GS business practices. The list of accusations was quite extensive: you stacked the deck against clients in the market slide of 2007; you set up your company's own securities to fail, secretly bet against those securities, and never told your buyers what you were doing; you dumped toxic mortgage assets on unwitting clients; etc. Several senators read aloud internal GS documents, in which these men boasted of how they had helped GS profit from the declining housing market, or described the firm's subprime deals in scatological terms. No matter; the Goldmanites refused to show any regret for their actions, and would not admit that they had behaved irresponsibly or had anything to do with the crash of 2008. A few argued that they were in fact the victims of this financial debacle. In fact, GS behavior continues much as before, as the subsequent Greek economic crisis, in which they played a key role, demonstrates.[10]

As disgusting as these companies, and these individuals, are, they are also, as we have seen, part of a long-range historical process that began more than four hundred years ago. It began in the spirit of enterprise, of self-confidence, but as Richard Henry Dana wrote (see the epigraph to this book), it inevitably became a very destructive force. That the hustling culture finally evolved into the thug culture, run by a gangster elite, is not that surprising. Pursued in a single-minded way, where else could it wind up? As Richard Powers shows in his award-winning novel *Gain*, the little soap and candle business in eighteenth-century Boston finally becomes the giant pharmaceutical firm in the late twentieth century that is polluting rivers, causing cancer, and trying to cover its tracks. What could be the psychology of an individual who thinks he needs a $9 million bonus on top of his already gargantuan salary? Hustling is a drug that admits of no limits, and has become the "vampire squid" that is killing us all.

"A financial system should be a means to an end," writes Nobel laureate Joseph Stiglitz, "not an end in itself." In saying this, he echoes John Maynard Keynes and even, in a way, the republicanism of John Winthrop. The fact is that given our own financial system, the greedy bankers were simply doing what everyone is doing, or aspires to do. They took advantage of the panic of 2008 "to take from the public purse to enrich their own." Their "moral depravity," their exploitation of the poor and the middle class, knew no bounds, because for them cash is "the end-all of life." "In Japanese society," Stiglitz continues, "a CEO who was responsible for destroying his firm, forcing thousands of workers to be laid off, might commit hari-kari [*sic*]. In the United Kingdom, CEOs resigned when their firms failed. In the United States, they are fighting over the size of their bonuses."[11]

All of this is true, but again, in a culture defined by hustling, cash is the end-all of life for literally everybody. This is why there is finally no use blaming Goldman Sachs or the corporate crowd exclusively, because Wall Street and Main Street pretty much converge. If you share the values of this culture, and act in concert with them; if you, like President Obama, admire Lloyd Blankfein and think his bonus was well deserved; if you shop like there's no tomorrow, and think the pursuit of affluence is what life is about; if you have no concern about the public sector or the commonweal, and regard Thoreau and Jimmy Carter as bad jokes; then you are, in your own little way, part of the gangster elite. There is something naive, or disingenuous, about putting the enemy completely "out there," on Wall Street or wherever—as culpable as those folks are. It's a little like complaining that "the traffic is awful today." The truth is, if you're on the freeway, you *are* the traffic. As George Walden writes in his aptly titled study *God Won't Save America: Psychosis of a Nation*, "The peculiarities of nations, good and bad, tend to reflect the temperaments and qualities of their peoples. As Plato remarked, where else would they have come from?"[12]

Meanwhile, the American people are back to spending, to the extent that they can. What else, indeed, is left to them, beyond work, if they can find it, and watching TV? Writing in the *Nation* in January 2009, political scientist Benjamin Barber tries to answer this question in a positive way; which means, of course, resurrecting the alternative tradition. He claims that what we need is a "revolution in spirit." The problem with Obama and his whole economic team, says Barber—and the whole country, for that matter—is that "No one is questioning the impulse to rehabilitate the consumer market as the driver of American commerce." What we need to do, he goes on, is take culture seriously. Establish a cabinet-level arts and humanities post to foster creative thinking, for example. "Imagine," he writes, "all the things we could do without having to shop: play and pray, create and relate, read and walk, listen and procreate—make art, make friends, make homes, make love." In short, "idealism must become the new realism." In fact,

Professor Barber has no suggestions as to how this might come about beyond exhortation and voluntary effort, and one gets the sense that he himself doesn't believe any of this will really happen. One can admire his Mumfordian sensibilities, but when I read the essay I frankly wondered what sort of high-grade weed the man was smoking. We are so committed to the primacy of private wealth over the public good that we can't even imagine what Europeans, Canadians, and Japanese (for example) take for granted: doctors making house calls, parents being paid to stay home and care for newborns, workers receiving several weeks of paid vacation every year, and paid sick leave as well. As for the life of the spirit, ours is not a population that reads much, walks much, places friendship ahead of career, or makes art. But Dr. Barber is no fool; he knows this—and so do you. We'll carry on hustling until we literally collapse from it (2008 being only a mild preview); this much is clear.[13]

Before I talk about the "end of days," so to speak, let me say a few words about the fallout from the hustling life—what has happened to the nation at the tail end of the whole experiment, as a result of living the way we do and rejecting the alternative tradition. To start with the immediate economic situation first: the housing and stock market crash of 2008 wiped out upward of $14 trillion in household wealth. Official statistics have it that 10 percent of the population is unemployed; in reality, it is probably closer to 20 percent. At the same time that Wall Street firms continue to award themselves huge bonuses, the former middle class is lining up at food banks and soup kitchens. "Millions of Unemployed Face Years without Jobs," announced the *New York Times* early in 2010. According to this article, labor experts say that "even a vigorous recovery is likely to leave an enormous number out of work for years." And as jobs have become as rare as hen's teeth, so has welfare: in forty-four states (this as of 2006) you are limited to $1,383 per month for a family of three to qualify for it. Millions of Americans have lost their homes. Meanwhile, the Obama administration, as we have seen, is busy funneling vast sums of money into the pockets of the rich; as always, the rest of us are left to fend for ourselves. Perhaps we should not be too surprised to learn that American children are more likely to die in infancy, or grow up in poverty, than the children in many other industrialized nations.[14]

The data on crime in the United States are quite startling as well: 25 percent of all the world's prisoners are locked up in American jails. In fact, if you count everyone caught up in the corrections system, including those on probation or parole, it amounts to 1 out of every 31 people! Between 1988 and 2008, spending on the prison system grew from 4 to 30 times the budget for public housing. The United States has the highest rate of homicide in the world (5.5 per 100,000 as of the year 2000), if countries caught up in serious political turmoil (such as Colombia) are excluded. It has four times the homicide rate of France and the United Kingdom and six times that of Germany. Also notable is the fact that while the homicide rate has been falling in Europe for centuries, the American rate has been higher than Europe's from the very start.[15]

It is not difficult to imagine that in a nation that is extremely acquisitive and competitive, and that enshrines a philosophy of You're on your own/Sink or swim, there would be a lot of crime and violence. One survey, for example, turned up the fact that 24 percent of Americans believe it is acceptable to use violence in the pursuit of one's goals. In addition, the work of Randolph Roth (*American Homicide*) and Gary LaFree (*Losing Legitimacy*) suggests that the high incidence of violent crime is a function of our politics, not just our culture. It seems that there is an inverse correlation between the crime rate and public faith in government. "The statistics make clear," writes Roth, "that in the twentieth century, homicide rates have fallen during the terms of presidents who have inspired the poor or have governed from the center of a popular mandate." This in turn might suggest that emphasis on the public good deters crime, while emphasis on private interest promotes it.[16]

To me, the worst type of fallout from the hustling life is the emotional climate in which American citizens are forced to live. It is one that generates, and reflects, a world of inner misery. I remember, a few years ago, being in the University of Maryland Hospital in Baltimore, and going to the men's room, only to find a man collapsed on the floor and someone else trying to lift him up. "Hang on," I said, "I'll go get help." The first person I encountered, outside the men's room, was a cop. When I explained what was going on, he told me he didn't work there and that I should go to the inpatient desk. The latter then sent me to Security, who told me they would call the Fire Department. I tried to show the Security officer which men's room I was talking about, and asked him if he would come with me . . . which he did, and then walked right by it, while I was calling to him, "It's here, he's right in here!" He never looked back, and the Fire Department never arrived. Not a single person I encountered was willing to spend five minutes to help someone who could have been dying, for all they knew; all of them just wanted to be left alone.[17]

Three years later, I watched a TV news report about a woman who collapsed on the floor of the waiting room of Kings County Hospital in Brooklyn, and lay there, face down, for an hour before anyone checked up on her, by which time she was dead. The video showed other people in the waiting room just sitting and watching her, not doing anything; and security guards occasionally looking in, then walking away. I wish I could have been able to interview some of the witnesses, ask, "What were you thinking when this woman fell off her chair and was lying face down on the floor?" But I know what the answer would be: "Nothing. I wasn't thinking anything at all." (Or possibly even, "Not my problem.") This numbness in the face of other human beings, my friends, is the essence of the American way of life.[18]

How did we get to this point? None of these things are aberrations of American life. That would be comforting, but it wouldn't be true. As noted above, a hustling culture cannot help but eventually evolve into a thug culture, and the thugs are not only on Wall Street; they also sit in hospital waiting rooms indifferently watching people die. Douglas LaBier, a psychotherapist in Washington, D.C., has a name for this type of behavior, which he says is rampant in the United States: empathy deficit disorder. Basically, it's just a fancy term for not giving a damn about anybody but yourself. LaBier claims that empathy is a natural emotion, but that Americans unlearn it from an early age because ours is a society that focuses on acquisition and status and avoids inner reflection. In my own experience of living in the United States, it constitutes an ambience or atmosphere; you can feel this kind of "autistic hostility" in the air, in the everyday interactions between people. It shows up as a kind of soullessness, of which Washington, D.C., is a perfect example (I lived there for eight years). "If you want a friend in this town," Harry Truman famously remarked, "get yourself a dog." But quite obviously, this is hardly limited to the nation's capital.[19]

What competition and acquisitiveness do is break down the likelihood not only of empathy, but also of human attachment *tout court*. How lonely Americans are! Between 1985 and 2004, the number of people who said that there was no one with whom they could discuss "important matters" tripled, rising to 25 percent. And more than 25 percent of American households, according to the 2000 U.S. Census, consist of only one person (in 1940 the figure was 7.7 percent). It is one of the highest rates of aloneness in the world, if not the highest, and the figure for

New York City is actually 48 percent. The problem with this is that the need for attachment lies at the center of the human psyche; it goes back to birth. Various studies show that social isolation tends to lead to early death, as well as depression— the rate of which has been growing steadily since 1960, while the suicide rate among the young tripled from 1960 to 2000. Thomas Lewis and his colleagues, in *A General Theory of Love*, conclude that happiness is achieved only by those who manage to escape the American value system. "Before our lives wither away into dust," they write, "we might ponder how much more prosperity human beings can possibly survive."[20]

In *Why We Hate Us*, Dick Meyer, the executive editor of NPR News, does a good job of describing the cultural effects of unlimited consumerism and the worship of wealth (both of which are actively promoted by the *New York Times*, as he points out). "Emotional malnutrition" leads the list, as Americans now suffer from a famine of interpersonal relationships. So boorish and aggressive have we become—road rage, obnoxious cell phone usage, violent song lyrics, indifferent vulgarity, etc.—that many Americans, perhaps most, have retreated into a posture of defensive living, preferring not to interact with the people around them. The culture has become hair-triggered, prone to quick argument and belligerent behavior. Public life, says Meyer, has become "subtly more malignant":

> You silently note a tattoo of "Fuck You" on a man's pumped-up bicep. You listen to the unembarrassable woman at the next table at a restaurant blather into her cell phone the details of her last gynecological checkup. You go to live theater among men in gym shorts, T-shirts, and baseball caps. At night, you hear people drive by with bass blasting so loudly that your liver jiggles. If you complain about this stuff out loud (or in print) you're a snob. Or a nut. Or a Behavior Nazi.[21]

This is daily fare now, in the U.S. of A.

One way Americans try to cope with this is through self-help manuals, but they are actually more of the same ideology. These best-selling psychological works, writes sociologist Zygmunt Bauman in his book on consumerism, urge us to invest in the self as a solo enterprise, to be detached and distrustful. What is being cultivated are people who don't need nurturance and who don't know how to nurture. The ideal is that of a private consumerist utopia, a place free for the solo self to acquire things. But it doesn't work; it is just not possible, says Dick Meyer, for a self to be "willfully constructed apart from tradition, community, and society." Studies of comparative world happiness show that Americans are not very happy, even in prosperous times; they typically rank well below other nations. And the Happy Planet Index, which includes factors such as health and environmental protection, ranks the United States 150th among all the nations of the world. It must surely say something when two thirds of the global market in antidepressants are purchased by Americans, and when, in 2008 alone, 164 million prescriptions were written for these drugs. The National Institute of Mental Health estimates that more than 14 million Americans suffer from major depression every year, which one psychologist, Gary Greenberg, argues is actually a sane response to a crazy world. Or a constantly hustling one, we might add.[22]

Perhaps the most disastrous result of this way of being is a pervasive absence of meaning, a condition that Chris Hedges calls "moral nihilism." He describes it as follows:

> We have trashed our universities, turning them into vocational factories that produce corporate drones and chase after defense-related grants and funding. The humanities, the discipline that forces us to stand back and ask the broad moral questions of meaning and purpose, that challenges the validity of structures, that

trains us to be self-reflective and critical of all cultural assumptions, have withered. Our press, which should promote such intellectual and moral questioning, confuses bread and circus[es] with news and refuses to give a voice to critics who challenge not this bonus payment or that bailout but the pernicious superstructure of the corporate state itself. We kneel before a cult of the self, elaborately constructed by the architects of our consumer society, which dismisses compassion, sacrifice for the less fortunate, and honesty. The methods used to attain what we want, we are told by reality television programs, business schools and self-help gurus, are irrelevant. Success, always defined in terms of money and power, is its own justification. The capacity for manipulation is what is most highly prized. And our moral collapse is as terrifying, and as dangerous, as our economic collapse.[23]

Sound familiar? It's all around us, and it is what we have come to after four hundred years of hustling. The corporate state, says Hedges, holds up the "manipulative character" (quoting Theodor Adorno) as the popular ideal. Who is this person, anyway?

The manipulative character has superb organizational skills and the inability to have authentic human experiences. He or she is an emotional cripple and driven by an overvalued realism. The manipulative character is a systems manager. He or she [is] exclusively trained to sustain the corporate structure, which is why our elites are wasting mind-blowing amounts of our money on corporations like Goldman Sachs and AIG.

These manipulative characters, people like Lawrence Summers, Henry Paulson, Robert Rubin,

Ben Bernanke, Timothy Geithner, AIG's Edward Liddy, and Goldman Sachs CEO Lloyd Blankfein, along with most of our ruling class, have used corporate money and power to determine the narrow parameters of the debate in our classrooms, on the airwaves, and in the halls of Congress while they looted the country.

This is America, then; this is where we all live, and to varying extents, who we all are. The data on depression, burnout, obesity, child suicide, heart disease, divorce, incarceration, debt, bankruptcy, etc., that form the shadow side of the American Dream have by now been chronicled in extenso by a great number of scholars, journalists, and analysts, and they make the results of living in this way quite clear.[24]

Let us, then, address the matter of the American decline. The disintegration of this country is an ongoing daily event, a factor in all our lives. We are witnessing the suicide of a nation, a nation that hustled its way into the grave. But what we need at this point is an outline of how this is taking place, beyond appeals to comparisons with the Roman Empire (accurate though they may be). In what follows, I am going to propose a specific model for what I believe is happening to us.

The first point is that affluence is always relative, not absolute. Human beings are social creatures, and it is by means of comparison that they feel happy or unhappy—which is obviously relative (and subjective) as well. This has, in fact, been a major problem with neoliberal economic theory, which assumes that what counts is absolute wealth, and therefore that people will make rational decisions about their economic situation. But as Keynes argued long ago, economics is fundamentally irrational; it is more a function of fear and desire than anything else. This is why study after study has confirmed that happiness does not rise with increase in per capita income. During 1945–91, for example, a period during which the GDP per capita doubled in the United States, there was no increase in average happiness, as far as surveys could determine. The data are similar for Europe as well as Japan. In a word, beyond a base level of material comfort, absolute amounts of cash have no impact on subjective well-being, a fact that led Derek Bok, in *The Politics of Happiness* (2010), to suggest that the United States abandon economic growth as a policy goal.[25]

If it is comparative or relative wealth that counts, then, it is easy to see how the mechanism operates: material aspirations rise with a society's income. Any positive effect is therefore offset by an upward shift to a new norm. In other words, as incomes rise, so do goals and aspirations, which vitiates the expected growth in happiness. The "growth process itself," writes Richard Easterlin (in *Growth Triumphant*), "engenders ever growing 'needs' that lead it ever onward." Each step upward on the economic ladder, he concludes, "merely stimulates new economic desires" that move the dynamic forward, one that can be best described as a "hedonic treadmill." As economist Robert Frank puts it, the driving force is one of "relative deprivation," the need to keep up with the Joneses. We are all caught in a "society wide arms race for goods." When you get down to it, the pursuit of affluence is a form of addiction.[26]

We now understand why there is not enough money in the world for Lloyd Blankfein: if it's an addiction, then the point at which satisfaction will be attained is infinity. This is why corporate executives have to have $20,000 bottles of wine or private jets, and why your next-door neighbor (or you) needs a subzero freezer or a granite countertop. With addiction, desire pursues a moving target; there is never an end to it. It is also why the American political system cannot change, except in superficial ways. It's not merely the weight and the momentum of the past, though these things are real enough; it's also the pull and the momentum of the future. The prospect of doing something radically different, of not pursuing more, is terrifying. A huge abyss opens before us: what would we be without the "hedonic treadmill"? In a lecture at New York University in October 2009, the historian Tony Judt posed the following question to his audience: "Why is it that here in the United States we have such difficulty even *imagining* a different sort of society from the one whose dysfunctions and inequalities trouble us so?" The answer should be clear: if the American Dream is really about unlimited abundance, and if we are addicted to that as a goal, then alternatives to that way of life are simply too scary to contemplate. Try telling a full-blown alcoholic to put down that glass of Scotch.[27]

Second point: addiction has a certain "systemic" pattern to it that is typically not self-corrective. Both capitalism and alcoholism are characterized by cycles of increasing dysfunction, "runaway," and breakdown, and the system can do this for a fairly long time. But it cannot do it forever; eventually some sort of crunch is unavoidable. This is why Dmitri Orlov, in *Reinventing Collapse*, writes of the crash of 2008: "We're in hospice care. The bailouts can be viewed as ever bigger doses of morphine for a patient that's not long for this world."[28]

One of the best analyses of addiction I'm aware of is the model proposed by the anthropologist Gregory Bateson in a classic essay he wrote back in 1971 called "The Cybernetics of 'Self': A Theory of Alcoholism." The irrational thing about addicts (whether of money or anything else) is that they always seek to maximize their stash, even though this is ultimately self-destructive. Reason would dictate that optimization would be a better strategy than maximization, but reason doesn't have much to do with it. Bateson claimed that "the ethics of optima and the ethics of maxima are totally different ethical systems," and that the ethics of maxima knows only one rule: more. The problem is that healthy organisms, societies included, tend to be homeostatic, i.e., designed to stay in balance. The attempt to maximize any single variable (e.g., wealth) will eventually push the system into "runaway," defined by the inability to control itself. To take a physiological example, we recognize that the human body needs only so much calcium per day to function. We do not say, "The more calcium I ingest, the better off I'll be," because we understand that past a certain point, any element is toxic to the system. If, however, we are calcium addicts, that understanding won't register. An American corporation doesn't say, "Okay, that's enough wealth for now; it's time to think in terms of distribution," or "it's time to think about inner meaning, and quality of life." And for the most part, the average American citizen doesn't think in these terms either. For both, wealth is an asymptote.[29]

Maximizing a single variable, said Bateson, can seem like an ingenious adaptation, but over time it turns into pathology. Think of the saber teeth of a tiger, which had short-term survival value but which ultimately weakened the animal's flexibility in certain situations that proved to be crucial. Eventually the species died out as a result. Bateson says that the system won't attempt to self-correct until it "hits bottom"—for example, the alcoholic has an experience so devastating that it acts as a kind of revelation, leading him to give up drink and start out on a new life. There is a surrender involved, as he realizes that the whole thing is beyond his control. (At the time of the 2008 crash, Alan Greenspan was the only economic adviser to demonstrate this kind of humility, stating publicly that his belief in the self-correcting properties of the market had been out of touch with reality. The rest of the neoliberal crowd, writes Thomas Frank, "repeat their incantations and retreat deeper into their dogma.") In Alcoholics Anonymous, this surrender is to a Higher Power;

God, if you will. The analogy in the case of the paradigm of affluence and the American Dream would be to admit that the market is not rational; that the pursuit of wealth needs to be set in a larger moral and social context; and that refusing to entertain other models, such as that of the alternative/republican tradition, has cost us dearly and needs to stop.[30]

Of course, a lot of alcoholics go on and off the wagon, or try to restrict themselves to beer and wine, or to drinking only on weekends, and so on. In fact, many addicts are able to dance around their addiction for years. But the overall trajectory is downward; time is not on their side. In fact, statistically speaking, most alcoholics don't recover; the tendency is to "hit bottom"—the other side of death. Radical change is always the exception, never the rule, and in this sense is kind of miraculous. No hyperbole is intended here: for the United States to seriously entertain the alternative tradition—not as some form of "ascetic chic," but as a kind of fundamental conversion experience—would require something on the order of an act of God. Or to put it another way, it would require the American people to suddenly wake up one morning and realize that they had the whole thing upside down: Ronald Reagan was a horse's ass, and Jimmy Carter a great man and a visionary thinker. Nothing of the sort is going to happen, of course. As Ralph Nader has pointedly remarked, "The progressive forces have no hammer." Indeed, they never have in the United States. And without real power, real political clout, nothing is going to change.[31]

This brings me to the third and final point I wish to make. In *Globalization and Inequality*, political scientist John Rapley points out that any functional regime has two components, distribution and accumulation, and to survive, it has to attend to both. The former Soviet Union, for example, was fairly successful at distribution but quite poor at accumulation. Eventually it went through an accumulation crisis from which it was not able to recover. The United States, on the other hand, is good at accumulation (until the system crashes) but weak in terms of distribution, and this generates instability in the system. In general, says Rapley, neoliberalism is an inherently unstable regime because it is based on a tension it can't resolve. The "trickle down" theory is an attempt to solve the problem of distribution by means of accumulation, which doesn't work. You only have to play the game "Monopoly" a few times before you realize that even though all the players have to go around paying rents, in the end one person will end up with all the money. In other words, the functioning of the accumulation element in this system depends on a dysfunctional distribution element. As a result, neoliberal regimes are plagued by crises. These crises can be managed temporarily, or even for a long while; but they ultimately cannot be resolved within the context of neoliberal economics. Over time they multiply and deepen, so the regime is condemned to a condition of permanent instability.[32] The upshot is that a nation such as the United States has only two options: replace the neoliberal regime with something else (which I personally don't believe is going to happen), or watch it get worse over time. For America, this can only mean a steady disintegration of its institutions, its culture, its infrastructure, and so on. This process will occasionally be punctuated by violent events, represented by 9/11 or the crash of 2008, for example, and there are certainly additional, and more catastrophic, events waiting for us down the road; of that we can be sure. But for the most part, daily deterioration will be the norm. Of course, changes of degree eventually turn into changes of kind, and it is likely that at some point—I'm guessing twenty or thirty years—we shall wake up to realize that we are living in a different country. Chris Hedges predicts that "America will be composed of a large dispossessed underclass and a tiny empowered oligarchy that will run a ruthless and brutal system of neo-feudalism from secure compounds."[33] This describes much of the Third World today, but we can already see the outlines of this shaping up here. Another possibility, which I'll deal with in chapter 5, is a secessionist breakup of the country—remote as that may seem today. As Bateson would say, these are the sorts of things that happen when you maximize a single variable. You really can't shoot heroin forever.

But we have tried, and the injections we keep giving ourselves have been technological innovations. As Joseph Schumpeter argued, this is the factor that keeps reinventing capitalism, and that, as a result, is the motor that drives the pursuit of affluence. In addition, technological innovation has provided the ideology, or even theology, that hustling alone could never do: "progress." For without specifying a clearly definable end point, this type of progress nevertheless contains a utopian vision, which says that in the fullness of time, humankind will be redeemed. How that eschatology has worked out is the next thing we need to look at.

3

The Illusion
of Progress

When scientific power outruns moral power, we end up with guided missiles and misguided men.

—Martin Luther King Jr.,
Where Do We Go from Here?

There is a time when the operation of the machine becomes so odious, makes you so sick at heart, that you can't take part; you can't even passively take part, and you've got to put your bodies upon the gears and upon the wheels, upon the levers, upon all the apparatus, and you've got to make it stop. And you've got to indicate to the people who run it, to the people who own it, that unless you're free, the machine will be prevented from working at all!

—Mario Savio,
Berkeley, California, December 3, 1964

The one who dies with the most toys wins.

—Popular American bumper sticker

THAT TECHNOLOGY IS the motor of the consumer economy is no great intellectual breakthrough; the evidence for this, from paper clips to iPods, is all around us. If the goal of American life is to accumulate as many objects as possible prior to death, then technology lies at the center of that life, because those objects exist only by virtue of technology and applied science. And historically speaking, economic and technological expansion have gone hand in hand. The word "technology" was coined by Professor Jacob Bigelow of Harvard University in 1829, the very same year when the first American railroad went into operation. By 1830, 73 miles of track had been laid; then 3,328 miles by 1840, 8,879 by 1850, and 30,636 miles by 1860—which was more than the combined total of the rest of the world. Between 1825 and 1850, 3,700 miles of canals were constructed. By 1850 as well, machine parts were being manufactured by other machines, ones that could reproduce an endless number of interchangeable parts—a technique that became known as "the American system of manufactures." Nearly 6,000 patents were issued in the United States during the 1840s; 23,000 were issued during the 1850s, and this latter figure was approximated or exceeded during *every single year* from 1882 on. At the same time that all of this was going on, the steel, petroleum, and electrical industries expanded so dramatically that by 1894 the value of U.S. manufactured goods was almost equal to that of Great Britain, France, and Germany combined. And should we be surprised that Philo Farnsworth, the first person to transmit a television picture in 1927, chose the dollar sign as the image he wanted to transmit? The synergy of all this is quite obvious.[1]

Less obvious is the role that technology has played in fueling the hustling life, which is as much a social phenomenon as an economic one. As indicated earlier, the geographical frontier was declared officially closed in 1890, leaving a psychological vacuum that got quickly filled by the technological frontier. Henry Ford pioneered the first moving assembly line in 1913, and the country was off and running; in 1926 alone, when the price of a Model T dropped to $260, Americans traveled 141 *billion* miles. Where's the fire? as the cop who stops you for a speeding ticket might reasonably ask.[2]

As we also noted in chapter 2 (citing Richard Easterlin), "the growth process itself engenders ever growing 'needs' that lead it ever onward." This "hedonic treadmill"—the situation in which every step you take in keeping up with your next-door neighbor "merely stimulates new economic desires"—is completely dependent on technological innovation. Technical novelty is integral to the hustling life because it ensures that there is a "ladder" to climb without end. As the philosopher Albert Borgmann points out, this expanding technological frontier keeps class antagonism at bay, in the same way that an expanding geographical frontier once did. The purpose of life is thus to keep hustling, but since there is no end to innovation (there is always another software or electric toothbrush variant), there is no end to hustling, which, like technological expansion, becomes its own purpose. Borgmann describes this rat-on-a-wheel lifestyle with uncanny accuracy:

> Inequality favors the advancement and stability of the reign of technology. The unequal levels of availability represent a synchronic display of the stages of affluence that many people can hope to pass through. What the middle class has today the lower class will have tomorrow, while the middle class aspires to what the rich have now. . . . The peculiar conjunction of technology and inequality that we find in the industrial advanced Western democracies results in

an equilibrium that can be maintained only as long as
technology advances.

As long as this arrangement remains unquestioned, Borgmann
goes on to say, "politics will remain without substance," for the
crucial dimensions of our life will have already been determined
by technology. The technological order is thus the real one; politics
merely exists on a metalevel. Appeals to republicanism, or to par-
ticipatory democracy, that fail to address this hedonic game and
the role that technology plays in it are therefore pointless. "One may
as well call for participation in pocket calculators," he concludes.[3]
   This is, in fact, about as deep as everyday discussion in
America gets. A few years ago, a friend of mine was taking the
train up the California coast, and decided to walk very slowly
through the train, from the last car up to the locomotive, so she
might get a sense of what people were talking about. Every single
conversation, she told me, was about technology: this new bit of
software or computer attachment, that new special function on a
cell phone, what is now available in TV screen sizes, etc. Consider
also the magazine *Wired*, which is one of the most popular and
sophisticated journals around. Its sole purpose is to chronicle
"progress," with essays on topics such as software that got created
and engineering problems that got solved. The November 2010
issue is a perfect example of what Americans regard as progress:
in addition to 3-D TVs and iPads, the issue deals with breast
implants, a Disney television cartoon, advances in sports betting,
methods for cheating at coin flipping, Ticketmaster, and a history
of the AK-47(!), complete (in the latter case) with illustrations
taken from clips from Hollywood films and video games. And
then we (well, a few of us) wonder how fundamentally hollow
individuals—Reagan, the Bushes, Clinton, Obama—who can be
trusted *not* to address the hedonic game and the role technology
plays in it, wind up in the White House. What a frivolous country this is, when you get right down to it: a nation of people who
throw their lives away for toys.

This brings me to my next point, namely that in the absence of real politics—of republicanism or any moral center for the country—technology moves in to fill the vacuum. It acts as a kind of hidden religion. Associated as it is with unlimited "progress," and therefore with utopia and redemption (more on this in a moment), it supplies the social glue that is lacking in the United States—a glue that hustling by itself is too shallow to provide. (Americans want to believe they have loftier goals than making money, even if they don't.) Indeed, since hustling is an every-person-for-themselves existence, it is basically a solvent, not a glue. As Zygmunt Bauman writes in *Consuming Life*, we live in a society that has been "pulverized into solitary individuals" and crumbling families. How we came to worship technology, then, is a topic of no small importance.[4]

The notion that technology is tied to unlimited progress, and the "perfectibility of man," is rooted in the French Enlightenment. By the end of the seventeenth century, for the first time, large numbers of people believed that progress had no bounds, and that by controlling the material forces of the world human beings could control their own destiny. To that end, the project of the *Encyclopédie* was launched, with the idea that it would contain the basic facts and principles of all knowledge. The first volume appeared in 1751 under the editorship of Denis Diderot, along with the *Preliminary Discourse to the Encyclopedia of Diderot* by Jean le Rond d'Alembert. The work of tradesmen and artisans was given special emphasis, because the editors believed that technology was the key to the current transformation, and in fact to happiness in general. To that end, the work contains fabulously detailed plates of tools, machines, and craft-industrial processes (eleven volumes of which appeared during 1762–72). All of this was a dramatic departure from French intellectual tradition, which saw mental activity as superior to manual labor. As Diderot explains in his

Prospectus to the work (1750), the editors sent designers to workshops to make sketches of everything, so they could illustrate exactly how the machines were assembled. Contributors to the articles on the mechanical arts—roughly seventy-two thousand entries in all—thus have a firsthand knowledge of the various trades being discussed. Subject matter, says Diderot, will include stonecutting, gardening, hydraulics, watchmaking, mineralogy, architecture, glassworks, brewing, dyeing, wood engraving, type-founding, sawmilling, and so on. The theme of unlimited progress was finally summed up in the *Sketch for a Historical Picture of the Progress of the Human Mind*, written by the marquis de Condorcet in 1793. The author promised a future utopia in which obstacles to progress, such as ignorance and tyranny, would be eliminated due to the impact of science, technology, and political revolution.[5]

Meanwhile, on the other side of the Atlantic, the Revolutionary generation was wasting no time getting on the Enlightenment bandwagon. Philadelphia merchant Tench Coxe addressed the Society for Political Enquiries at the home of Benjamin Franklin in 1787, and also delivered the inaugural address for the Pennsylvania Society for the Encouragement of Manufactures and the Useful Arts a few months later, at the request of Benjamin Rush. These lectures, which emphasized the importance of manufactures for America's future, constituted "a prophetic vision of machine technology as the fulcrum of national power." In fact, says Leo Marx, they prefigured "the emergence of the machine as an American cultural symbol." Except in the South, the idea that the aims of the United States would be realized by means of machine production was fast becoming an official ideology, closely linked to progress. Technology, adds John Kasson, was increasingly seen as an instrument of republican virtue, a defender of liberty, and something essential to democratic civilization. From the 1820s on, Americans identified

the progress of the nation with the progress of technology.
In his 1831 essay "Defence of Mechanical Philosophy," Cincinnati
lawyer Timothy Walker expounded on the doctrine of unlimited economic development based on technology, and in fact
viewed technological progress as part of a divine revelation. The
machine, he wrote, represents the possibility of universal abundance, and is the one thing that can fulfill the egalitarian aims of
the nation. William Henry Seward, the New York politician who
would eventually become Lincoln's secretary of state, caught the
prevailing mood when he declared that "popular government
follows in the track of the steam-engine and the telegraph." As
the railroad, steam engine, and (after 1844) the telegraph became
national obsessions, writers elaborated on this idea, and popular
magazines such as *Harper's Weekly* were filled with progressive-
republican rhetoric, along with illustrations of blast furnaces and
cotton presses. As Leo Marx tells us, the underlying assumptions
were those of the Enlightenment, and "the awe and reverence once
reserved for the Deity . . . [were] directed toward technology, or
rather, the technological conquest of matter." By 1850, he concludes, the machine had become a transcendent symbol endowed
with metaphysical significance. Americans "grasped and panted
and cried for it," and foreign travelers recorded the nation's obsession with it. Even Emerson (who changed his mind only later)
got into the act, telling his audience in 1844 that machinery and
Transcendentalism went hand in hand and that "railroad iron is a
magician's rod." Currier & Ives turned out romantic lithographs of
railroads (done as ads for railroad companies), and Walt Whitman
wrote a quasi-religious song to the locomotive in 1876:

> Type of the modern—emblem of motion and power—pulse
>   of the continent,
> For once come serve the Muse and merge in verse, even as
>   here I see thee, . . .

In his poem about the Centennial Exposition of the same year in Philadelphia, Whitman made this explicit: "sacred industry," he wrote, after sitting in silence in front of the Corliss steam engine for half an hour.[6]

The new power, says Marx, was seen as a means of realizing the original aims of the Republic; indeed, it was regarded as a validation of national "greatness." Only a few understood what was going on, saw that technology was not just technology but something much more than that—an ersatz religion. "It would seem," wrote Thoreau, "that there is a transcendentalism in mechanics as well as ethics."[7]

Fanatical devotion to technology is something that the great historian of Puritanism, Perry Miller, identifies as a quintessentially American characteristic. Early Americans, writes Miller, were not "a simple, ascetic, and pious rural people who suddenly had their idyllic way of life shattered by a barrage of mechanical contrivances." Rather, the American mind "positively lusted for the chance to yield itself to the gratification of technology. The machine has not conquered itself in some imperial manner against our will. On the contrary, we have wantonly prostrated ourselves before the engine." During the period of Tocqueville's visit, he adds, "democracy itself was identifying its innermost being with the vibration of this triumphant utility." Tocqueville himself, says Miller, "could not comprehend the passion with which these people flung themselves into the technological torrent, how they ... cried to each other as they went headlong down the chute that here was their destiny, here was the tide that would sweep them toward unending vistas of prosperity." "The age was grasping for the technological future, panting for it, crying for it." Technology, he concludes, is "the veritable American religion."

The religious nature of American technoworship is the focus of an important study by a student of Leo Marx, David Nye, titled *American Technological Sublime*. The sublime, according to Nye, is an overwhelming feeling of grandeur or power; applied to technology, it is the sense of awe or astonishment one might be seized with on encountering, say, the Corliss steam engine, or the Golden Gate Bridge. Year in and year out, he says, Americans have demonstrated their adoration of technology, from the Erie Canal and the first railroads to the space program of the 1960s and '70s. Thus the artist Joseph Stella recorded how he would stand on the Brooklyn Bridge, feeling as though he were "on the threshold of a new religion or in the presence of a new DIVINITY." In reality, technology has been a sacrament for this country, "an outward and invisible sign of an ideal America." (I shall never forget the crazed fanaticism that greeted the "unveiling" of Windows 95 by Microsoft, in Seattle, when I lived there in the 1990s. There was actually a countdown to the "launch.") Projects such as these enable the citizen to see himself or herself as part of a moral vanguard, leading the entire world toward democracy. Nye argues that the Revolutionary generation had to invent new forms of civic virtue, in the face of a citizenry motivated by pecuniary objectives. The technological sublime, he contends, moved in to fill the void, serving as a crucial element of social cohesion—"a transcendental ideal that constituted the glue of American culture for more than two centuries." When you have more than a million people turning out for the Apollo XI liftoff on July 16, 1969, and the rest of the nation watching it on TV, you get some idea of how the technological sublime functions socially, culturally, and politically. Cape Kennedy (Canaveral), Nye contends, is in effect an American holy place, the focus of pilgrimage.[8]

In this regard, a comparison with Europe is very instructive. The European nations have a social glue dating back to the Middle Ages; they do not need to find sublime experiences or national purpose in machinery (although, as we have seen, the

French in the eighteenth century came pretty close). Europeans never embraced the vertical city of the skyscraper, they banned or restricted electric signs, they did not see atomic explosions as tourist sites, and they rarely took trips to see rockets going off into space. All these things are necessary in a country where the social glue is weak and community life practically nonexistent.[9]

This matter of religion, transcendence, and utopia as being central to the belief in technological progress, however, is deserving of closer attention. It turns out that it has a deeper and more complex pedigree than the Enlightenment thinkers of eighteenth-century France. How modern were these folks, really? In a stunning reversal of the classic interpretation of the Enlightenment (secular, modern), the historian Carl Becker, in 1932, argued that the "progressive" and utopian aspirations of the movement were actually the conversion of Christian eschatology into a kind of secular fundamentalism. As Christianity declined, wrote Becker, its core of revolutionary utopianism morphed into a secular variant. Nor should this be particularly surprising: Western civilization is, after all, a Christian one, and that means it has been dominated by millennarian thinking. What we really have in the *Encyclopédie* and the *Sketch* of Condorcet, said Becker, is a form of secular salvation: *The Heavenly City of the Eighteenth-Century Philosophers*.[10]

In more recent years, the British philosopher and social critic John Gray has gone over this territory in his book *Black Mass* and concluded that Becker correctly fingered the central contradiction of Enlightenment thought: it is basically religious. Progress via technology, the notion that the evil of the world can and will be eradicated by means of reason and applied science, is ultimately Christian eschatology in modern dress. After all, there is absolutely no evidence whatsoever that technology is taking us to a better place; in fact, there is a lot of evidence to suggest the contrary. Theories of progress, says Gray, are not scientific hypotheses but rather myths, which—like the Christian myths of redemption and the Second Coming—answer to the human need for meaning. This is why we refuse to let them go, regardless of what the evidence might suggest. It is also why, in the United States, the commitment to technology goes much deeper than fueling consumerism, lubricating the socioeconomic system, and keeping a lid on class conflict. Without this belief system, Americans would have literally nothing, for it lies at the heart of the American Dream and the endlessly vaunted American way of life. Strip away the illusion of unlimited growth and the country would suffer a collective nervous breakdown. (This is key to why Jimmy Carter had to go: he was pushing the limits of American psychological tolerance, asking a nation of addicts to confront their dependency and change course.) Globalization, along with neoliberalism, according to Gray, is merely the latest incarnation of this illusion, and its deep religious roots account for the ferocity of its adherents, even after the crash of 2008 gave the lie to the notion of unlimited development through the free market economy. We want to believe that the future will be better than the past, but there isn't a shred of evidence to back this up. In particular, as I shall discuss below, scientific progress doesn't translate into moral progress; one could reasonably argue that just the opposite is the case. Truth be told, concludes Gray, we are even more superstitious than our medieval forebears; we just don't recognize it. Nor is it likely that we shall abandon these beliefs. It's utopia or bust, even if the odds are heavily weighted toward bust.

If, as we saw in chapters 1 and 2, consumerism and the pursuit of affluence didn't have too many critics along the way, it can surely be said that the religion of technology has had even fewer. Ultimately it amounted to little more than a handful of disaffected intellectuals. "Let your life be a counter friction to stop the machine," wrote Thoreau in 1849, in an uncanny anticipation of Mario Savio (see his epigraph to this chapter). In *Walden*, Thoreau calls the new machinery "an improved means to an unimproved end." Leo Marx comments that Thoreau's real enemy was a culture pervaded by a technological outlook, which he referred to as an antilife. Nor was Thoreau unaware of whom all this was intended to benefit. "The principal object," he wrote, "is, not that mankind may be well and honestly clad, but, unquestionably, that the corporations may be enriched." As for Emerson, a note of skepticism began to creep into his attitude toward the machine culture as early as 1839, when he wrote that it could establish "a new Universal Monarchy more tyrannical than Babylon or Rome." In an address he gave in Concord in 1851, he asserted that the United States was metaphysically debilitated, and that locomotives and telegraphs couldn't compensate for this. In general, Emerson came to see that the attempt to use technology as a substitute for republican ideals was doomed to fail.[11]

The self-destructiveness of the hustling, techno-driven way of life was a theme of America's greatest writers at about this time. One can see it metaphorically in the stories of Edgar Allan Poe, for example (most particularly in "The Pit and the Pendulum"), or in *Moby-Dick*, where Ahab's monomaniacal obsession with the whale leads to the destruction of the *Pequod* (more on this in chapter 5). As the ship is rammed by the whale and pulled under, writes Leo Marx, the vagabond sailor Ishmael survives, but as a kind of orphan, "floating helplessly on the margin of the scene as society founders." Nathaniel Hawthorne also emphasized the dangers of the narrow-minded pursuit of a science divorced from conscience in stories such as "Ethan Brand" and "The Procession of Life." In the latter he writes that "the demon of machinery annihilates the soul." In a lighter vein, Hawthorne satirized the blind faith in technology that he saw all around him in "The Celestial Railroad" (1843), in which passengers believe they are on a train to the "Celestial City." Their guide, "Mr. Smooth-it-away," rides with them to dispel any doubts they may have; he also turns out to be a major stockholder in the corporation. Along the way, the passengers observe two dusty travelers walking alongside the train. "The preposterous obstinacy of these honest people in persisting to groan and stumble along the difficult pathway rather than take advantage of modern improvements," writes Hawthorne, "excited great mirth among our wiser brotherhood." But the wiser brotherhood proves to be a pack of fools. For Smooth-it-away is actually the devil, and he leaps off the train before it arrives at its real destination: hell. The voyage of salvation promised by modern technology, it turns out, is a complete illusion.[12]

The great spokesman for this point of view in the early twentieth century was Henry Adams (great-grandson of John), especially in *The Education*. Like Thoreau, Adams saw through the game; he understood that the order advanced by the technological narrative of progress was an imaginary one. For Adams, such beliefs were mere vanity, and he posed the issue most starkly in chapter XXV, "The Dynamo and the Virgin." Adams was struck by the power of the dynamo at the Gallery of Machines at the International Exposition in Paris in 1900, and was led to compare this with the statue of the Virgin in Chartres Cathedral. Worship of the machine, said Adams, is as nothing in the face of true spiritual belief. For Adams, comments Jackson Lears, "The worship of technological force ended in a solipsistic blind alley, a worship of ourselves." Adams was not a Catholic, but he saw the Virgin as representative of true faith, and worship of the dynamo as sterile, a dead end.[13]

Again, we need to be clear as to how marginal all of this literature was to mainstream American thinking. In the nineteenth century as well as the twentieth, it made absolutely no difference for the actual behavior of the American public. In fact, as Leo Marx points out, outside of the South the Luddite position had no social or political clout at all. Opponents of the new religion of technology were regarded, then as now, as "a small cult of literary dreamers beyond the fringe." While the rhetoric of the technological sublime wound up in mainstream publications such as the *North American Review* or *Scientific American*, the writings of its opponents got published in the papers of small organized minorities, groups that had no visibility and no ability to change anything. "The dissenters," writes Perry Miller, "were at best minor voices and . . . were sadly ineffectual. They provide us . . . with no usable programs of resistance." Today, the religion of technology is so entrenched that critics of it are largely invisible, associated with hippies (if there are any left), the environmental movement (such as it is), a few university professors, and assorted "techno-cranks," including Theodore Kaczynski, the notorious Unabomber. In this way, technological civilization manages to escape any widespread fundamental critique of its premises, which are basically self-congratulatory and self-confirming.[14]

Of course, the twentieth century's greatest critic of American techno-civilization was Lewis Mumford, some of whose work we have already discussed. As Mumford pointed out in an anniversary review he wrote in 1959 of his pioneering work *Technics and Civilization*, the really remarkable thing about the book was that no one, down to 1934, had thought to undertake an extended historical and critical study of technology—in the English language, at least. Mumford ends the review by saying that the book "still unfortunately possesses its original distinction: it stands alone, an ironic monument if not an active influence."[15]

This was hardly an idle observation. The fact that technology was so single-mindedly celebrated in the United States made it virtually invisible as a possible target of criticism, even as late as 1959. It would be like criticizing the air, in a way, which didn't begin to happen until the next decade. Indeed, when Mumford published the first volume of *The Myth of the Machine* in 1967, *Time* magazine characterized it as a call to return to Neolithic culture. The fog of techno-civilization is so dense in this country that any suggestion that a technological culture might be something of a mistake will only be met with blank incomprehension or dismissive sound bites.[16]

Mumford began pursuing his central theme—the rise of the machine and the mechanistic outlook in the West—as early as 1922, in *The Story of Utopias*. Reviewing the Western utopian tradition from Francis Bacon's *New Atlantis* to Edward Bellamy's *Looking Backward*, Mumford couldn't help but notice how one-dimensional these visions were. They were essentially machine-age utopias, he observed, relying on technology to bring about the good life. Both (economic) liberalism and socialism, quite clearly, subscribed to the same vision, in which "progress," defined as technological innovation, would lead to ever-increasing material expansion. This critique was developed further in *Technics and Civilization*, which argued that the flaw in this sort of "progress" was that it required human beings to submit to the cult of the machine. During the Middle Ages, said Mumford, technics (i.e., the industrial arts, but including the habits and goals of a society with respect to technological innovation) were used in the service of life—to build cities, say, or cathedrals. This was a balanced civilization; but in the "paleotechnic era," starting with the Industrial Revolution of the eighteenth century, the defining idea was to bring all of human experience under a technological regime. Oddly enough, Mumford believed we could turn all this around; that since this regime was a product of our values, we could change society by changing our values. A mental revolution, in short, would bring about a "neotechnic" civilization, in which the machine would be directed toward human purposes once again.[17]

The second volume of *The Myth of the Machine*, titled *The Pentagon of Power* (1970), elaborates on this theme, arguing that the American "megamachine" was based on a kind of bribe, namely that the individual can get to enjoy the benefits of the technocapitalist way of life if he or she gives the system unquestioning allegiance. The answer, then, was obvious: reject the bribe, the myth of the machine, and the whole structure will collapse like a house of cards. "The gates of the technocratic prison will open automatically," wrote Mumford, "as soon as we choose to walk out." But as his biographer, Donald Miller, comments, by this time the optimism came as a kind of afterthought, and had a false ring to it. Mumford hardly believed Americans would turn their backs on technology, and frequently stated (if not in print) that only a miracle could save us. "I think, in view of all that has happened in the last half century," he wrote to a friend in 1969, "that it is likely the ship will sink." His increasing pessimism, as already noted, was understandable: "he was living in a culture that rejected completely the values and ideals he stood for." Mumford's life work was comprehensive, brilliant, and desperately needed, but (given the context) unfortunately quixotic: he was un-American in the finest sense of the word. As indicated in chapter 1, his call for a redefinition of progress in human rather than technological terms was totally ignored by a nation that couldn't really grasp what he was talking about.[18]

Despite the depth and originality of Mumford's work, he cannot be said to have been operating in a vacuum. In particular, his emphasis on the "balanced" (steady-state) civilization of the Middle Ages, and its disruption by the rise of an "imbalanced" (ever-expanding) industrial economy, with attendant loss of meaning, has a long intellectual pedigree. Before we look at the various critiques of technology that arose in the 1960s and after, we need to have some sense of this tradition, because the conflict between the "technical order" and the "moral" one, as it has been called, lies at the heart of virtually all contemporary critiques of the technological society.

The notion that there is a way of life characteristic of modern (or industrial) societies that is qualitatively different from the way of life of premodern (or folk) societies goes back, at least, to the German sociologist Max Weber. Modern societies, said Weber, are governed by bureaucracy; the dominant ethos is one of "rationalization," whereby everything is mechanized, administered according to the dictates of scientific reason. Weber famously compared this situation to that of an "iron cage": there was no way the citizens of these societies could break free from their constraints. Premodern societies, on the other hand, were permeated by animism, by a belief in magic and spirits, and governance came not through bureaucracy but through the charisma of gifted leaders. The decline of magic that accompanied the transition to modernity Weber called *die Entzauberung der Welt*—the disenchantment of the world.[19]

The distinction between these two fundamental types of social orders emerged in a variety of studies in the decades that followed. Thus another sociologist, Ferdinand Tönnies, saw the two in terms of gemeinschaft (community) vs. gesellschaft (society, especially the culture of business), noting that whereas the former was characterized by bonds of kinship or friendship, the latter is notable for the preponderance of impersonal or contractual relations. Linguist Edward Sapir, in turn, cast the dichotomy in terms of "genuine" vs. "spurious" cultures, arguing that the activities of the former were imbued with spiritual meaning, whereas the latter are discordant and empty. Finally, the American anthropologist Robert Redfield would relabel the dichotomy as the moral vs. the technical order, asserting that in traditional or folk societies meaning was given, whereas in modern ones it had to be constructed. Individuals had a sense of belonging in the moral order, he wrote; indeed, that's what a moral order *is*. In the technical order, on the other hand, people essentially feel lost, cosmically orphaned. Ultimately, Redfield believed that while the human race had made great advances in the technical order, it had made virtually no progress in the moral order—the knowledge of how to live, as it were—and that because of this, the human prospect was rather dim.[20]

At the heart of Redfield's anthropological research was the conviction that technological progress by itself was sterile. In the technical order, he maintained, human beings are bound by things or are themselves things. If this regime were to be adopted by (or more likely, forced upon) traditional societies, it would tear those societies apart—which is, of course, the historical record. "Every precivilized society of the past fifty or seventy-five millenniums," he wrote, "has a moral order to which the technical order was subordinate." Over time, however, this equation was reversed. The consequences, he concludes, are obvious.[21]

Two things deserve comment here. The first is that the dichotomy of moral vs. technical is a bit too stark, based (as Redfield acknowledged) on "ideal types." As the Norwegian anthropologist Thomas Hylland Eriksen points out, there are significant differences between traditional societies. And yet, he adds, it is not off base as a first approximation: life in medieval Europe or in a remote village in Melanesia was/is vastly different from life in contemporary New York. Thus the following things have become scarce in hypermodern society:

Slow time; silence
Security; predictability
Sense of belonging, and of personal identity

Coherence; understanding
Organic growth
Real experiences (i.e., ones not mediated by the mass media)
Recognition that death is a part of life

Whereas the items below are new and constantly in your face:

Chips and computers
Ubiquitous mobile telecommunications
Genetic engineering
Electronically integrated global financial markets
Interlinked capitalist economy embracing the entire planet
Majority of urban labor force working in information processing
Majority of planetary population living in urban centers[22]

The second point is that it is not at all clear that those of us in the technical order feel more in control of our destinies than those in the moral order did, even though technology is (ironically enough) specifically about control. Indeed, if we frame this difference in terms of the preceding two lists, what sane human being could possibly find a sense of belonging in the world of the second list? And yet, as Lewis Mumford's life demonstrates, you can't get taken seriously if you point this out. What is left out of public discussion, writes Zygmunt Bauman, is "the role that almost every single 'modernizing' measure has played in the *continuing decomposition and crumbling of social bonds and communal cohesion.*" Or as *New Yorker* staff writer Adam Gopnik once put it, "There is the feeling that something vital is passing from the world, and yet to defend this thing is to be immediately classified as retrograde." What can possibly be done to save a culture that thinks iPads represent "progress," while everything humanly valuable is going down the drain? What are the chances that this culture might ever be able to rethink its definition of progress? What is the point of these rhetorical questions?[23]

In many ways, it was Vietnam that brought all of this to a boil in the United States. Not that sixties radicals spent a whole lot of time reading Redfield; but the so-called counterculture was definitely attuned to the notion of a technical order that was obliterating the moral one, as it was conveyed through the work of a number of serious, yet popular, writers: Herbert Marcuse (*One-Dimensional Man*), Arthur Koestler (*The Sleepwalkers*), and Jacques Ellul (*The Technological Society*), to name the most prominent. In the context of a hypertechnological society pounding a peasant culture into the dirt with napalm and cluster bombs, some of the younger generation began to make the obvious connections. This surely accounts for the huge popularity of Theodore Roszak's work, discussed in chapter 1, and a limited but nevertheless vocal revulsion against science and technology, which were now regarded by a small segment of the population as inherently inhumane. This is a crucial point, and one to which I shall return in a moment.

As noted in chapter 1, it was partly the debacle of Vietnam that catapulted a most unlikely candidate, Jimmy Carter, into the presidency. He was hardly unaware of these currents in popular culture, especially as they were taken up by the environmental movement; and as a man trained as an engineer, he was sensitive to technology-related issues. I already mentioned that he was a follower of the economist E. F. Schumacher, and invited the latter to the White House in 1977. As with his attempt to redirect Americans away from the hustling life, so was he interested in getting them to think differently about technology. In his enormously influential *Small Is Beautiful*, Schumacher advocated what he called "appropriate technologies"—ones that would operate in local, decentralized contexts, a proposal that had a crafts-oriented, Mumfordian flavor to it. Such technologies, he held, would be nonintrusive—ecologically sensitive and respectful of the communities in which they were embedded. They would employ simpler equipment, for example, and involve the creation of workplaces that were located where people lived; they would be inexpensive, and suitable for small-scale application; and they would enable the use of simple techniques and local materials. Following this vision, Carter saw to it that the U.S. Agency for International Development received $20 million to set up an AT program (as it was called), and a National Center for Appropriate Technology also was established. All of this was quickly dismantled soon after Reagan's assumption of the presidency in 1981. In effect, the AT movement died before it was born.[24]

Yet the failure of the movement had deeper roots than Reagan's opposition to it. As historian Carroll Pursell points out, despite state and federal initiatives for AT during the Carter administration, there was great resistance to shifting economic subsidies from nuclear to solar power, for example. It's not likely that Carter, or the environmental movement, could take on agribusiness, private utilities, major manufacturing firms, as well as the military-industrial complex, and win. But beyond the issue of vested interests, Pursell believes that the forces behind "hard" as opposed to "soft" energy options "were committed to a certain kind and understanding of technology which operated as a hegemonic culture." There was a way of life, a symbolism, at stake, in other words; AT was seen by the dominant culture as subversive, a very different kind of value system— "feminine," perhaps one could call it. "In attempting to redefine technology," writes Pursell, "advocates of Appropriate Technology were directly challenging the power of those who shaped the hegemonic notion of that subject." In a word, switching to a kind of crafts-based technology (or indeed, merely advocating it) was as great a mental shift as Carter's 1979 suggestion that Americans find fulfillment in spirituality rather than consumerism. It never had much of a chance.[25]

Of course, AT didn't fit into the category of a technology that was inherently inhumane. As indicated, it was more craft than technology, and its specific objective was to enhance the way of life already present in any given context, not radically alter it. The same cannot be said of the dominant technological mode of industrial societies, but for psychological and cultural reasons it has been hard for people to grasp this. In particular, it would seem almost impossible for individuals living in societies such as ours to entertain the notion that technology is not neutral. Ingrained in the popular mind is the idea that technology operates much like a razor blade: you can choose to shave with it, or you can cut your wrists. In this presumably commonsense view, technology is nothing more than a tool—value-free—and it is up to human beings to decide how to use it. It can be used in a positive way (peaceful nuclear energy, say) or a negative one (atomic bombs); the decision is ours.

The only problem with this theory is that it is wrong. From Robert Redfield to Lewis Mumford to Marshall McLuhan to the Frankfurt School for Social Research (which includes Herbert Marcuse) to the technocritics of today, the one thing they all agree upon, and have been able to substantiate in various ways, is that the "tool" theory of technology is hopelessly naive. It ignores the fact that most technologies are not appropriate; rather, they carry with them a mindset, a way of life, that once introduced into a culture changes that culture forever. As Redfield discovered, if you start vaccinating cows in a small Mexican village, the tradition of magic, of native healing, begins to disappear. Similarly, McLuhan, in books such as *The Gutenberg Galaxy*, *Understanding Media*, and *The Medium Is the Massage*, which catapulted him to celebrity status in the sixties, argued that communications technologies radically changed the societies into which they were introduced. Believing that such things are neutral, wrote McLuhan, is a form of "somnambulism." Thinking that it is strictly the use of the technology that is the issue, he went on, "is the numb stance of the technological idiot." A medieval oral culture, for example, is radically different from a modern print culture, which is in turn different from a postmodern screen culture. The medium is not only the message, it is also the *massage*—it molds the culture in powerful ways. Hence the popular adage that the man who is given a hammer suddenly relates to everything as though it were a nail. Print culture pushed the auditory and sensuous world of the Middle Ages to the margins, just as digital/virtual culture is now doing to the inward and contemplative world of print culture—as Sven Birkerts demonstrates quite convincingly in his aptly titled *The Gutenberg Elegies*. And what modern technology does (and not just media technology) is translate everything into mechanism (including cybermechanism)—people and human life included. If you live in a hustling society, everything is a commodity; if in a technological one, everything is a means, an instrument. There is nothing "neutral" about this.[26]

This one powerful, and accurate, thesis runs through the writings of literally every critic of technocivilization of the McLuhan-Mumford era and beyond: Paul Goodman, Theodore Roszak, Langdon Winner, Jerry Mander, Kirkpatrick Sale, Wendell Berry, Albert Borgmann, Neil Postman, Theodore Kaczynski (the Unabomber), and twenty-first-century critics of the virtual information society such as Christine Rosen and Nicholas Carr.[27] It will, therefore, not be necessary to review the work of all these writers because for the most part what we find are variations on a theme. Winner, for example, who has been writing on the politics of technology since the seventies (*Autonomous Technology, The Whale and the Reactor*), states repeatedly that technologies imply whole ways of life, and that ways of life are hardly neutral. Ignorance of this fundamental reality—which (echoing McLuhan) he refers to as "technological somnambulism"—lies at the root of the mess we are in. It should be a vision of society that determines the course of technological innovation and distribution, he argues, rather than (as is now the case) the reverse. Technological development needs to be guided in advance "according to self-conscious, critically evaluated standards of form and limit." Winner does not believe, à la Mumford, that we can return to an older tradition of small-scale technics and craftsmanship, for "the world that supported that tradition and gave it meaning has vanished." What, then? The fact is that beyond exhortation and appealing to our (nonexistent, in my view) better sensibilities, Winner, no more than any of the other writers on the subject, has no specific, credible program for bringing this about. Furthermore, he fully understands this. "The idea," he writes, "that civilized life consists of a fully conscious, intelligent, self-determining populace making informed choices about ends and means and taking action on that basis is revealed as a pathetic fantasy." This, of course, raises the question of how things are likely to finally play out, a topic I shall deal with in chapter 5.[28]

Something similar can be said about the work of Neil Postman (*Technopoly*), which provides an excellent analysis of how America lost its moorings ("The Surrender of Culture to Technology"). Postman divides cultures into three types: tool-using cultures, technocracies, and technopolies. Until the seventeenth century, he tells us, all of the world's cultures fell into the first category. Tools were invented to solve specific problems (e.g., the windmill) or to serve symbolic purposes (e.g., the cathedral). They continued the traditions of the cultures in which they were invented. In such cultures, "technology is not seen as autonomous, and is subject to the jurisdiction of some binding social or religious system." Of course, occasionally there were long-range, unintended consequences. Thus the mechanical clock of the fourteenth century went from being a "tool" of religious observance to one of commercial enterprise. But for the most part, inventions were not intruders; they were integrated into the culture in ways that didn't significantly contradict its worldview. They were, in a word, appropriate.[29]

The same cannot be said of technocracies. In a technocracy, tools play a central role in the worldview of the culture. Rather than being integrated into the culture, they attack it—they bid to *become* the culture. The printing press and the telescope fall into this category. It was technocracy, says Postman, that gave us the idea of progress and that speeded up the world. Still, it is typical for technocracy to coexist, for a time, with its tool-using predecessor, as was the case in nineteenth-century America. With the rise of technopoly, however, the earlier culture disappears. Technopoly is "totalitarian technocracy," or "technological theology"; it eliminates everything else.

Postman dates this latter development to the emergence of Henry Ford and Frederick W. Taylor as pivotal figures on the American scene. As already indicated, the moving assembly line debuted in 1913; Taylor's *Principles of Scientific Management* rolled off the press two years earlier. Taylor saw efficiency as the goal of human life; his book, and his industrial time-and-motion studies, constituted the first clear statement that society is best served when people are subordinated to technology rather than the reverse. "In the past," he wrote, "man has been first; in the future the system must be first." Whereas in a technocracy, it is understood that people must sometimes be treated like machines, this never rises to the level of a philosophy. In a technopoly, it does. Technopoly, says Postman, is "the submission of all forms of cultural life to the sovereignty of technique and technology." It's essentially a form of madness, and it creates a culture lacking in moral foundation. (We should not be entirely surprised that Taylor was greatly admired by both Hitler and Lenin.) The culture tries to use technology itself as a source of direction and purpose, but this is doomed to failure: it's like making the disease the cure. As in the case of Winner, Postman has no real remedies to suggest. A statement in his last chapter is also exhortatory: "You must try to be a loving resistance fighter." It comes off more wistful than inspiring.[30]

The best example of a *non*loving resistance fighter in recent years is Theodore "Ted" Kaczynski, more commonly known as the Unabomber. His case is extremely illuminating in terms of where America is vis-à-vis the role of technology in modern life, both in terms of his *New York Times/Washington Post* "manifesto" and in terms of how he was perceived by the American public. After killing three people and injuring twenty-three more by means of homemade letter bombs, Kaczynski wrote the *New York Times* on April 24, 1995, that he would desist from any further attacks if the *Times* or the *Washington Post* agreed to publish his "manifesto" regarding technological civilization, "Industrial Society and Its Future." It subsequently appeared in both newspapers on September 19, 1995.

From one angle, one wonders what all the fuss was about, apart from the fact that it was written by someone who was ostensibly deranged and had spent the past sixteen years randomly selecting targets for assassination. The text—which is leaden and tedious—is largely a pastiche of environmental clichés and pop psychology. It is digressive, rambling, and poorly argued, and it offers a potted version of a host of writers such as Weber, Marcuse, Ellul, and Aldous Huxley without ever mentioning them. The "problem" here (if there really is one) is that from my point of view, at least, there isn't that much in the manifesto to disagree with. Consider the opening paragraph:

> The Industrial Revolution and its consequences have been a disaster for the human race. They have greatly increased the life-expectancy of those of us who live in "advanced" countries, but they have destabilized society, have made life unfulfilling, have subjected human beings to indignities, have led to widespread psychological suffering (in the Third World to physical suffering as well) and have inflicted severe damage on the natural world. The continued development of technology will worsen the situation. It will certainly subject human beings to greater indignities and inflict greater damage on the natural world, it will probably lead to greater social disruption and psychological suffering, and it may lead to increased physical suffering in "advanced" countries.

If the system survives, the author goes on to say, it will do so "only at the cost of permanently reducing human beings and many other living organisms to engineered products and mere cogs in the social machine."[31]

Given the fact that turning people into "cogs in the social machine" was the express purpose of Frederick Taylor a hundred years ago, and that this goal has pretty much been achieved, it's hard to regard Kaczynski's analysis as dramatic or unprecedented. In addition, the notion that the Industrial Revolution has been an unmitigated disaster for the planet is coin of the realm among most environmental groups. They would certainly agree with Kaczynski's statement that techno-civilization offers human beings no real stability; that it breaks down community and family ties; that it has shattered ancient cultures; and that it is taking us in the direction of a dystopian nightmare. The thesis really boils down to two points: one, that technological society greatly constricts human freedom, and two, that it will survive only if it gains enough control over human behavior (by means of psychoactive drugs, for example). If it doesn't, the system will break down, says Kaczynski, probably within a few decades.

The point, however, as Kirkpatrick Sale wrote in an article about the manifesto in 1995, is that while this way of thinking is au courant in most environmental circles, the majority of Americans are not familiar with it, and therefore that these issues need to be popularized and made the focus of public debate. (Note that on this side of the Atlantic, the Green Party is trivial in both strength and following.) Even environmentalists, I would add, are not really clear on the thesis of technology being value-laden, which is why they can be counted on to buy the latest electronic gadget along with the rest of the population, as though these things were not seamlessly woven into the industrial way of life they condemn. Kaczynski himself was not that naive, noting at one point that while each technological innovation by itself may seem desirable, and a source of increasing freedom, taken as a whole these "advances" (mistakenly regarded as "progress") actually narrow our freedom, and put increasing power into the system and the corporations that are running it. Meanwhile, he adds, people become more dependent on these devices with every new advance—in effect, enslaved.[32]

As an interesting exercise, the reader might want to take the "quiz" offered online that reproduces quotes from the manifesto alongside quotes from Al Gore's book *Earth in the Balance*, and asks you to sort out which is which. A couple of examples:

We retreat into the seductive tools and technologies of industrial civilization, but that only creates new problems as we become increasingly isolated from one another and disconnected from our roots.

Modern industrial civilization, as presently organized, is colliding violently with our planet's ecological system. The ferocity of its assault on the earth is breathtaking, and the horrific consequences are occurring so quickly as to defy our capacity to recognize them, comprehend their global implications, and organize an appropriate and timely response. Isolated pockets of resistance fighters who have experienced this juggernaut at first hand have begun to fight back in inspiring but, in the final analysis, woefully inadequate ways.[33]

Which of these was penned by the Unabomber? Neither, as it turns out. Both were written by the former vice president and Nobel laureate. There are a total of twelve quotes; as I began taking the quiz, I realized that my responses were purely arbitrary—I had no idea who said what, and wound up with a humiliating score of 33 percent, worse than random guessing would likely have gotten me.

But the notion of the manifesto as being a cliché among environmental groups, or the fact that it is occasionally difficult to distinguish it from the writings of Al Gore, should not deceive us as to what is going on here. The *New Yorker* once remarked that there was a little of the Unabomber in all of us, but what does this really mean? As I said, the idea of technology not being a neutral tool has very little currency in American society, and the condemnation of industrial civilization by environmentalists is not necessarily matched by concrete daily behavior. I actually knew a bigwig in the "voluntary simplicity" movement years ago who owned a Porsche, and I doubt that she was all that idiosyncratic; it's very easy to be schizophrenic about modern technology. We are in a situation similar to the early sixties, in which millions devoured Vance Packard's books and then ran out and bought a ton of consumer goods; or that of the early eighties, in which the huge popularity of *Small Is Beautiful* or *The Whole Earth Catalog* of the previous decade ultimately counted for nothing at all. If Americans, by their daily actions, can be seen to be fierce advocates of the consuming way of life, the same can be said of their behavior with respect to technology. It really doesn't matter how much Al Gore or Bill McKibben you read; if you interrupt a conversation with a friend to take a cell phone call, you are not only rude; you are also doing your bit to tighten the grip of technology around your own throat and that of society. When push comes to shove, virtually the entire country is on the side of technological civilization, and basically ignorant of what is at stake.[34]

For this reason it was imperative for the news media to paint a portrait of Kaczynski as insane. He wasn't. His court-appointed lawyers wanted to use the insanity plea, presumably because this would be much more easily understood or accepted than an intellectual critique of industrial society. In general, Americans classify anyone who is opposed to the American way of life—the 9/11 attackers, for example—as insane by defini-tion, for what rational person could possibly not want what we have? But terrorists are not necessarily insane; they may just be dedicated enough to follow up on the logical consequences of their beliefs. Thus Sale writes of the manifesto, "It is the state-ment of a rational and serious man, deeply committed to his cause." Of course, one might legitimately wonder how clearly Kaczynski was seeing things if he believed that sixteen years of random bombing, without public explanation of that cause, would serve to "get the message out," as he claimed to be try-ing to do. Nevertheless, when someone provided the FBI with a sketch of him at one point, the Unabomber suspended his activities for a full six years so as not to push his luck—hardly the behavior of a lunatic. And the manifesto comes across not as insane, but sophomoric (and badly in need of a good editor). But the news media were heavily invested in branding the guy a total nut job, and in this they succeeded. This is also the way the American public preferred to see him. Because the alternative— that he was drawing on a long-standing, and quite respectable, tradition of critique of the technological society and the American way of life—is something we shall never collectively acknowledge as legitimate. If that critique does flit across our consciousness, it gets dismissed almost immediately as being outside the realm of serious consideration. I very much doubt that Kirkpatrick Sale's call for public attention to these issues will ever be heeded, because ironically enough, if it were, this would be a very different country and probably not even need such a public forum in the first place. We are strangling on our own catch-22.[35]

Kaczynski's vision is what I call the *Pequod* theory of the course of American civilization, according to which it was Melville, our greatest writer, who got the meta-narrative of the nation correct. The obsessive pursuit of the whale, in short, will end with the ship being smashed to pieces. Kaczynski believes that the likely scenario is a dialectical one: our commitment to this way of life, the exacerbation of it, will generate enough instabilities and self-destructive tendencies to eventually bring about its collapse. I don't regard this as mad; I regard it as obvious. Indeed, the process is well underway.

As an illustration of this, it might be helpful to look at specific instances in which technology is failing in its own terms— making things less efficient rather than more, for example. This phenomenon might best be described as a "technological boomerang." Thus Thomas Hylland Eriksen points out that while the period from 1980 saw an enormous development in so-called time-saving technologies, the truth is that we have never had so little free time as we do now. The Internet has made possible a huge expansion of available information, and yet the data show an increasingly ignorant population. (Books such as *The Dumbest Generation*, by Mark Bauerlein, that document this, are becoming increasingly common.) Air travel is now so heavily congested that by the year 2000, 50 percent of the flights connecting major European cities were delayed. In the United States, road traffic tripled during 1970–2000, and the average speed involved in getting around decreased every year. In fact, the average speed of a car in New York City in 2000 was about seven miles per hour, and we can guess that it is even less today. You get the idea.[36]

Another example of the techno-boomerang is the alleged socialization function of the Internet, the promise of virtual communities (a variant of McLuhan's "global village," perhaps). We were all going to be happily wired into each other, having hundreds of friends instead of just a handful, and creating new, intimate connections. And, of course, the Net now includes Facebook, YouTube, MySpace, Twitter, etc.—an embarrassment of riches. Except that "poverty" is much closer to the truth. All of this cyberactivity has led to social isolation, because if you are at home alone with a screen, that's where you are. (Michael Kinsley of *Slate* magazine calls these sites "vast celebrations of solipsism.") "Virtual community" is pretty much an oxymoron, because friendships online don't typically involve physical proximity or genuine intimacy. In 1998, for example, a research team at Carnegie Mellon University published an empirical study titled "Internet Paradox," demonstrating that within the first year or two online, people were experiencing less social engagement and poorer psychological well-being. The researchers also found that greater use of the Internet was associated with less family communication, a reduction in local social circles, an increase in loneliness, and higher rates of depression. The authors of the study concluded by suggesting that by using the Net, people were "substituting poorer quality social relationships for better relationships, that is, substituting weak ties for strong ones," with consequent negative effects.[37]

A more recent study, conducted at the University of Michigan for the period 1979–2009, revealed a 48 percent decrease in empathy among college students during this time, and a 34 percent decrease in the ability to see things from another person's perspective. Most of these declines, it turns out, occurred over the past decade, and the general interpretation was that this was related to the isolation involved in the use of personal technology and popular social networking sites that have become so much a part of student life. The study suggested that this was not surprising "in a world filled with rampant technology revolving around personal needs and self expression." But it is also the *nature* of the technology that is at issue, because (see below) the Internet and other electronic media are based on speed and distraction, on rapidly shifting attention. The higher emotions, such as empathy and compassion, emerge from neural processes that are inherently slow. Various studies have shown that the more distracted we become, the less able we are to experience such emotions, or to see things from the perspective of others. Put briefly, these technologies may be undermining our moral sense. At the very least, it becomes hard to argue that they are promoting community.[38]

Another example of the boomerang phenomenon is the crash of 2008. In "The Financial Crisis and the Scientific Mindset," Paul Cella argues that for the past twenty years capital investment in the United States has been driven by a very intricate structure of speculative debt known as shadow banking, "a technological innovation amalgamating computing power and probabilistic modeling to vastly expand the various world markets in debt securities." The technology involved slicing and dicing and repackaging pools of loans to generate huge profits (for a few) while it was actually creating a debt culture that put the entire economy at risk. Credit derivatives, credit-default swaps, leveraged buyouts—these were technical products of computerized mathematical models that resulted not in more wealth, the ostensible purpose of it all, but in economic collapse. Nor are these practices a thing of the past, crash be damned. Cella writes, "much of the reckless grandiosity of modern technological civilization is evident in the peculiar features of the finance crisis."[39]

In truth, the techno-boomerang is really a particular subset of a much larger pattern, that of negative fallout from technology in general; what might appropriately be labeled "techno-blowback." As in the case of political blowback—i.e., terrorism (what some have called the price of empire)—these results are not side effects; rather, they are integral to the way the system functions. When Winner or Postman or the Unabomber argue that the system is doing itself in, they are talking about this type of blowback. Illustrations of this could, and do, fill many volumes; I'm going to cite only a few examples.

The most significant types of techno-blowback at the present time are due to the rapid diffusion of telecommunication devices (TDs, for short). A review of the literature analyzing the impact of screens, cell phones, and related gadgets suggests two themes in particular: the creation of a different type of human being, partly as a result of the neural rewiring of the brain engendered by these devices; and the emergence of a different type of society, concomitant with that. These are frequently hard to separate in real-life situations, but let me start with the impact of the new technology on individual consciousness and behavior.

One activity that is particularly encouraged by the proliferation of TDs is multitasking—doing several things at once. It is not uncommon to call someone up these days and realize, in the course of the conversation, that they are simultaneously checking something out online and watching television, for example. Whereas you might regard it as rude and annoying, more often than not they think it's good use of their time, despite the fact that they are only half-listening to the conversation. Multitasking was initially hyped (everything in the TD world seems to be hyped) as the key to future productivity and efficiency, and as far as I know is still the rage. But the truth proved to be otherwise. In 2007 Jonathan Spira, a leading business analyst with the research firm Basex, estimated that multitasking was actually costing the American economy $650 billion a year in lost productivity. It turns out (this from a 2005 University of London study) that workers who are distracted by e-mail and cell phone calls suffer a drop in IQ of more than twice that experienced by pot smokers. Research conducted by the University of Michigan further revealed that multitasking causes short-term memory loss. In switching back and forth between tasks, you lose focus; you have to keep "revving up" to get back to what you were doing every time you switch. In typical techno-boomerang style, multitasking *reduces* efficiency.[40]

"Multitasking," writes Walter Kirn, "messes with the brain in several ways." The constant switching of attention has a negative effect on those areas of the brain related to memory and learning. In this way, it slows down our thinking; it interferes with our ability to analyze things (which requires a continuous, linear thread of attention). Screen technology, of course, is a big part of this, whether we are talking about televisions, cell phones, or laptops; and recent neurological research has discovered that "screen people" are exposing themselves to large amounts of dopamine, which can result in the suppression of activity in the prefrontal cortex. Multitasking also boosts levels of stress-related hormones (cortisol, adrenaline) and wears down the system, resulting in premature aging. All in all, he concludes, "multitasking is dumbing us down and driving us crazy."[41]

Much of the evidence for this has been collected and expanded upon by Nicholas Carr in his recent book *The Shallows: What the Internet Is Doing to Our Brains*. The problem goes way beyond multitasking, writes Carr; it's the use of TDs in general. McLuhan had argued that the brain takes on the characteristics of the technology it uses, and we now see this in the cultural shift from print media to screens. For the Internet's emphasis is on searching and skimming, not on genuine reading or contemplation. As a result, given what we now know about the relative plasticity of the brain, the ability to reflect or to grasp the nuance of a situation is pushed to the margins. The Net, he says, is literally rerouting the pathways in our brains, making our thought processes increasingly shallow. It breaks up the content of a text into searchable chunks and surrounds it with other content. This is why a page online is very different from a page of print. The concentration and attention factor are high for the latter, low for the former. Then there are links, which encourage us not to devote our attention to any single thing but rather to jump from item to item. Our attachment to any single item is thus provisional and fragmented. The Net is basically an "ecosystem of interruption technologies."[42]

Print, on the other hand, has a quality of calm attentiveness. "The quiet was part of the meaning," as the poet Wallace Stevens put it. When a printed text is transferred to an electronic device, says Carr, it turns into something like a web site; the calm attentiveness disappears. Instead, the Net delivers repetitive, intense, and addictive stimuli, promoting very superficial understanding. Basically, you don't really read on a screen; it's a different kind of activity: browsing, scanning, keyword spotting, and so on. And the better you get at multitasking, the less able you are to think deeply or creatively. We are, he concludes (quoting the playwright Richard Foreman), turning into "pancake people"—spread wide and thin.[43]

The lack of interest in printed material, and the corresponding upswing in interest in TDs, is especially pronounced among the young. In 2009 the average American teenager was sending or receiving 2,272 text messages a *month*. I remember watching an interview on TV (sorry) with two sixteen-year-olds who each said that they exchanged more than two hundred such messages per day (they were quite proud of this). Meanwhile, the amount of time the average American between twenty-five and thirty-four years of age devoted to reading print in 2008 was forty-nine minutes a week. As Maryanne Wolf of Tufts University cogently puts it, "the digital world may be the greatest threat yet to the endangered reading brain as it has developed over the past five thousand years." Collectively, adds Christine Rosen, this is the end point of the tragedy we are now witnessing:

> Literacy, the most empowering achievement of our civilization, is to be replaced by a vague and ill-defined screen savvy. The paper book, the tool that built modernity, is to be phased out in favor of fractured, unfixed information. All in the name of progress.[44]

As the Googlification of society proceeds apace, we might want to take note of the fact that the "religion" of the Google corporation, according to Carr—that is, its intellectual ethic—is Taylorism: "progress" personified. The prime value here is efficiency, even in thought. The company itself has said that its goal is to get users in and out quickly; in fact, its profits are tied to that process. Prolonged engagement with an argument or narrative is their enemy. "The last thing the company wants is to encourage leisurely reading or slow, concentrated thought," writes Carr. "Google is, quite literally, in the business of distraction."

Following Frederick Taylor, Google believes that intelligence is merely the output of a mechanical process. There is little room in this world, Carr points out, for "the pensive stillness of deep reading or the fuzzy indirection of contemplation." In Google's Tayloresque world, he goes on to say, "Ambiguity is not an opening for insight but a bug to be fixed." The cultural impact follows upon the individual one, then: what we are witnessing is the replacement of a complex inner diversity with a new kind of self, one devoid of any sense of cultural inheritance. It may not be too much to say that TDs are generating a nation of buffoons.[45]

Buffoon behavior, as the reader well knows, is particularly encouraged by the use of these devices. Much of this is intentional—passive-aggressive behavior—but it also (again) lies in the nature of the technology, which is extremely addictive. As Dick Meyer writes in *Why We Hate Us* (already referred to in chapter 2), "People touch their portable devices like rosary beads. They are compelled to check their e-mail when they could be talking to you face-to-face." These "techno-boors," he continues, are oblivious to others in public space, all of which has created a "rude zombie world." Wireless technology, he maintains,

> allows people to hook into the Internet umbilical all over, so coffee shops, airports, parks, and bookstores are populated by laptop hooligans. An expert can commandeer a large space. This kind of behavior signals an egomaniacal message like "I'm very, very important. I am more important than you. I must be connected at all times."

Thus someone on a cell phone in a store doesn't have to thank the cashier or even acknowledge their existence, and this kind of social disrespect has actually become acceptable (you see it every day). What this amounts to, Meyer concludes, is "techno-aggression," hugely destructive of common decency and the social capital of our society.[46]

Christine Rosen, in her article "Our Cell Phones, Ourselves," contends that TDs function as what psychologists call "transitional objects" from childhood—the blanket or teddy bear. This is undoubtedly the source of their enormous addictive power, rooted as they are in issues of deep psychic insecurity. "We are constantly taking them out, fiddling with them, putting them away, taking them out again, reprogramming their directions, text messaging." Cell phones enable us to advertise our (ostensible) emotional fulfillment to everyone in the environment: "Look how much I'm in demand, how full my life is." (Incredibly sad, when you think about it.) Rosen agrees with Meyer regarding the boorish aspect of it all, because the use of the phone (again, inherent in the technology) enables us to dominate public space, to violate it, in effect, and thus demonstrate to others (now rendered invisible) that there is absolutely nothing they can do about it. Kenneth Gergen has called this behavior "absent presence," in which your body is there but your mind is somewhere else. It's a way of treating the world as a backdrop, of effecting a "radical disengagement from the public sphere," and of devaluing those around you. And it's everywhere now: across the nation, cell phones interrupt movies, concerts, lectures, and theater performances. At any given moment, at least 25 percent of the people you see walking down the street have them glued to their ears, oblivious of their surroundings. "The language of wireless technology itself," says Rosen, "suggests its selfishness as a medium." The vulgarity and narcissism of such a society can hardly be overestimated.[47]

The fact that individual brains are changing under the impact of TDs results in yet another cultural change: the general "frenzy" of technological society, in Heidegger's telling phrase.

The collective effect of these devices is that the hustling quality of American life increases exponentially—and as we have seen, it was pretty high to begin with. In the pathological climate of "techno-social Darwinism," as Rosen calls it, there is no time for stillness. All of these brave new people lack the ability to be alone with their thoughts or to appreciate the importance of silence. The buzz of all this crap drowns out everything else. Some time ago I was riding around Mexico City with a colleague of mine when we saw a huge billboard ad for some cell phone, with the caption, in three-foot-high block capitals (in English, for some strange reason), KILL SILENCE. "Well," I said to him, "at least they are being honest about it." "Oh," he quipped, "you are fixated on technology." True, this is a guy who is on his Blackberry 24/7; but I couldn't help thinking how even the brightest people don't get it, and typically have no idea what George Steiner meant when he called modernity "the systematic suppression of silence." Silence, after all, is the source of all self-knowledge, and of much creativity as well. But it is hardly valued by societies that confuse creativity with productivity, and incessant noise with aliveness. In reality, it is *society* that is fixated on technology, but since it practically constitutes the air we breathe, the fixation seems "normal." As a result, we don't notice that fundamental aspects of being human are disappearing. During his time at Yale, William Deresiewicz asked his students what place solitude had in their lives. In response, they seemed to be puzzled that anyone would want to be alone. "Young people today," he concluded, "seem to have no desire for solitude, have never heard of it, [and] can't imagine why it would be worth having. In fact, their use of technology . . . seems to involve a constant effort to stave off the possibility of solitude." The world of creativity, of imagination, of depth of the self, is closing down. The society envisioned in *Brave New World* is clearly on the horizon.[48]

This brings us to the only question that really matters, as far as technology is concerned: what *is* progress, when you finally get down to it? Some years ago the Swiss artist Jörg Müller created a portfolio of eight plates called *The Changing City*, illustrating the "evolution" of a typical Swiss or German town over the period 1953–76. Under the pressure of technology and market forces, the gemeinschaft of the original town is slowly transformed into the final gesellschaft nightmare: a collection of elite hotels, superhighways, and parking lots, with hardly a human being in sight. The place that was originally imbued with character and purpose now has none at all; it's completely soulless. Who in their right mind would label this "progress"? But the answer to that is easy: Americans.[49]

Octavio Paz, in *The Labyrinth of Solitude* (1950), observed that for Americans, progress was basically novelty. "They enjoy their inventions," he wrote, but "their vitality becomes a fixed smile that denies old age and death but that changes life to motionless stone." Progress hardly, in the United States, has much to do with quality of life. Rather, it's just about "the impertinent dynamic of 'more,'" as Joyce Appleby characterizes it; more of anything, of everything. There is no point to it at all, on this definition; it's basically mindless. Hustling, fueled by the religion of technology, has taken us to an impoverished place devoid of meaning. The critics of this way of life are completely ignored; the airwaves are filled with exhortations to keep doing what we are doing. Yet underneath the frenetic activity is a great sadness, which hustling and technology are designed to repress—which they do, but they probably won't be able to do it forever. As the above discussion suggests, the facade is already breaking up.[50]

It is sobering to realize that in American history, there has been only one political opponent of any consequence to bourgeois liberalism and the driven way of life, and that has been the

American South. Because of the stigma of slavery—and I don't wish to play it down in any way—there has been a huge resistance, outside of the South, to recognize the value of the South as an alternative way of life. The truth is that although the Civil War was fought over slavery, the conflict went much deeper than that; it represented a "clash of civilizations." Of course, Southerners could not have anticipated men such as Frederick Taylor and Lloyd Blankfein; but in a way, they did. They knew the type, so to speak. With the election of the Lincoln Republicans in 1860, they understood that the hustling that increasingly characterized the North, with its misguided notion of progress and its inability to appreciate the leisurely life, could only get worse, and that the outcome of all this would be to reduce the South to the status of an economic colony. And so— they "took their stand."

4

The Rebuke of
History

The past is always a rebuke to the present . . . it's a better rebuke
than any dream of the future.

—Robert Penn Warren

Since 1865 an agrarian Union has been changed into an industrial empire bent on conquest of the earth's goods and ports to sell
them in. This means warfare, a struggle over markets, leading,
in the end, to actual military conflict between nations. . . . [This]
has brought upon the social body a more deadly conflict, one
which promises to deprive it, not of life, but of living; take the
concept of liberty from the political consciousness; and turn
the pursuit of happiness into a nervous running-around which
is without the logic, even, of a dog chasing its tail.

—Andrew Nelson Lytle, "The Hind Tit"

[The Southern heritage] is far more closely in line with the
common lot of mankind than the national legends of opulence
and success and innocence. The South once thought of itself as
a "peculiar people," set apart by its eccentricities, but in many
ways modern America better deserves that description.

—C. Vann Woodward, "The Search for Southern Identity"

THERE IS, THEN, an illusion created by progress—which includes technology and the hustling way of life—that problems can be solved, and our situation dramatically improved, by just a little more of the same. More economic expansion, more technological innovation—perhaps just one more technological "fix"—and we'll be on the right track, have the type of society we really want. As a belief system, it's quite mesmerizing; except that there was one section of the country that did not buy into it: the South. As already noted, the American South is the one example we have of an opponent of this ideology that had real political teeth, and for this reason, in the mind of the North, it had to be vanquished.

When you think about it, nearly everything in modern American history turns on the Civil War, because the ideology I have been describing (which can be more accurately described as a mythology, or grand narrative) requires us to "fix" traditional societies and eliminate obstacles to progress. With the Civil War these two goals converged, making it the paradigm case of how we carry out, or attempt to carry out, these two projects. What the North did to the South is really the model of what America in general did and does to "backward" (i.e., traditional) societies, if it can. You wipe out almost the entire indigenous population of North America; you steal half of Mexico; you literally vaporize a large chunk of the Japanese population; you bomb Vietnam "back to the Stone Age" (in the immortal words of Curtis LeMay); you "shock and awe" Iraqi civilians, and so on. In what follows, then, I want to look at the War Between the States in a completely different way than the one found in the typical American history textbook. This is not to justify slavery, which I don't believe can be justified; but rather to say that the conflict was a lot more "cosmic" than most of us realize. At stake was nothing less than the definition of what a meaningful life was finally about. This, in fact, is what generated the energy that led to a four-year battle and the death of 625,000 individuals. What follows is an elaboration of this argument.

Let's start with the view of the South as seen from the North. The popular image of the antebellum South, as it was presented in American history textbooks and classes when I went to high school in the North, was pretty much the same then as it is now. That is to say, we were taught that the South, as the home of slavery, was a backward and immoral place, and that its refusal to abandon that institution was the cause of the Civil War. Under the leadership of Abraham Lincoln (pretty much depicted as a saint), the virtuous Union armies defeated the evil Confederate ones, and the slaves were finally set free. Mutatis mutandis, this remains the politically correct version, as well as the liberal academic version, of the war down to the present time. While many historians have modified it in significant ways, the notion of the conflict as having been at root a moral one is preserved in the titles of leading history texts—as James McPherson's *Battle Cry of Freedom*, the most popular one-volume history of the Civil War, would indicate.[1] And although I don't recall any of my teachers saying this explicitly, the image of the South that somehow came through to us was that it was dumb. These people spoke with a drawl, were barely coherent, and—given their supposed inbreeding and their diehard opposition to racial integration—were often referred to as "crackers" or "rednecks." From a Northern point of view, the South was regarded as a national embarrassment.

There is no question, of course, that slavery was a barbaric system and that the South sought to defend that system to the bitter end. The problem with the popular image, however, is that the causes of the Civil War are quite complex, and amount to something much larger than the singular issue of slavery; that the South had an intellectual tradition that was quite rich; and that it also had a virtue all its own—one that was in some ways superior to the supposed virtue of the North, slavery notwithstanding. These ideas may be startling to most of us (they were to me, quite frankly), but as it turns out, there are a number of very talented historians (and not only from the South) who have defended them quite skillfully. In fact, a closer look at the South, one that goes beyond the list of negative stereotypes outlined above, reveals a very nuanced picture, one that says a great deal about the character of the nation as a whole. Much of the problem here is that Americans are far more interested in slogans than they are in nuance—as my high school education would tend to suggest—and this has made sophisticated insight into the character of the nation rather exceptional. But if there is one event in American history that cannot be understood in simple black-and-white terms (literally or metaphorically), it is the War Between the States.

I do understand, however, the attraction of slogans in this particular case. The literature on the Civil War is so vast, so labyrinthine, and ostensibly so inconclusive that after a few months' study of it the temptation to vigorously beat one's head against a wall for an hour or two (without interruption) becomes very strong. Summarizing this literature a little more than fifty years ago, David Potter wrote:

> Perhaps the most pervasive quality which it all has in common is that it continues to be explicitly or implicitly controversial. Not only have historians failed to agree as to whether slavery furnished the basic motive

for the war or whether it provided a smoke-screen for concealing the basic motives; they have also disagreed as to the nature of the society of the Old South, the nature of slavery, the motivation and character of the anti-slavery movement, and the interpretation of every link in the chain of sectional clashes which preceded the final crisis. The irony of this disagreement lies in the fact that it persists in the face of vastly increased factual knowledge and constantly intensified scholarly research.[2]

As already noted, this chaotic situation seems to have been resolved in our own time by means of a politically correct, liberal academic focus on the moral dimensions of the slavery issue. The resolution is not just that the South immorally protected the institution, but that the North bravely sacrificed hundreds of thousands for the sole purpose of liberating black people from servitude. But it is a false resolution, not only because the arguments for other factors (economic motives, the desire to preserve the Union, the fight over states' rights, etc.) cannot be ignored, but also because even historians such as James McPherson and Eric Foner, who are identified with the "growth of freedom" position, suddenly modify that position in favor of a larger "clash of civilizations" argument at the very end of their major works (see below). This suggests to me that the latter argument, which is far more complex, could be a much more sophisticated analytical structure for understanding all the other elements. As Foner tells us, "none of these elements can stand separately; they dissolve into one another, and the total product emerges as ideology."[3] The crucial questions for us, then, are What ideology? What is this "clash of civilizations" I am referring to? and, How does it work as an explanation for the Civil War?

Before we can answer these questions, however, we need to consider the possibility that slavery, as a moral issue, was *not* a fundamental factor in bringing about the war. There were some Confederate historians who argued this during and after the war, maintaining that the conflict was actually about states' rights or economic goals, rather than about slavery as a moral question. Much of this comes off as Southern apologetics; but as Thomas Pressly points out, prior to the Emancipation Proclamation (January 1, 1863), the North had proposed no change in the status of the Negro as a result of the war. This does lend some weight to the Confederate claim (made by Jefferson Davis, among others) that the real goal of the North was not abolition, but the attempt by the North to dominate the South. More dramatically, the Marxist historian Charles Beard (in *The Rise of American Civilization*, 1927) saw the war as a struggle between two conflicting economies, the watershed division between the agricultural era and the industrial era in American history. For him, slavery was not a significant factor, being more a kind of footnote to the war than anything else. After all, said Beard, the most obvious result of the war was the ascendancy of Northern capitalism, and the emergence of a plutocracy in the United States. It was not for nothing, he argued, that planters such as John Calhoun had predicted that it would be a disaster if those forces got control of the federal government—the "triumph of business enterprise."[4]

This is an argument with a lot of merit to it, but as the historian John Ashworth points out, Beard unfortunately couched it in rather simplistic terms. He made the mistake of thinking that in order to make an economic argument, he had to simultaneously argue that slavery was not part of the equation. In practice, however, slavery is integral to the economic argument because it was the basis of the Southern economy. Those who attacked or defended slavery did so for a variety of reasons, says Ashworth, with economics often being paramount. As James McPherson tells us, without slavery there would have been no Republican Party to threaten the Southern way of life. Beard's dichotomy—either it's economics or it's slavery—is thus a false one.[5]

Nevertheless, most Northerners also believed, at least initially, that the war was not about slavery as a moral issue; and if we look at what Lincoln said about it, we see that this is true: the North did not go to war to free the slaves. "I have no purpose," said the president in an address to a special session of Congress on July 4, 1861, "directly or indirectly, to interfere with slavery in the States where it exists," repeating what he had already said in his inaugural address earlier that year. Secession, he went on, was the real issue, for the Union must be preserved at all costs (the Union Congress passed resolutions endorsing all of this). Lincoln had already made it clear that he did not favor social and political equality for blacks "in any way," and was in fact a major proponent of colonization—repatriating them to Central America. In addition, it turns out that large and influential sections of the population, in both the North and the South, shied away from taking a radical position either for or against slavery; and for some Republicans, moral opposition to slavery was a nonissue—it didn't figure into their political outlook.[6]

As for the Union soldiers, McPherson notes that they saw themselves as fighting for the Union, and against what they regarded as treason. Only a minority, he says, had an interest in 1862 in fighting for black freedom. A popular Northern wartime ditty captured the mood pretty well:

A willingness to fight with vigor,
For loyal rights, but not the nigger.

Thus in the case of "contrabands"—slaves who escaped from their masters during the war and sought refuge in Union army camps—the typical Yankee response to these refugees was indifference or even cruelty. The Northern soldiers often used them as de facto slaves, making them do all the fatigue work for them. Occasionally the women were raped or abused.[7]

Although Lincoln personally believed that slavery was morally wrong, his primary motivations were social and economic. His vision was a nation of unlimited economic opportunity and upward social mobility—"free labor," or what would later be known as the American Dream. He had no particular prejudice against the South, write Eli Ginzberg and Alfred Eichner in *The Troublesome Presence*; his goal was to halt the further spread of slavery in the territories (the West—that is, our present Midwest) so that white people could build a better life for themselves through their own efforts. For a few, of course, it was not enough: abolitionists such as Horace Greeley (editor of the *New York Tribune*) rebuked him in 1862 for not taking a stronger stand. Lincoln's reply ought to clear up any doubts as to where he stood on the matter, at least at this point in time:

> My paramount object in this struggle *is* to save the Union, and it is *not* either to save or to destroy slavery. If I could save the Union without freeing *any* slave I would do it, and if I could save it by freeing *all* the slaves I would do it; and if I could save it by freeing some and leaving others alone I would also do that. What I do about slavery, and the colored race, I do because I believe it helps to save the Union; and what I forbear, I forbear because I do *not* believe it would help to save the Union.[8]

In a word, the moral argument cannot be pushed too far as a cause of the war, even though it served as a focal point around which the other factors managed to coalesce. All the evidence suggests that the North's "nobility" in fighting slavery was a long-after-the-fact justification, an attempt to portray the conflict as a victory of morality and equality over depravity. It's a thesis that gets people all worked up, but it finally doesn't wash.

What about the economic argument, then? This is where things get especially difficult, in exactly the way Eric Foner describes: you can't talk about one thing without talking about everything else, and finally things get melted down into a kind of stew pot, from which ideology—the clash of civilizations—emerges. In other words, the conflict between an agrarian slave economy—neo-feudal or "prebourgeois," as some have called it (and to which many others have objected)—and an industrial capitalist one, had direct implications for the sectional debate (whether slavery should be extended to the western territories) as well as for the theme of modernization (the replacement of a traditional, gemeinschaft way of life by a business-oriented, gesellschaft one). From here it is but a half step to the conclusion that the Civil War was fundamentally about a contest of worldviews. As I said, both McPherson and Foner seem to come to this conclusion almost in spite of themselves. Here is Foner's version of it: all the factors in the "stew pot," he writes, added up to the

> conviction that North and South represented two social systems whose values, interests, and future prospects were in sharp, perhaps mortal, conflict with one another. The sense of difference, of estrangement, and of growing hostility with which Republicans viewed the South, cannot be overemphasized.... An attack not simply on the institution of slavery, but upon southern society itself, was thus at the heart of the Republican mentality.[9]

Foner notes that Avery Craven had written (in *An Historian and the Civil War*, 1964) that by 1860, slavery had become a symbol or metaphor, a carrier for sectional conflicts; and he adds that as far as the issue of the extension of slavery into the territories went, it was really part of a more comprehensive ideological struggle. Each ideology, the Northern and the Southern, contained "the conviction that its own social system must expand, not only to insure its own survival but to prevent the expansion of all the evils the other represented." The conflict had become Manichaean; only the aspirations of one of these sides could prevail. To have remained in the Union after Lincoln's election, says Foner, "the South would have had to accept the verdict of 'ultimate extinction' which Lincoln and the Republicans had passed on the peculiar institution [slavery]." Secession, he adds, was "the only action consistent with its ideology." Or as the Italian historian Raimondo Luraghi puts it, "no society can ever be expected to commit suicide."

I shall return to the clash-of-civilizations argument in a moment. For now, I just wish to reiterate that it is almost impossible to discuss the various factors that led to the war in isolation. As a result, I shall try to navigate the "stew pot" as best I can, keeping in mind that the dish that finally gets served is that of two irreconcilable weltanschauungen and ways of life. Each side, by the 1850s, looked at the other's way of being in the world and found it nothing less than reprehensible.

So once again, the economic argument. Charles and Mary Beard set the stage here: the Southern economy was agrarian, the Northern one industrial, and over time they increasingly came into conflict. Skipping ahead a few decades, Barrington Moore, in *Social Origins of Dictatorship and Democracy*, notes that after the 1830s cotton ceased to dominate the economy of the North, which had basically become a manufacturing region. North and West (again, this refers to the Midwest) came to depend less on the South and more on each other; and the Northern manufacturing output was more and more heavily marketed to a rapidly growing West. Northern business interests, says Moore, were hardly advocates of war for the sake of

the Union. Although it is a scenario that historians have subsequently modified, the economic conflict appears to be one of
plantation slavery in the South versus industrial capitalism in
the North. What other outcome besides war could we expect?
As Moore puts it, "It is difficult to find a case in history where
two different regions have developed economic systems based
on diametrically opposed principles and yet remained under a
central government that retained real authority in both areas."
Perhaps even more to the point is the comment (once again) of
Raimondo Luraghi: "nowhere," he writes, "has the industrial
revolution . . . ever been achieved except by compelling agriculture to pay for it."[10]

Let's do the math, then, as the saying goes. Between 1800 and
1860 the proportion of the labor force engaged in agriculture
in the North dropped from 70 percent to 40 percent; in the
South, the proportion held fast at 80 percent. One tenth of
Southerners lived in urban areas; 25 percent of Northerners did.
For those engaged in business, the North to South ratio was
three to one; for engineers and inventors, six to one. In 1850,
only 14 percent of the national canal mileage ran through the
slave states. Those states represented 42 percent of the country's
population but only 18 percent of its manufacturing capacity.
The city of Lowell, Massachusetts, operated more spindles in
1860 than all eleven of the future Confederate states combined.
Economically, then, the North was racing ahead of the South in
no uncertain terms.[11]

Meanwhile, it might be instructive to look at what Mr.
Lincoln was up to during the latter part of this time. In
Lincoln and the Economics of the American Dream, Gabor
Borritt demonstrates quite convincingly that the Illinois poli-
tician's economic (and technological) views were central to his
political philosophy. Lincoln, he tells us, first came to promi-
nence in rural Illinois as an advocate of better transportation.
As a (Whig) member of the Illinois House of Representatives,

he supported the creation of numerous private companies engaged in river, canal, turnpike, and railroad construction, as well as the establishment of a state bank in 1835. His vision, according to Borritt, was that of endless material progress; the American Dream, as we have said. *"Since the central idea of America was economic,"* writes Borritt, *"the measure of the nation's success had to be economic, too."* The extension of slavery thus had to be opposed, in Lincoln's eyes, because it flew in the face of this economic objective, and had the potential to cut it off at the knees. By far, Lincoln's most determined defense of the Union was an economic one; to him, it "formed an indivisible economic unit." In socioeconomic terms, Lincoln regarded "unobstructed upward mobility [as] the most important ideal America strove for." In summation, says Borritt, Lincoln devoted more attention to economic issues than to any other question.[12]

All of this integrates quite well with Foner's classic study of Republican Party ideology. The central argument of *Free Soil, Free Labor, Free Men* is that the Republican Party was united by the idea that free labor was socially and economically superior to slave labor and that "the distinctive quality of Northern society was the opportunity it offered wage earners to rise to property-owning independence." Their political pitch throughout the 1850s was that freedom meant prosperity, progress, and upward social mobility, while slavery was an obstacle to all of these things. If slavery were to expand (that is, into the western territories), they argued, freedom—that is to say, free labor, the "class" of independent workers—would contract. Lincoln was the perfect representative of this group—and indeed, offered himself as an example on the campaign trail in 1860—because his life embodied the ideology of the self-made man, an ideology that would be carried on in the next century by means of Horatio Alger stories and the self-advertising of Andrew Carnegie, Bill Clinton, Bill Gates, and Oprah Winfrey, to name but a few. The free labor ideology, which was basically an idealized world of successful, independent entrepreneurs, was seen as key to an expanding capitalist society. "The universal desire for social advancement," writes Foner, "gave American life an aspect of almost frenetic motion and activity." Lincoln, he says, summed up the competitive character of Northern society when he spoke (in the 1850s) of the "race of life." He and the Republicans held that today's laborer was tomorrow's capitalist, and that if a man failed to rise above this status he had only himself to blame. It was never, said Lincoln, the fault of the system. (The legacy of this, as John Steinbeck pointed out many years later, was that in America the poor regard themselves as "temporarily embarrassed millionaires.")[13]

Now it turns out that in the antebellum period, let alone much later, the myth of the self-made man, of rags to riches, was just that—a myth. For example, during that period 4 percent of the inhabitants of New York City controlled 50 percent of the city's wealth; only a tiny percentage of the wealthy were truly self-made. Social mobility was, in short, pretty limited; the vast majority of wealthy individuals were born into rich families. As far as free labor (autonomous or entrepreneurial labor) goes, the reality was that it included wage labor (factory or other types of employment); and wage labor is "free" only if one chooses not to eat. Lincoln asserted, in 1859, that wage labor didn't amount to more than an eighth of the workforce, but this was certainly incorrect: almost 60 percent of the workforce was employed, not economically independent (self-employed). By the late nineteenth century, observes Foner, Lincoln's argument that wage labor was but a temporary stage on the road to free labor could not be maintained, and in fact the labor movement argued that coercion was as inherent to industrial capitalism as it had been to slavery. "Wage slavery" was a popular phrase during the Gilded Age—a concept that Southerners were bandying about decades earlier. "Your whole class of manual laborers and operatives, as you call them, are slaves," declared South Carolina senator James Hammond.[14]

In a word, Southerners found the Lincolnesque vision of a "race of life" grotesque; why would any reasonable person want to live that way? They looked North and saw a society of frenetic activity, selfishness, and greed—of hustling, in short—and wanted no part of it. They were, as the *New York Times* told its Northern readers in 1855, "content with things as they are"—which its Southern readers (if there were any) certainly would have taken as a compliment. Traveling through the South at about this time, Frederick Law Olmsted commented that the Southerner "enjoys life itself . . . [and] is content with being," whereas the Northerner couldn't be happy unless he was doing something, making some sort of "progress." For the most part, the North, when it looked South, saw a "dead society," as the *Cincinnati Gazette* put it in 1858: lazy, decadent, and absent of industry. But such a judgment not only confirmed Southern fears about the North; it also expressed the essence of the American imperial outlook: we know what's best for you—namely, the hustling life—and if you refuse to get on board with it we'll be forced to remake you in our image. Even beyond that, we need you to do this so we can develop an overseas empire and spread American influence throughout the world. In that way, our national greatness can be realized. (William Henry Seward explicitly stated this in the late 1850s.)[15]

In reality, the treatment of the South by the North was the template for the way the United States would come to treat any nation it regarded as an enemy: not merely a scorched earth policy, but also a "scorched soul" policy (the destruction of the Native American population was, of course, a preview of this). From Japan to Iraq, the pattern is the same, to the extent that we have been able to impose it: first destroy the place physically (in particular, murder huge numbers of civilians, as the

North did to the South during the Civil War—fifty thousand of them by 1865), and then "Americanize" it. Humiliation, the destruction of the identity of the defeated party, has always been an important part of the equation. Thus we have the *Cincinnati Gazette* (once again), in 1858, declaring that the South had to be regenerated, and that the only way to do this was to introduce "the Northern system of life" into it. (Later, of course, this would be changed to the American way of life, to be imposed on any nation foolish enough not to want to be just like us.) Two years earlier the *New York Tribune* called for an influx of "Northern capitalists, manufacturers, and merchants" into Virginia—basically, the Southern definition of hell. Lincoln himself told an official in the Interior Department in 1862 that as of 1863, "the character of the war will be changed. It will be one of subjugation. . . .The South is to be destroyed and replaced by new propositions and new ideas." There was an incessant repetition of the theme of how it was necessary to "Northernize the South" so it could finally enter the modern world. Thaddeus Stevens, leader of the radical faction of the Republicans in the House of Representatives, believed that this would have to "involve the desolation of the South," and in his speeches of 1865 he said that Southern institutions "*must* be broken up and *relaid*. . . . This can only be done by treating and holding them as a conquered people." The slave economy, said Charles Sumner a few years before that, prevents the example of the United States "from being all-conquering," whereas the nation had a responsibility to "renovate the condition of mankind." And if mankind chose to decline this generous offer, what then? The truth is that the South was right on the money in its assessment of Northern psychology and of what a "Northernized" America would mean for the nation and possibly the rest of the world. Slavery notwithstanding, it was hard for the South to regard the North as an ethical society. And, of course, vice versa.[16]

William Tecumseh Sherman's march from Atlanta to Savannah in 1864 was a deliberate policy of scorched earth and scorched soul. It was, writes James McPherson, retribution for secession (not for slavery), a war of plunder and arson. Sherman himself said that his aim was to terrorize the state of Georgia, demoralize it. As for the physical damage inflicted by the war in toto, by 1865 the South was "an economic desert." A quarter of the Confederacy's white men of military age perished, along with 40 percent of Southern livestock. The war also wrecked 50 percent of Southern farm machinery and thousands of miles of railroad. And whereas in 1860 the South had 30 percent of the national wealth, in 1870 it had only 12 percent.[17]

Some idea of the "clash of civilizations" involved in this is already apparent from what we said above, but before elaborating on it, we need to have a brief look at the sectional controversy that led to the war, and also the process of modernization—keeping in mind, once again, Foner's admonition that everything bleeds into everything else. In terms of the sectional controversy, it boiled down to what would happen to the new territories opening up to the West. Both Woodrow Wilson and Frederick Jackson Turner believed that the "view from the West," and the issue of the advancing frontier, constituted the proper perspective from which to understand American history. They thus rejected the archetypal dichotomy of dynamic North/stagnant South by adding the West as the crucial third dimension. Slavery itself, Wilson maintained, would not have disrupted the Union; its real importance (with which Lincoln certainly agreed) was that it had become intertwined with the national acquisition of new lands. Hence, rather than showing signs of disappearing, it was becoming more and more of a problem. Turner, in fact, argued that had there been no western area of expansion, slavery would have probably died off on its own.[18]

This is, in fact, pretty much the argument of McPherson's major study, that the cause of the war was a sectional conflict over the future of slavery. Were these territories, comprising two million square miles west of the Mississippi River, to be free or to be slave? For it was westward expansion that was making the slave issue so explosive. Expansion, as both Turner and William Appleman Williams have taught us, was the lifeblood of the nation. The West represented the future, and so it was Manifest Destiny that was heating the argument to the boiling point (the acquisition—i.e., theft—of half of Mexico in 1848 was a major part of this, obviously). This is why the conflict wouldn't go away, and why it kept recurring with the Missouri Compromise, the Wilmot Proviso, the tariff debates, the Dred Scott decision, etc., until war was finally the only way to settle it. John Calhoun implied as much in his "Southern Address" of 1849—that if the South was not given the right to expand slavery into the whole of American territory, the slave states would have to secede for their own protection. This is also why Jefferson Davis' famous remark "All we ask is to be let alone" was ultimately disingenuous. If the Northern capitalist system was an expansive one, so was the Southern slave system. The fight was at least in part a conflict of two expansionist systems, and it was not possible for both of them to win.[19]

Let's go a bit deeper. Turner did not invent his 1893 frontier thesis out of thin air. In the years leading up to the Civil War, the basic Republican answer to urban poverty was westward migration, which the Republicans regarded as a safety valve. It protected Northern labor from the degradation associated with European workers and Southern slaves. In addition, a slave influx into the western territories would put the kibosh on the social mobility that was the hallmark of Northern society: an economy of independent farmers would obviously be undercut by a flourishing slave economy. From the Southern side of the fence, expansion of the slave system was equally important, because agriculturally it needed virgin territory to survive. According to Eugene Genovese (in *The Political Economy of*

Slavery), the one-crop plantation system exhausted the soil and made fertilization and crop rotation nearly impossible. The Northern attempt to limit the expansion of slavery in favor of market capitalism and free labor thus threatened the entire Southern economy (although the conflict was not just an economic one). At this point, says Genovese, not seceding would have amounted to political suicide. For this and other reasons (for example, the increasing amount of trade between North and West), the focus on new states became intense: the admission of a slave state or a free one would tip the balance of power one way or the other. Both sides thus became hypervigilant regarding anything that might increase the advantage of the other side. All in all, then, an important cause of the war was the attempt of the South to arrest Northern expansion into the territories, and vice versa.[20]

We are almost at the threshold of the clash of civilizations now; the missing link is the factor of modernization. In many ways, it subsumes the issue of sectional conflict; in fact, some historians have argued that we may have taken the Civil War too seriously as an historical divide, and that from a more global perspective it was essentially an "episode" (if a dramatic one) in the modernization process. In other words, Reconstruction was already in the works; it was the culmination of a bourgeois revolution, a struggle over the nation's transition to modern society. At issue is the difference between gemeinschaft and gesellschaft referred to earlier, the difference between a dynamic, capitalist society and a traditional, neo-feudal one. These polar opposites function as ideal types; no society is wholly one or the other, and the original dichotomy between North and South as modern vs. traditional has been modified significantly over the past few decades. But something of the original polarity remains, certainly in the antebellum period. By way of comparison, we might note that while Maori or Mayan villages in New Zealand or Mexico (say) have access to television, life in those places is still very different from what it is in New York or Paris. Let me then sketch out a somewhat classic picture of this dichotomy before attempting to modify it—as, for example, Genovese has done with his own work over the years.[21]

What Genovese originally argued, in any case, was that the Old South was premodern, possibly even neo-feudal, and appalled by the modernization under way in the North. Southerners seceded specifically, he wrote, "to evade a modernity that would crush them." In a similar vein, a few decades earlier, the Southern historian Frank Owsley contended that it was the express goal of the North to destroy the South because "it impeded the progress of the machine." In his book on modernization, Richard Brown contrasts the aristocratic ethos of Southern society with the bourgeois ethos of the North. While deferential behavior, for example, was common in the former, in the latter the labor force was pursuing technological innovation. Northern literature romanticized technological progress, competitive behavior, and capital accumulation; the South regarded all of this as ungentlemanly. As opposed to the hustling life, it argued for honor and tradition. Sherman's march to the sea sought to destroy the Southern traditional way of life, and it succeeded. After that, says Brown, the Northern vision became the national one, while the traditional vision was equated with the "lost cause," the supposed feudal fantasy life of the South (hence the phrase "whistling 'Dixie'"). The good life was now about individual achievement, competition, and social mobility. The Confederacy, Brown maintains, was the last stand of the leisurely, organic, hierarchical way of life. Thereafter, "the ideal of a traditional society was erased from national life." While it is true that the South had been modernizing as well, it was far outdistanced by the North; and it was this gap, the speed of Northern changes and the propaganda that accompanied them, according to Brown, that threatened the South and led to the Civil War.[22]

Raimondo Luraghi sees all this as part of a global process of industrial colonialism, claiming that something similar happened during the unification of Italy. Basically, industrial expansion requires huge capital investment, which ultimately involves modernization: banking systems, railroads, a common currency, a unified system of weights and measures, tariffs, taxes, and typically, military occupation and even terrorism, to carry the modernization process to its logical conclusion. The old feudal order is deeply committed to localism, so it has to be destroyed. In the case of Italy, the southern part, or *mezzogiorno*, was reduced to the status of a colony. As the industrial revolution expanded worldwide during the nineteenth century, there was an accompanying attack on agrarian societies. The destruction and reconstruction of the American South was part of this general process; it, too, became an economic colony of the North.[23]

Earlier I talked about how James McPherson's "growth of freedom" position, as evinced in *Battle Cry of Freedom* (1988), got transmuted into a "clash of civilizations" position at the end of the book. It was, however, not without precedent in McPherson's work, for he had previously developed this idea in a brilliant essay in 1983 on "antebellum Southern exceptionalism" (some of which is repeated verbatim at the very end of *Battle Cry*).[24] Southern exceptionalism, says McPherson, is the belief that the South has a separate and unique identity that was out of the mainstream of American experience. Many historians, he points out, have argued that the root cause of the Civil War was that the North was threatening that sense of identity. Thus Genovese argues that the Southern ruling class had an antibourgeois spirit with mores that emphasized honor, family, and ease—things that set it apart from the mainstream of capitalist development. Even David Potter, who tried to argue against the notion of Southern distinctiveness, wound up saying that the South was characterized by a folk or gemeinschaft society, as opposed to the gesellschaft ideology of the rest of the country.

The former, said Potter, was about tradition, rural life, patterns of deference, and codes of honor and chivalry, whereas the latter was impersonal, bureaucratic, meritocratic, commercial, industrial, mobile, and rootless. In addition, many antebellum Americans, says McPherson, believed that North and South were two separate nations, with values and ideologies that were totally incompatible. As one congressman from Ohio put it, the struggle was "between systems, between civilizations." This sentiment was quite widespread on the eve of the war.

At this point McPherson revives the argument of his mentor C. Vann Woodward that the truth is that on a world scale, it was *America* that was exceptional, not the South.[25] However, Woodward was talking about the *post*–Civil War period. McPherson, in a sense, did his teacher one better, using the exceptionalism argument for the antebellum period to make a strong case for the clash of civilizations theory. Asking if the South was exceptional, says McPherson, is the wrong question. "It was the *North* that was 'different,'" he writes, "the North that departed from historical development." We should, he goes on, speak of *Northern* exceptionalism. For it wasn't the South that changed in the decades before the Civil War, it was the North. In most respects, he points out, "the South resembled a majority of the societies in the world more than the changing North did." Much of the world, for example, had an unfree or quasi-free labor force. Worldwide, most societies were rural, agricultural, and bound by traditional networks of family/kinship/hierarchy. It was gemeinschaft and tradition, not gesellschaft and modernization, that was the norm. "The North—along with a few countries in northwestern Europe—hurtled forward eagerly toward a future that many Southerners found distasteful if not frightening." So when secessionists argued in 1861 that they were acting to preserve a way of life, traditional rights and values, they were being honest. McPherson continues:

The South's concept of republicanism had not changed
in three-quarters of a century; the North's had.... The
accession to power of the Republican party, with its ideology of competitive, egalitarian, free-labor capitalism,
was a signal to the South that the Northern majority had
turned irrevocably toward this frightening, revolutionary future.

Secession was thus a preemptive move, and Jefferson Davis
was hardly off base when he asserted that *we* are the conservatives in this dispute; *you* are the revolutionaries. The Union
victory ensured that the Northern vision would become the
American one, but until 1861 "it was the North that was out
of the mainstream, not the South." "When did the northern
stream become the mainstream?" asks McPherson. Who is
really the anomaly here?[26]

I shall return to the question of anomaly below, because there
is one important way in which the South can also be regarded
as anomalous in 1860. Be that as it may, I find the Woodward-
McPherson argument extremely compelling. Sure, the war was
about slavery; it was hardly a minor issue. But it was part of a
much larger one about two very different and incompatible civilizations, and a fixation on the moral question of slavery can
blind us to the larger (world) context of the Civil War, which
was really the American version of the global modernization
process. No, I have no wish to live in a slave society; I regard
it as an abomination. But the South saw a different type of
abomination on the horizon, one that is now with us; and quite
frankly, I have no wish to live in that one either. This is what
books such as *Brave New World* are really about (Max Weber's
iron cage meets *American Idol* might be one way of putting it);
and the question of where contemporary "Southerners" can go
to escape this dystopia is no small point. I shall return to this
question in chapter 5. For now, we need to revisit the Old

South and get a clear, non-starry-eyed assessment of what that society was finally about. To be sure, it wasn't about moonlight and magnolias and *Gone with the Wind*; but it also wasn't *not* about those things, either.

The classic exposition of the Southern way of life was written by W. J. Cash in 1941 and titled *The Mind of the South*. A Southerner by birth, Cash had a love-hate relationship with the place that finally drove him to suicide shortly after the book was published. It is a book of stereotypes, and has been modified greatly in the seventy years since it first appeared. Nevertheless, it's still worth reading. Cash captured some essential aspects of the region that were true enough of the antebellum period and beyond, and he was hardly unaware of the Southern tendency to romanticize its own way of life.

While it is certainly the case that there are many Souths, wrote Cash, there is also, he asserted, only one South as well. One can, in other words, trace a definite mental and social pattern across the region: the "Savage Ideal." We can thus speak of a cultural unity, or collective temperament, which included vigilante justice, an eye-for-an-eye ethic, and a Manichaean division between good and evil. Throughout Southern history, we find (among whites) a desire for power, pride, and prestige, and a corresponding distaste for the acquisition of money for its own sake. It was "a world singularly polished and mellow and poised, wholly dominated by ideals of honor and chivalry and *noblesse*." The very marrow of this tradition, said Cash, "was a sort of immense kindliness and easiness," a graciousness of style that was part of the working code of the Old South. Manners were informed by the aristocratic ideal, so that among yeomen farmers there was "a kindly courtesy, a level-eyed pride, an easy quietness, a barely perceptible flourish of bearing, which, for all its obvious angularity and fundamental plainness, was one of the finest things the Old South produced." The (classical republican) habit of tailoring your behavior to the social good, he went on, was "passed down through the whole of Southern society and became a characteristic Southern trait." It amounted to a "simple tradition of uprightness." In contrast to the zeal for money that characterized the North, the South was guided by ideals of honor, courage, generosity, amiability, and courtesy. As a result, he argued, the South is "another land, sharply differentiated from the rest of the American nation, and exhibiting within itself a remarkable homogeneity." If it was not quite a nation within a nation, he concluded, it was "the next thing to it."[27]

All of this, however, had a very large, dark shadow. For example, the South, according to Cash, displayed a deep anti-intellectualism. The Southern gentleman, he said, was interested in dogs, guns, and horses, not books, ideas, and art. The dominant mood of the place was "one of well-nigh drunken reverie," and the mode of discourse was one of rhetoric and oratory, things that appealed to the emotions rather than the intellect. Laziness and hedonism characterized the region, said Cash, not curiosity or intellectual exploration. While there is some truth to this particular stereotype, it is vastly overdrawn here, and has for the most part been debunked by the historian Michael O'Brien in a study of the intellectual life of the Old South that runs to nearly fourteen hundred pages.[28]

Then there was the Southern tradition of honor. This characterization has a lot more validity to it. The tendency to take offense at the slightest insult (or perceived insult) made for a rather volatile society. As W. E. B. DuBois said of Southern whites, "Their 'honor' became a vast and awful thing, requiring wide and instant deference." The result was that the use of physical force was endemic to the South. Duels, tarring and feathering, and lynching (more than 90 percent of which was done by whites to whites during 1840–60, according to Cash) were the order of the day. And if Southern society was easygoing and gracious, there was no getting around the fact that it was based on slavery, on brute force. White supremacy was everything, and "The lash lurked always in the background." If, as McPherson and Woodward argue, the North was the anomaly, worldwide, and the traditional society of the South the norm, it is nevertheless the case that by 1861 much of the Western world had abolished slavery, and the South was in the anachronistic position of embracing the institution at the very time that virtually everyone else was giving it up. As Eric Foner notes, there was "something decidedly odd," in 1861, about an independent proslavery nation. Or as Tocqueville put it in a letter to the Boston newspaper the *Liberty Bell* in 1856, "I am pained and astonished by the fact that the freest people in the world is, at the present time, almost the only one among civilized and Christian nations which yet maintains personal servitude." After all, it's not that hard to have a leisured, non-hustling society when you've got four million slaves to do most of your work for you.[29]

Cash also held that the Southern habit of looking down at the Yankee as crass and money-grubbing was a defense mechanism; that secretly, the Southerner was envious of Northern capitalist success and that this had led to a nostalgia about an imaginary past, including a fascination with medieval chivalry, Sir Walter Scott, and the like. Yet as we already saw, he does credit the difference between these two types of societies as being fully real, adding that the desire to make everyone like themselves (that is, modern and progressive) was "the most fundamental drive behind the Yankee's behavior." This brings to mind a conversation Tocqueville had with a lawyer in Baltimore, in which the latter told him:

> What distinguishes the North is the spirit of enterprise, and what distinguishes the South is the spirit of chivalry. A Southerner's manners are frank and open; he is excitable, irritable even, and extremely touchy on points of honor. A New Englander is cold, calculating,

and patient. When you stay with a Southerner, he makes you welcome and shares all the pleasures of his home with you. As soon as the Northerner has received you, he starts to consider whether he might be able to do business with you.

Regarding the latter, Tocqueville jotted in his notebook, "Coldly burning spirit, serious, tenacious, egotistic, cold, frozen imagination, respectful of money, industrious, proud, a reasoner."[30]

This is the real clash of civilizations, it seems to me, and what the Civil War was finally, at root, about. Slavery was the focal point, but the heart of the matter was that the North wanted to give the South a modern "makeover," and the South had no interest in this project. Discussing Charles Frazier's famous novel *Cold Mountain*, Louis Menand says that the book basically argues that the result of the war was "the defeat of the crafted by the machine-made, the hearth by the factory, the folk by the mass." As Inman, the Confederate soldier gone AWOL and making his way back home to North Carolina states at one point, "One man I knew had been north to the big cities, and he said it was every feature of such places that we were fighting to prevent." "When we say Yankee thought and Yankee mind," observes Cash, "we are in effect saying modern thought and the modern mind." The South was having none of it.[31]

The subject of Southern honor, briefly alluded to above, is something that also highlights the differences between the two civilizations. The topic has been extensively explored by the historian Bertram Wyatt-Brown, who approaches it almost anthropologically. The shame/honor culture, he points out, is the oldest ethical system in human history. Negotiations with such cultures—for example, those of the Middle East—require that the stronger party never display disrespect for the weaker one. Symbols of parity must be offered so the latter can save face, and it was precisely this, he says, that the North was not willing to do with respect to the South. Indeed, as we have seen, the tendency was to regard the South with open contempt, to ridicule and humiliate it, both before and after the war. Rightly or wrongly, white Southerners were certain their cause was justified by a prehistoric honor code. (Both the Old and New Testaments, for example, sanction slavery at a number of points.) The threat to the South was loss of honor, according to Wyatt-Brown, no less than the loss of slavery; the loss of a whole way of life. It was honor, he says, that called for secession in 1860–61, and there weren't too many Southerners who were willing to break this code.[32]

The issue of honor also can be viewed through the lens of modernization. By the 1830s, the North was replacing communal justice with a legal apparatus. Honor in the North was becoming increasingly identified with civic respectability. From this perspective, dueling and vigilante justice were regarded as barbaric; but if slavery were an anachronism in the Western world by 1860, the traditional honor code was not (at least not yet). A gemeinschaft culture focuses on honor and community; a gesellschaft one thinks in terms of conscience and secular economic activity. The modernization process was pushing the North in an accelerated gesellschaft direction, one the South found repugnant. As McPherson and Woodward argue, the South was not exceptional in this regard.[33]

The clash of civilizations was the special focus of a group of Southern intellectuals loosely associated with Vanderbilt University in Nashville in the 1920s and after (including Allen Tate and Robert Penn Warren), who produced a defense of the South in 1930 with the deliberately provocative title *I'll Take My Stand*. The book, and its enduring popularity, bear witness to the fact that the clash of civilizations hardly ended with the Civil War. (Faulkner: "The past isn't dead, it isn't even past.") The Southern Agrarians, as they are known, were out to show that Northern "progress" had proven to be a huge mistake and that the Southern agrarian way of life, slavery excepted, was needed now more than ever. For the Northern culture of production and consumption, they argued, had no intrinsic meaning; it was little more than a treadmill, an "infinite series," going nowhere. The historian Willard Gatewood comments, "Theirs was a protest against the material acquisitiveness, spiritual disorder, lack of purpose, destruction of individual integrity, and other trends in modern society that they associated with industrialism." The latter was for them a malevolent force, and they regarded the South "as the last substantial barrier against mass dehumanization and the philistinization produced by industrialism." Gatewood notes that Sheldon Hackney (like James McPherson, another Woodward student) referred to the South at one point as "the nation's largest and oldest counterculture," which to my mind hits the nail directly on the head. *I'll Take My Stand* did not sell well initially, and critics accused the group of romanticizing the Old South, ignoring slavery, and attempting to roll back progress—all of which were true. And yet, as time passed, the book came to seem increasingly prophetic, a pre-Vance Packard-Mumford-Marcuse-type warning about the dangers of sacrificing aesthetic values for economic ones. Far from being a reactionary text, wrote one reviewer in 1982, *I'll Take My Stand* is now celebrated as a forward-looking work. As Robert Penn Warren told the *New York Times* in 1977, the Agrarians could be characterized as a kind of fifth column in the dominant culture, similar to Transcendentalists, ecologists, and hippies. Except that the South was a geopolitical entity, not just a fad or an intellectual tradition. It had real power, and it was prepared to use it.[34]

It would thus be fair to say that the subject of the book is the subject of this one as well: What might be an alternative, historically speaking, to the hustling life? Why has America basically been about only one thing? Why did those who were averse to capitalism never have a chance? Allen Tate pointed out that there *was* an alternative, at least in theory, from the country's earliest days: a simple, nonacquisitive existence, which he believed was a rebuke to the dominant culture, to a society that had been obsessed with wealth and power from day one. While the book emphasized agriculture as the economic basis of this alternative way of life, the agrarian bias was dropped by the group in the ensuing years, since the real focus of the book (to put it in Marxist terms) was the superstructure, not the base. Thus in 1942 Tate wrote to his fellow poet Donald Davidson that the book was "a reaffirmation to the humane tradition, and to affirm that is an end in itself. Never fear: we shall be remembered when our snipers are forgotten." As an Amazon reviewer put it more recently, "It is a book with an old-fashioned humanism and dignity that is seldom encountered anymore." Thus the Southern historian Louis Rubin claims that the book is not really about the revival of the South, or about agrarian society, but about human life, and what that should be. The twelve authors held up an admittedly idealized image of the Old South as if to say, *This was what America could have become, but didn't.* The book, says Rubin, functioned as a critique of the modern world: "in contrast to the hurried, nervous life of cities, the image of the agrarian South was of a life in which human beings existed serenely and harmoniously." *I'll Take My Stand* thus remains "a rebuke to materialism, a corrective to the worship of Progress, and a reaffirmation of man's aesthetic and spiritual needs."[35]

One of the contributors to the volume, the poet John Crowe Ransom, framed the contrast in terms of Europe vs. America and argued that "The South is unique on this continent for having founded and defended a culture which was according to the European principles of culture." (The Southern states, wrote the playwright Thornton Wilder, constitute "enclaves or residual areas of European feeling.") Europe had a maturity of mind, he said, whereas most Americans were "in a state of arrested adolescence." They worshipped progress, even though "Progress never defines its ultimate objective"; it just goes on and on, brutalizing our lives. They spoke of ambition, said Ransom, but what it really came down to was belligerence, the endless striving for personal success. Real community was not possible under these conditions—a prediction that has proven to be tragically true. As another contributor, the novelist and editor Andrew Nelson Lytle, observed (echoing what the Baltimore lawyer said to Alexis de Tocqueville), social gatherings in the North invariably have an agenda. Socializing in this context always has some ulterior motive lurking behind it, and that motive is business. As the comedian Chris Rock once put it, "When you're talking to someone [in the United States], you're not talking to that person, you're talking to their agent." As for progress, wrote Lytle, it was basically a "whitewash metaphysics."[36]

The topic of progress, so-called, was the particular focus of the contribution of the psychologist Lyle Lanier. The word, he argued, was little more than a slogan, a public anesthetic. This was the psychology of the system, he wrote, and since it amounted to little more than business and "noisy social ferment," we would do well to stop using the word. "The only intelligible meaning of progress," he asserted, "implies social institutions for producing psychological effects just the reverse of those so outstanding in our machine age." There is no humanized living in such a system, he added; the drab existence of those "caught in the throes of these convulsions of a predatory and decadent capitalism . . . will bear mute testimony that our century of Progress lies below the cultural level of the Pyramids." The contrast was put very clearly by Stark Young of the *New Republic* when he wrote of the Southern ideal:

> This way of life meant mutuality of interests among
> more people, an innate code of obligations, and a

certain openness of life. It meant self-control that implied not the expression of you and your precious personality, not the pleasures of suffering or of denying your own will; you controlled yourself in order to make the society you lived in more decent, affable, and civilized and yourself more amenable and attractive.

To the South, wrote Frank Owsley, the philosophy of the North was "the religion of an alien God."[37]

As the years passed, however, it became clear that sectional identification was not the primary issue. Tate acknowledged this in a footnote in the book itself, that the writers were talking about a certain spirit, and that this spirit may have lived elsewhere, not just in the South. Thus Paul Murphy, in *The Rebuke of History*, argues that the book was "an affirmation of universal values," and a defense of an older European civilization—really, a defense of the humanistic tradition of the West. The authors, he says, regarded the South as the "true" Western civilization, and the hustling bourgeois civilization of the North as a rupture with that tradition. Even Marshall McLuhan got drawn into all of this, writing an essay in 1947 for the *Sewanee Review* (edited by Tate) titled "The Southern Quality," in which he argued that the South, in its exemplification of a humanist culture, possessed a lesson for the rest of the world. McLuhan, along with Southern conservatives such as Richard Weaver, regarded the dropping of atomic bombs on Japan as the final discrediting of the Northern notion of progress via science and technology. "We all stand today at Appomattox," wrote Weaver, we all have surrendered to a world governed by scientific "reason." Many on the Left, such as Dwight MacDonald, C. Wright Mills, and Lewis Mumford, were making similar arguments around the same time; and years later Eugene Genovese would assert that the tradition of Southern conservatism was the most convincing American critique of bourgeois individualism we had.[38]

I have already referred to Genovese at several points, in a rather desultory fashion, but his work really deserves a separate discussion all its own. Although, given the political correctness of the times, he is rather out of fashion these days, his work is probably the most important contribution to our understanding of the antebellum South that we have. No study of the Civil War can possibly ignore it; the *Atlantic Monthly*, a few years ago, referred to him as "This country's greatest living historian"— an assessment that can't be too far off the mark.[39]

Once again, Genovese's original argument, in *The Political Economy of Slavery* (1965), was that the slaveholding class—the planter elite—was essentially precapitalist, or semifeudal (he would later refer to it as "prebourgeois"). Its wealth and power were based on land and on slave labor; the owners didn't really understand much of capitalism as a system. Genovese argued that Southern society, "in its spirit and fundamental direction, represented the antithesis of capitalism." While it is true that the planters traded in international markets, were dependent on bankers for credit, and were ineluctably tied to Northern capitalism, it is nevertheless the case, he wrote, that a few capitalist features do not amount to a capitalist system. For example, the planters tended to consume profits rather than reinvest them; or to invest them in land and slaves, rather than in new industrial enterprises.[40]

Since the publication of that book (and even before), there have been numerous studies of the Southern economy arguing that it was fully integrated into the larger American capitalist system; even, that it was more profitable than the free-labor system of the North. This is a hot-button topic, because if the Southern slave economy was actually a flourishing capitalistic one, then the Civil War and the death of 625,000 men was probably justified, in that without the war, slavery might have lasted another fifty years or so. If, on the other hand, the slave economy was weak, or on its last legs, as others have argued, then the institution probably would have petered out on its own; in which case the war was pure folly, a tragedy full of sound and fury, signifying nothing.

In any case, given the evidence for varying degrees of capital-ism in the South, Genovese felt compelled to modify his argu-ment somewhat over the years, but he has nevertheless been able to defend the claim that the Southern economy and soci-ety (and certainly, mental outlook) constituted a very different creature than the one up North; that North and South were, indeed, two distinct civilizations. His essential pitch (and that of his late wife, Elizabeth Fox-Genovese) is that the Southern economy was a kind of hybrid—"in but not of the capital-ist world." As already noted, the slaveholders sold their crops and accumulated capital in the world market, but they did not invest in that market to improve the system. In other words, antebellum Southerners were not members of a capitalist class who also happened to own slaves, because these men regarded the free-labor (capitalist) system as a source of evil, which they identified with the North. The master-slave relationship is very different from the employer-employee relationship, no mat-ter how benign the former, or exploitative the latter, might be. Social relations in the former were defined by "paternalism," as Genovese put it—that is, by authority and (at times) benevo-lence; in the latter, they were defined by cash. In addition, says Genovese, commerce should not be mistaken for capitalism; otherwise capitalism would have existed in Sumer and Babylon (a point also made by Joyce Appleby). The slave economy thus had a Janus face, somewhere between feudalism and capital-ism. The South had a market economy in a restricted sense; but it definitely did not have a market *society*—something it was hell-bent on making sure did not find its way below the Mason-Dixon line. Once again, we have an anomaly, or hybrid: a slave-holding country within a bourgeois nation-state and a world capitalist market; a modern slave society, in short.[41]

This sorting out of the ambiguous nature of the Southern economy constitutes, to my mind, a crucially important contribution to our understanding of the American South and the origins of the Civil War. But perhaps equally significant is Genovese's appreciation of the culture of Southern society, and the significance of that culture for American history in general. This is, of course, a sensitive issue, because (as Genovese notes) to speak positively about the Southern tradition at all "is to invite charges of being ... an apologist for slavery and segregation."[42] But what do you have when the best features of a society grow out, as it were, of the worst features of that society? After all, Athenian democracy depended (at one point) on having more than a million slaves working the silver mines, yet by and large we are great admirers of Athenian democracy. The Greeks are our heroes—and rightly so. True, slavery in the ancient world was coin of the realm, not an anachronism, as it was in Alabama in 1860, and perhaps that makes it a bit more acceptable. But does it? If millions suffered so that a few could sit around discussing the ideal nature of the state, or the essence of virtue, doesn't that come off as rather ... grotesque? On the other hand, doesn't that, in many ways, describe contemporary life as well? And in addition, what would Western civilization really be without Plato and Aristotle? We in the West have understandably not wanted to throw out the baby with the bathwater.

I know of no way of resolving this, at least for the South, except to say that if it is possible to admire and discuss Athenian democracy, slavery notwithstanding, then it seems to me equally possible to admire and discuss the cultural and political achievements of the South, even while recognizing the socioeconomic basis on which they rested. In fact, for reasons that will become obvious (or perhaps should already be), I think we have an obligation to do so. It finally comes down to Sheldon Hackney's point about the South being the nation's only serious counterculture. As one Genovese student, David Chappell, has put it, the argument is that the South is "*the* anticapitalist tradition in America—the one that, although it was defeated in the war, gave capitalism a harder run for its money than any other anticapitalist tradition in America." No mean achievement, that, in the grander scheme of things. In effect, the South was the only muscular opposition to the American definition of the good life as hustling; this is finally why, from a Northern perspective, it had to go. Reviewing the work of Genovese, historian James Livingston comments, "The only opposition to North American capitalism that ever combined ideological coherence and material consequences—both words and deeds—was . . . the opposition of the slave South." As already noted, the other countercultural traditions we have discussed in this book were essentially about words. The Southern countercultural tradition was also about deeds.[43]

"The northern victory in 1865," writes Genovese,

> silenced a discretely southern interpretation of American history and national identity, and it promoted a contemptuous dismissal of all things southern as nasty, racist, immoral, and intellectually inferior. The northern victory did carry out a much too belated abolition of slavery. But it also sanctified northern institutions and intentions, which included the unfettered expansion of a bourgeois worldview and the suppression of alternate visions of a social order.

That suppression was a great loss, says Genovese, because the Southern critique has much to offer us. The Southern vision is—again—an older humanist ideal, one that sees the flowering of the personality within a communal or societal structure. This is a "social bond individualism," one rooted in family and community and civic responsibility, and very different from

modern bourgeois individualist ideology, which is about ego-
centrism and loss of civic discipline, and is devoid of any moral
basis. Southern conservatives today, remarks Genovese, argue
that their society grew out of a people who settled Virginia and
the Carolinas *not* to build a city on a hill. (How refreshing!)
Instead, we got the alternative, one that "makes the market
the arbiter of our moral, spiritual, and political life," and at the
same time expects us "to live as civilized human beings." The
happy dream of free market advocates, of a "well ordered international economy of morally indifferent affluence for many and
misery for those who cannot compete . . . is becoming a reality."
It is, he concludes, a "brave new world of affluent depravity."[44]

Genovese sees it as ironic that the defeat of the South, of slavery, opened the doors to an imperialism that imposed "unprecedented misery and mass slaughter on the world." "The defeat
of the slaveholders and their worldview," he writes, "opened
the floodgates to the global catastrophe their leading spokesmen had long seen a-borning." It also made sure that the cash
value of things would be the only value of things. In *The Mind
of the Master Class* (2005), he and Elizabeth Fox-Genovese show
the graciousness, generosity, courage, openness, and sense of
ease that were common to that class, a class that had a learned
relationship to classical culture and Christian civilization. They
thus argue for the need to see beyond the slave issue, if we can;
to realize that the South was trying to hold off the coming tide,
namely the destructive forces of capitalism, especially in terms
of what it does to human relations. The slaveholders saw how
bourgeois social relations dissolved family and community ties
and made the market the ultimate determinant of human life.
Their objection was not to a market economy as such—they
were embedded in one—but to its tendency to become the
essence of society, such that everything became a commodity.
In its flawed and tragic way, the Old South stood for values
that we finally cannot live without if we are to remain human.

The tragic part of this, the maddening part, is that now, looking back, it is impossible to separate the horror of slavery from the positive features of that society, except in a theoretical sense. One has to wonder if these are the only choices available.[45]

As for the debate over slavery vs. capitalism and the economic viability of the Southern economy, referred to briefly above, this issue never really got resolved. Nobody "won" the argument in any clear and definitive way; basically, it just petered out (for more on this see n. 41). (It also moved to a more global context—some historians have begun to look at the role of the South in the entire capitalist world system, not just in America.) The most recent historiographical review of the subject, *Debating Slavery*, by Mark Smith (1998), muddles through to a kind of middle ground. In short, no decisive conclusions were ever reached, which means, of course, that the question of whether the Civil War was worth it never got resolved either. I can't help thinking back to that comment of David Potter, quoted at the beginning of this chapter, that such basic questions have not gotten sorted out "in the face of increased factual knowledge and constantly intensified research." It's enough to turn one into a postmodernist, really, because if we cannot say with any degree of certainty whether the slave economy was a boom or a bust, and therefore whether the Civil War—*the* defining event in American history, beyond the Revolutionary War—really needed to be fought, then one has to wonder what the past fifty years of research finally amounted to. Personally, I agree with the Genoveses when they write, in *The Mind of the Master Class*, that there is simply no way to make the case that a society based on servitude would ever have led to one that was more humane and just. For slavery was not just an economic institution, quite obviously; it also was a psychological phenomenon, deeply woven into the whole unconscious of the South. On this, at least, Smith is definitive: "the holding of slaves," he writes, "was important for southern whites' definition of personal freedom." Along with Tocqueville, I believe that only a war could have dislodged it, in the end. But this is only an educated guess on my part, just as the clash-of-civilizations argument strikes me as the most likely explanation of the war itself. These issues finally seem to be "beyond facts."[46]

Speaking of postmodernism, and of the larger issues that surround the war, the two got combined a few years ago in a book by Walter Hixson titled *The Myth of American Diplomacy*. Hixson believes that the civilizational clash we have been talking about is in fact much greater than one of modernization, which is a relatively recent phenomenon; that it can be traced to the emergence of modernity itself, a long-term pattern going back to early modern Europe. This might sound a bit like the lawyer in a play by Molière, who attempts to prove the innocence of his client by deducing it from the history of the world ("Skipping to the Flood, Your Honor . . ."); but Hixson seems to have captured something essential here. In the sixteenth and seventeenth centuries, Euro-American history developed within the framework of modernity. That is to say, these nations defined themselves as modern, in contrast to those they labeled "backward"; and colonialism and imperialism followed from a worldview that apotheosized the new mode of existence. On this schema, those peoples who lived in accordance with different realities were viewed as unenlightened, and thus fair game for Western (Occidental) control. The United States, says Hixson, became the epitome of modernity, and central to this was Turner's definition of the frontier as the "meeting point between savagery and civilization." (One is reminded of Claude Lévi-Strauss' distinction between the raw and the cooked.) "In here" is civilization; "out there" is savagery, which must be converted, subdued, or (typically) exterminated. (This is why the Unabomber had to be pictured for the American public as a lunatic, a wild, unkempt "mountain man" living alone in a cabin in Montana like some kind of animal. If you seriously disagree with the American notion of progress, you must be a madman or a savage.) The result, says Hixson, is a continuous history of violent conflict, wherein, to quote the eminent Americanist scholar Sacvan Bercovitch, the United States engages in "a rhetoric of holy war against everything un-American." This is what happened in the "winning of the West" (the Indian genocide), the destruction of the American South (perceived by the North as backward and barbaric), the Cold War (think of the "gooks" and "slopes" of Vietnam), the so-called war on terrorism, and so on. Starting with Native Americans, these Other were not perceived as being fully human; they were merely obstacles in the way of modern-ist "progress." For deep psychological reasons I have explored elsewhere (the need to give yourself an identity through oppo-sition), and which Hixson explores from a somewhat differ-ent angle (the psychoanalytic theory of Jacques Lacan), war is at the center of U.S. history and of American identity. There is simply no stopping the "beacon of liberty" concept, the "march of progress" concept, or the "triumph over savagery" concept. These notions lie at the heart of the frontier encoun-ter with the Other, which involves, says Hixson, "an especially violent form of identification." This is why the Southern way of life had to go, and why our approach to our supposed ene-mies—then, before, and since—is always one of scorched earth and scorched soul. American military campaigns are incredibly violent; the enemy is always a collection of *untermenschen* and therefore must be completely destroyed.[47]

My own take on this vortex of violence is that from an early point, America had no real content. Hustling, after all, hardly qualifies as content; indeed, it can only generate an anti-society, which we now see all around us. In addition, in breaking away from England and Continental Europe, America acquired what Hegel called a "negative identity," one that was defined by what it was not, what it was opposed to. Hixson, following

Louis Hartz, argues that our belief that we are special came out of not having, in contrast to Europe, a long history of feudalism and religion to endow us with a solid identity. And without the sense of a long historical tradition, America became dependent on representation—on an image of itself to organize consent and coherence. This is why the boundless expansion of the frontier and the ideology of progress (as against the "savage," who is unprogressive) are so closely tied together and why our behavior toward perceived enemies is so extreme—pathological, in a word.[48]

It is also why there is so little tolerance for substantive dissent, or fundamental critique, in America. Since our identity is in fact quite brittle, we have to be constantly telling ourselves how fabulous we are. Thus Tocqueville wrote of America that "the least reproach offends it, and the slightest sting of truth turns it fierce; one must praise everything, from the turn of its phrases to its most robust virtues.... Hence the majority lives in a state of perpetual self-adoration."[49]

And finally, this is why the thesis that slavery as a moral issue was the cause of the Civil War is so popular: it fits completely with the narrative of the national identity as the growth of freedom. It is a lot more flattering (except in the South, of course) to think of the war in terms of "Glory, glory, hallelujah!" than in terms of a clash of civilizations, or a product of the long-term rise of modernity, or a pathological drive to stamp out a backward, nonprogressive Other. The war, says Hixson, got papered over with a sacred imagery that endures to this day. He writes:

> The kaleidoscope of Civil War imagery—the bloody lane and cornfield at Antietam, the Emancipation Proclamation, Mathew Brady's photographs, the "Battle Hymn of the Republic," Lincoln at Gettysburg, Sherman's march to the sea, Grant and Lee at Appomattox, and the final Shakespearean

tragedy at Ford's Theater—all redefined and ultimately "hallowed" the meaning of America.[50]

To paraphrase that great humanitarian Donald Rumsfeld, you
don't always get the country you want. But in this case, we
did—at least most of us did.

And what about the rest of us? Ah, that's where this country
really missed the boat. It chose to vilify the South, as a result
of which—Genovese and the Southern Agrarians notwithstanding—it never got to understand the positive aspects of
that way of life, the possible alternative to a life of endless hustling. Donald Davidson wrote that "the Lost Cause might not
be wholly lost after all. In its very backwardness the South had
clung to some secret which embodied, it seemed, the elements
out of which its own reconstruction—and possibly even the
reconstruction of America—might be achieved."[51]

Of course, this never came to pass. The importance of
the Southern experience for the rest of the country, and the
failure of America to come to terms with it, is for C. Vann
Woodward the real tragedy of the century following the Civil
War. In an essay he wrote in 1953—so prescient it is sometimes breathtaking—Woodward spelled this out in some detail.
Unlike the South, he wrote, America has never known defeat
(remember, this was in 1953). In fact, it has been dangerously
isolated from the common experience of mankind, believing
that it can accomplish anything; whereas the South did not
share "the national faith in unlimited progress, in the efficacy
of material means, [and] in the importance of mass and speed."
This type of illusion "has fostered the tacit conviction that
American ideals, values, and principles [will] inevitably prevail
in the end. . . . And the assumption exposes us to the temptation
of believing that we are somehow immune from the forces of
history."[52]

Dominating the world, Woodward continues, has not worked out for us, and we are bitter because we see ourselves as innocents. As a result, "there is the danger that America may be tempted to exert all the terrible power she possesses to compel history to conform to her own illusions. The extreme ... expression, would be the so-called preventative war." Our celebration of laissez-faire market capitalism, he says, is central to these illusions, for we have allowed "our whole cause, our traditional values, and our way of life to be identified with one economic institution." We have even identified "the security of the country with the security of that institution."

All of this, he goes on to say, involves us in "a moral crusade on a world-wide scale," and people so involved typically concede no validity to the opposing point of view. "Expressed in military policy and war aims these passions overwhelm reason and find no bounds short of complete submission, unconditional surrender, and total domination of the defeated people." The irony of all this is that it shatters "the foundations of the political and moral order on which peace has to be built." What America needs, he concludes, is an understanding that only the South (America's shadow, in effect) can give it an understanding of "the tragic and ironic aspects of man's fate." The South could also teach us the futility of "imposing the ideals of the conquerer upon defeated peoples by force of arms"; that "economic systems, whatever their age, their respectability, or their apparent stability, are transitory and that *any nation which elects to stand or fall upon one ephemeral institution has already determined its fate.*" [Emphasis mine.]

America, of course, paid no attention to any of this, any more than it paid attention to the South (or the Transcendentalists, Herman Melville, Lewis Mumford, Jimmy Carter, etc.) before or after the Civil War. Anything out of the hustling, technological, expansionist, and basically bellicose mainstream is regarded as heresy. America's historical amnesia is, of course, legendary, but this should shock even the most jaded reader: the most significant aspects of possibly the most important moment in our national history can simply be discarded, or disregarded. Listening to the South, understanding its history from *its* point of view, could generate a degree of maturity that the United States sorely lacks. But for reasons already indicated—above all, the brittleness of the American psyche, the shakiness of its identity, the emptiness at the core—we shall never do that, any more than we attempted to understand anyone opposed to, or critical of, the American way of life. As Woodward realized, even in 1953, our fate is already determined; we are not immune to the forces of history, as events since 1953 have shown.

5

The Future of the Past

"Ah, monsieur!" [the old monk] exclaimed, "I think I must be dreaming when I recall the state of minds in my youth—the vivacity, the sincerity of opinions, the respect for oneself and for public opinion, the disinterested political passion. Ah, monsieur! . . . in those days we had a cause; now there are only interests. There used to be bonds between men; now there are none. It is sad indeed, monsieur, to outlive one's country!
> —Alexis de Tocqueville, letter to Freslon, March 16, 1858

God help thee, old man, thy thoughts have created a creature in thee; and he whose intense thinking thus makes him a Prometheus; a vulture feeds upon that heart for ever; that vulture the very creature he creates.
> —Herman Melville, *Moby-Dick*

We have made a shoddy merchandise of our souls.
> —Wendell Berry, *A Continuous Harmony*

IN 2006, AFTER COMPLETING *Dark Ages America*, I left the United States. It was hardly a sudden decision. In the course of writing the book, its analysis of America seeped into the marrow of my bones. There was no denying the essential character of the place, and the relationship between that and its ongoing disintegration. "Character is destiny," wrote Heraclitus eons ago, and it is as true now as it was then. I had, in effect, outlived my country; there didn't seem any point in sticking around.

The truth, however, as Sacvan Bercovitch has argued, is that the nation was "blind from birth."[1] There has been a lot of discussion among American historians about how republicanism and the acquisitive life were locked in an early struggle for the soul of what would become the United States (see chapter 1), or how Americans resisted becoming frenzied consumers for much of the twentieth century (see, for example, Gary Cross' *An All-Consuming Century*); but the evidence really doesn't back much of this up. Consumerism was already rampant by the mid-eighteenth century, and Walter McDougall's assessment of the country as a collection of hustlers from the get-go remains valid. Alternative ways of life were basically marginal and exhortatory, and religious objections to the hustling life were easily converted into religious *approval* of the hustling life, ironically enough.[2] How one sees all this depends on one's value system, of course; but given mine, I should have left the United States long ago. On a visceral level, I had always felt like a stranger in a strange land. The competition, the aggressiveness, the lack of interest in

human connection, the confusion of goods with the good life, the
deep antagonism to the life of the mind—this is the dominant
ethos, and I could never fit in. I stayed and struggled because
I believed in a different America, but that belief proved to be a
mirage. The South excepted, there really has never been a different America. And even that, as we know, had a terrible dark
side to it.

The best guide to the future, of course, is the past. Not that
change does not occur, but for the most part it tends to be evo-
lutionary, and characterized by great continuity with what came
before. Hustling, the pursuit of affluence, technology, and "progress," have amounted to a huge steamroller in American history,
a steamroller that is now going off the edge of a cliff. And our
ingrained optimism has not helped much in this regard; indeed,
it has blinded us to what is going on. Given this native demand
for "solutions," even when there are none, books of this sort, or
any book about the United States, is required to conclude on a
positive note, showing how things can be fixed, how they will
be different in the future if only "we" (which is who, exactly?)
take matters into our own hands and create a different outcome.
But this is fantasy. History doesn't work that way, and I am not
going to join the legion of authors out there who out of naïveté
or a desperate kind of hope (or maybe just a desire for sales)
attempt to pull a rabbit out of a hat at the eleventh hour. There
is no rabbit, and the hat is coming apart at the seams.

If this book is a tragedy, it can be schematized as having
three acts:

Act I: "The Steamroller" (chapters 1–3)
Act II: "The Steamroller Destroys the Opposition" (chapter 4)
Act III: "Eventually the Steamroller Self-Destructs" (chapter 5)

It is simply not possible for Act III to be "The Steamroller
Has an Identity Crisis but Emerges New and Improved." As

I said, this is the note most books on Troubled America end on, because the authors believe this or believe that this is what the public wants to hear. This is true for the most part. Having lived in fantasy all of their lives, most Americans want it to continue even if they are out of work, have had their homes foreclosed, see plainly that the government is doing very little for them or anybody else (except the rich and the well connected), watch helplessly as the country is bogged down in meaningless wars it cannot win, understand on a gut level that their lives have no real purpose, etc. But personally, I can't write such a book, because I regard the fantasy of a recovered future as pure drivel. As a result, I have to write about what is likely to occur, but that probably guarantees a readership of at most a few thousand people, if that. It's not really a problem for me: life is not a popularity contest, and I have a genuine affection for that minuscule fraction of the American public who prefer truth to illusion. False comfort is, in my opinion, a terribly indecent thing to peddle, and genetically speaking, I'm not wired up to do it. I do see an Act III(a), however, which is the continuation of the alternative tradition in its marginal and politically ineffective capacity—what I described as the "monastic option" in an earlier work—with the possibility of it appealing to greater numbers of people as the self-destruction proceeds; but I'm guessing that is thirty to forty years away, at best. I'll talk about that a bit later. My job right now is to expand on what I talked about briefly at the end of chapter 2: the hows and whys of our collapse.

Be clear, however, that that collapse is not some sudden, dazzling event awaiting us down the line. Something like that happened with the Mayans and the Soviets, but that is not the typical pattern. It's more common to go out with a whimper rather than a bang, in a long, strung-out process of disintegration; and that is what we are currently engaged in. American life is many things, but ultimately it's a life without a heart, not really a life for human beings—something I suspect many or even most of us feel, if only on an unconscious level. The sensation is one of being haunted, and the core of this is the vapidity, the utter meaninglessness, of this way of life. A country whose purpose it is to encourage its citizens to accumulate as many objects as possible, or to export "democracy" at the point of a gun, is a ship without a rudder. Meanwhile, the ship is slowly sinking out of sight.

The metaphor of a sinking ship was given a more dramatic treatment by Herman Melville in that greatest of American novels, *Moby-Dick*. Ezra Pound once said that artists were the antennae of the human race but that the bullet-headed majority would never learn to trust them. The monomaniacal quest of Captain Ahab, the destruction of the *Pequod* by the great white whale, and the sucking of the entire ship and its crew into a huge vortex down under—all of this was an eerie, unconscious metaphorical description of the course of American history, the future included. The fanatical pursuit of goods, money, power, technology, and "progress" in effect created the whale that is currently ramming the ship to pieces; and if the suction of the vortex is slower in real life than in Melville's novel, it is nevertheless steady and unrelenting. Our foreign policy generated 9/11, from people who had had it with the United States attempting to control their destiny. Our domestic (economic) policy precipitated the crash of 2008. And our whole way of life has dialectically led to the collapse of that way of life, which is a way of life that cannot give people what they truly need. It's a life without a drop of love in it, with techno-toys and bombast covering up the void. There is such a thing as karma, and we are now seeing the results of our actions on a daily basis. Not surprisingly, not too many people, worldwide, are shedding tears for America's plight or for America's end. As for Americans themselves—all in all, not a very bright collection of individuals, as Perry Miller pointed out fifty years ago[3]—they are angry and depressed, thinking themselves innocent victims of events supposedly beyond their control, when they themselves live (or try to live) in such a way that makes those events inevitable. When Vann Woodward wrote in the 1950s that Americans were a "peculiar people," he had no idea of how right he was.

Let's talk about "blind from birth," then. In books such as *The Puritan Origins of the American Self* and *The American Jeremiad*, Sacvan Bercovitch demonstrates that it was more the rhetoric of the Puritans than the specific content of their ideas that created the American ideology, amounting to a single comprehensive vision—a mythology, in a word. The language used invested America with a sacred history, in which the land was analogous to Canaan, and the Puritan settlers to the ancient Hebrews who crossed the river Jordan. America would be God's New Israel, or New Jerusalem. It was essentially, observes the historian David Harlan, a "theocratic prophecy." Thus Cotton Mather wrote that the salvation of the Massachusetts Bay Colony was the salvation of the individual American soul. The American, says Bercovitch, "had to justify himself by justifying America," and therefore "To be an American is to assume a prophetic identity."[4]

Whew! Strong stuff, eh? No wonder Turner was motivated to call the frontier the boundary line between savagery and civilization. The Puritan legacy is a deeply Manichaean one, and any criticism of the fundamental premises of America is practically regarded as treason in the United States. This hegemonic consensus, writes Bercovitch, exercises a domination "unmatched in any other modern culture." As Harlan points out, Louis Hartz had said something similar, attributing the monolithic way of life and thought in America (economic liberalism) to the influence of John Locke. Hartz believed that the Lockean legacy could be transcended, however, whereas Bercovitch feels there is no recovery from the cultural mythology bequeathed by the Puritans, which operates on a subliminal level. For, he says, American history possesses no counterforces that are working to shatter that mythology; the myth is simply too powerful, too all-encompassing in its scope. The United States, he writes, is "a secular modern nation living a dream," "the example par excellence of a collective fantasy."[5]

Alexis de Tocqueville understood much of this 150 years before Bercovitch, as it turns out. "I know of no country in which, speaking generally, there is less independence of mind and true freedom of discussion than in America," he wrote. "One might suppose that all American minds had been fashioned after the same model, so exactly do they follow along the same paths." Tocqueville called this the "new despotism," noting that it worked by inner conditioning rather than by overt force, thus providing the illusion of freedom. As Leo Damrosch tells us, Tocqueville's description of this power was downright Orwellian:

> It would resemble paternal power if its object was to prepare men for adult life, but it seeks on the contrary to keep them in permanent childhood. It likes citizens to enjoy themselves, so long as all they think about is enjoyment. It labors willingly for their happiness, but it wants to be the sole agent and arbiter of their happiness.... The sovereign power doesn't break their wills, but it softens, bends, and directs them. It rarely compels action, but it constantly opposes action. It doesn't destroy, but it prevents birth; it doesn't tyrannize, but it hinders, represses, enervates, restrains, and numbs, until it reduces [the] nation to a mere flock of timid and industrious animals, with government as their shepherd.

The result of this, as one philosopher notes, is America's "heartless inability to recognize the real otherness of the other."

The American way of life (free-market capitalism in particular) is the only permissible narrative.[6]

If you have made it this far into this book, you know what I'm talking about. A couple of anecdotes to illustrate the point. Some time ago I turned a friend of mine, the dean of a major medical school in the United States, on to the work of Joyce Appleby, in particular her discussion of the changing definition of virtue in the 1790s (see above, chapter 1). He was very taken with her analysis of the shift from virtue as public service to virtue as private gain, and wanted to share it with some of the faculty members at his university. But he discovered that whenever he tried to discuss her thesis with his colleagues, their eyes would glaze over within thirty seconds and they would change the subject. This is symptomatic of the subliminal cultural mythology that Bercovitch is talking about, the brainwashing, really, that goes on in this country, such that the nation's most intelligent citizens cannot tolerate even a casual examination of the country's structural premises. "Love it or leave it" is not merely the slogan of the redneck patriot.

My second example is a very public one, although by now long forgotten. In 1988 George H. W. Bush announced, "I never apologize for the United States of America. I don't care what the facts are." This came after a U.S. warship shot down an Iranian Airbus (supposedly mistaken for an F-14 fighter jet), killing all 290 people on board. Philosopher Ronald Wright comments that it is hard to imagine a prominent statesman of any other country saying such a thing, let alone getting elected president in the wake of remarks like these (four months later). "That his words did not wreck, or even hinder, his political career," observes Wright, "raises questions about American culture that the country and the world must address." Of course, the world is in the process of addressing it; America is not. When President Bush subsequently declared, after the Gulf War of 1991, "What we say goes," the rest of the world found this grotesque; the American public just took it as the natural order of things. Despite our subsequent failure in Iraq and Afghanistan, there is virtually no widespread, fundamental reassessment of the modus operandi of this nation from within.[7]

And there never will be. The British historian Eric Hobsbawm once wrote that "the alternative to a changed society, is darkness"; but if America has been blinded from birth, as seems to be the case, darkness is the only option for her now. What could possibly give her sight at this point? A changed society is clearly not a possibility, for precisely the reasons we have been discussing.[8]

How to penetrate the fog? It's not exclusively a question of intelligence in the IQ sense of the term, for brainwashing goes way below the cognitive level to the limbic one, the ontological one—as the med school faculty example I gave above would indicate. There are a fair number of books like Hixson's (see the conclusion of chapter 4), or Bercovitch's, around; at least we can say that truly serious and courageous critics do exist in the United States. But there is no need to censor such works, because the cultural fog is so thick. The argument of some critics, such as Noam Chomsky or Michael Moore, that the American people have had the wool pulled over their eyes, and that once the wool is removed, we will move forward to a socialist or progressive or truly democratic future—this is fantasy. For the wool *is* the eyes. The consent may indeed be manufactured, but it is no less real for that. I doubt that there are two hundred thousand people in the whole of the United States who could grasp, let alone tolerate, an argument such as (say) Walter Hixson's; who can see, as though with X-ray eyes, the skeletal structure of American history: the Puritan legacy, the frontier savage/civilized dichotomy, and the enemy-other narrative so central to our identity. After all, what does it say when we butcher three million Vietnamese peasants and torture tens of thousands, and the American public is more upset about what antiwar protesters are doing than about what the U.S. military is doing? What an irony that in the end, the real savages are— *us*. "Having the wool pulled over their eyes" is a kind of "rape" theory of American history, in effect; "consensual sex" is a much more accurate description. There will be no seeing through the fog, let's be clear about that.[9]

Even beyond that, most of American society is wallowing in trash; it has no interest in questions of this sort, doesn't even know they exist. The culmination of a hustling, laissez-faire capitalist culture is that everything gets dumbed down; that all significant questions are ignored, and that every human activity is turned into a commodity, and anything goes if it sells. A trashy culture even trashes its own sacred sites. During 2010, plans were in the works to build a resort hotel and gambling casino half a mile south of the Gettysburg battlefield. The lead developer was the owner of a local motorcycle dealership; he was backed by state representative Harry Readshaw (a Democrat) in this endeavor. One critic of the project, Dave Cohen, suggested, with heavy irony and some degree of bitterness, that the casino be put on the very spot where Lincoln delivered the Gettysburg Address:

> Whereas in the past Gettysburg has served as a powerful symbol of our desire to be better than we are . . . we now have an opportunity to invest Gettysburg with a new meaning more fitting to the times we live in. . . . Let this . . . casino be a powerful symbol to future generations of what an open, running, rancid sewer the United States had become by 2010. It is altogether proper that Gettysburg remain an unwavering emblem of who we are, and what we aspire to. Let us resolve today and henceforth to give a New Meaning to Gettysburg.[10]

Political conservatives, of course, try to have it both ways: they fume at the trashiness of American culture, but are perfectly happy with the corporate-commercial-consumerist economic base that gives rise to it, that has destroyed decency and community and just about everything else. There is no longer a "vibrant, living tradition and community to be born into, to inherit, or to bequeath," writes Dick Meyer in *Why We Hate Us*. There has been "an erosion of socially shared ways of treating others respectfully, the ties that make community possible." In fact, "Boorishness and vulgarity are sanctified by public culture and [are] thus omnipresent." In popular music, Meyer points out, violence and drugs are glorified; women are routinely referred to as "bitches." He quotes from the song "Drips," by Eminem:

> All these bitches on my dick
> That's how dudes be getting sick
> That's how dicks be getting drips
> From these bitches on our dicks

What would be a *forbidden* lyric in American culture today? Meyer asks. The fact that we tolerate such cultural toxins, that millions find them entertaining, goes to the heart of our cultural collapse. It is what Islam rightly finds repulsive about American society—a society, says Meyer, that has lost the confidence and capacity to impose standards. The Southern critic M. E. Bradford wrote that the typical Southern conservative "cherished a clear sense of what Southern grandmothers have always meant in admonishing children, 'we don't do that.'" Where is Grandma now?

Eminem (aka Marshall Bruce Mathers III) is really a synecdoche for American culture at large, and has in fact been referred to as the "spokesman of his generation." His album of 2000 "The Marshall Mathers LP" is the best-selling hip-hop record in history (it has sold more than ten million copies in the United States alone). A review of his work in the Mexico City newspaper *El Universal* commented that his success "serves to illustrate the brutal emptiness that exists among the young people of contemporary societies, black holes that need to be filled with anything, but above all with hatred. This is the entry point for all the Eminems, and for all the Eminems to come."[11]

Black holes that need to be filled with anything. This is surely the logical end point of the hustling society, the vortex Melville was talking about. For there is a limit to how many new cars, computers, and DVD players, or how many wars against mythologically scripted enemy others, can fill that yawning abyss. If there were more than two hundred thousand individuals in America who understood the game, who saw through it, we might have a chance; but there aren't. To paraphrase Dylan Thomas, we shall go stupidly and unconsciously into that good night.

I want to return to that Southern grandmother in a moment; but before I do that, we need to ask, Who is doing better than this (not that it would take all that much)? In *Europe's Promise*, Steven Hill suggests that the European Union has deliberately turned its back on the American way of life and come up with something very different. I'm not entirely convinced of this, but his portrait of contemporary European society is definitely worth looking at.[12]

Since the end of World War II, says Hill, a quiet revolution has been occurring in Europe, a development model that breaks with the ones being pursued by America, China, and India. It is a "workfare" state, not a welfare state; not socialism, but capitalism with a strong social safety net. Or to put it another way, it is a security revolution rather than a socialist one, and was in fact conceived by conservative politicians— Winston Churchill, Jean Monnet, and Konrad Adenauer. The idea is to combine the wealth-generating capacity of capitalism with a more broadly shared prosperity, which it does via invest-ment in health care, education, child care, housing, and mass transit. Doctors actually do house calls in Europe; workers receive nearly two months' paid vacation, sick leave and unem-ployment compensation, and generous retirement benefits. This is a "social capitalism" that helps people, not a Wall Street casino capitalism that takes advantage of them. In general, the Europeans are wrapped in an economic security blanket; they don't live in fear of being wiped out by illness or stock market crashes or job loss. For Americans, these fears are present for most of their working lives.[13]

The comparison between the two socioeconomic orders is perhaps the most impressive part of Hill's book. For example, scores of studies have shown that societies with great inequal-ity, such as the United States, have more violence and crime, and less trust and community life. Whereas Europe regards economic growth as a tool, "America is suffering the slow, cor-rosive deterioration of having the wrong values, misplaced pri-orities, and inadequate . . . institutions that are producing this unequal society." Hill produces a table of comparison between the two systems, institution by institution—politics, media, economy, energy, and "workfare"—and the picture of America that emerges is fairly appalling. What we have is domination by corporate media, politics via poll-driven sound bites, a foreign policy based on unilateralism and preemptive strikes, a failing newspaper industry, a poorly informed citizenry, the unem-ployed winding up destitute, weak (or no) mass transit sys-tems, and a health care system that ranks thirty-seventh in the world. Basically, the United States has run out of steam; it has very few new ideas, if any, and quite frankly, it's not clear why any American reading Hill's list would want to remain there. "The American system and its animating ideology," he asserts, "have no future. The American Way is in its endgame." Well, no great revelation there.[14]

The psychological differences of the two ways of life are particularly striking. What does it mean, asks Hill, not to live in constant fear? What impact does it have on the psyche to know that the basics will be taken care of because you are a *member* of your society? "Certainly it is hard for an American," he writes, "raised as an atomized individual in the 'ownership' (i.e., 'on your own') society, to step into the shoes of a European and imagine what that sense of security and support must feel like and how it affects your overall outlook." This lack of security, he suggests, is why America is so violent: when the basics are taken care of, it decreases each person's anxiety and aggression. In essence, it means not having to hustle all the time. Hill continues:

> A society in which . . . individuals on the middle rungs don't have to constantly scamper so fast up the ladder to maintain their place in the world, is a society that can be built more on cooperation, non-violence, and solidarity. That psyche becomes the foundation for a more consensual society instead of the winner-take-all, "if I win, you lose," dog-eat-dog society we have in the United States.

"In the United States," Hill concludes, "violence of all kinds . . . has become a way of life, the sea in which we swim."[15]

Nevertheless, we should not be confused into thinking that this is some sort of American South without the slavery, or a traditional, gemeinschaft society. Europe is a capitalistic, high-tech, mass consumer society. It is hardly neofeudal or prebourgeois. It has found a way to do capitalism better, not do away with it; the goal remains material comfort, and the spiritual dimension is basically optional. Hill's comparison between Europe and the United States reveals the latter to be sclerotic and oppressive, but not ideologically discontinuous with the former—at least not in a truly

profound way. Thus it is easy to list Europe's capitalistic achievements, which are fairly mind-boggling:

• Europe has one of the highest levels of productivity in
the world, with more goods and services cranked out per hour
worked than nearly any other economy. There is wide access to
electronic gadgets and appliances, and the system is designed to
stimulate consumer spending.

• With only 7 percent of the world's population, the EU
accounts for 29 percent of the world's economy. Its GDP is $16
trillion, the largest economy in the world—nearly as large as those
of the United States and China combined. It is the largest foreign
investor in the United States and the largest trading partner with
China, and also corporate America's biggest target for foreign
investment (affiliates of American companies in the fifteen core
EU nations showed profits of $85 billion in 2005). Of the global
Fortune 500 rankings for 2009, 179 of the top 500 companies were
European (140 were American); and of the 60 largest companies
in the world, half were European (18 were American). European
companies were at or near the top in oil, food products, airlines,
telecommunications, the chemical industry, and automobiles.

• This applies to the cultural field as well. For example,
Vivendi, a French company, owns the Universal Music Group,
which produces 50 Cent and Eminem.

• European centers have become leaders in the high-tech
industries, notably Finland and the regions around Munich,
Geneva, and Milan.[16]

This hardly sounds like a nonhustling society. What we have
in the case of Europe, really, is a sort of "restrained hustling,"
a quasi-socialist society, at best. But it is not a traditional society by a long shot; it remains a modern mass consumer society,
and it is not clear what the purpose of it all is, beyond providing
material comfort.

But not so fast. Hill's seventh chapter, titled "The European Way of Health," makes a good case for Europe as a modern civilization trying to avoid hustling, capitalistic success notwithstanding. In this particular area, it is clear that Europe does preserve some major features of traditional societies (it did emerge from a feudal background, after all). Health in Europe, Hill observes, is about bike paths and walking trails and health spas, about organic food and "slow food." It's about lingering in cafés, living an unhurried life. Everywhere you go, you see senior citizens walking and cycling, making trips to small grocery stores. Whereas walking and cycling account for less than a tenth of all urban trips in American cities, the figures are a third for Germany and a half for Holland. Pedestrian zones are common, as is the central town square, which corresponds to longing for community and contact, for "shared, womblike physical space as opposed to atomized and individual space," such as is typical of the United States. In Italy, the Slow Food movement is very popular (they took the snail as their official symbol), and it is the antithesis of the American fast food industry and way of life. The founder of the movement, Carlo Petrini, says,

> The art of living is about learning how to give time to each and every thing. But if I have sacrificed my life to speed, then that is impossible. . . . Ultimately, "slow" means to take the time to reflect. It means to take the time to think. It is useless to force the rhythms of life.

European life includes slow food, slow pace, and long siestas and dinners, says Hill. It reflects a philosophy that values the quality of life, and it has created a physical and social infrastructure to support that. People who have a sense of the importance of the quality of life create Siena; hustlers create Dallas.[17]

Hill also notes—shades of the Southern Agrarians—that an agrarian outlook is still very much a part of the European identity. The countryside is gorgeous. Encircling urban zones will be a patchwork of community and individual garden plots with flowerbeds, fruit trees, and vegetables, which foster an "urban-agro sensibility" that is both charming and practical. You typically see Europeans working in their gardens in an unhurried way. All in all, he concludes, Europeans

> enjoy unhurried pleasures, whether food, drink, art, architecture, saunas, or strolling or bicycling along their meandering pathways. While Europe is fully modern, sometimes it feels as if it is caught in a nineteenth-century time warp. . . . Living environments are more humane and well planned, with their magnificent public plazas that create such a sublime sense of openness.[18]

So what's the problem? That this is significantly better than the American way of life seems obvious enough; but as noted above, we are not talking about a traditional society here. It may be the best a modern mass consumer-oriented society can do, but it would still seem to lack a larger sense of meaning. Hill calls the economy "steady-state," but this is an error. The steady-state economies of the feudal age were no-growth, whereas growth is certainly central to the EU's concerns. In addition, the fact that a French company is cranking out CDs by Eminem and 50 Cent ought to give us a moment's pause. You can hear hip-hop music practically everywhere in Europe, in fact; and if the techno-boorishness and trashy behavior documented by Dick Meyer is not quite as blatant as it is in the United States, it is hardly absent from France or Germany or Italy. Or Spain. I recall being on the metro in Barcelona a few years back, and a man of about thirty throwing an apple core on the floor of the car. No one said a word, because, as in the United States, no one had the confidence or the authority to do so; and it would have triggered a fight in any case. There was no Southern grandmother present to take him aside and tell him "we don't do that," any more than there is on the New York subway system, where teenagers routinely put their feet on the seats, wear their pants below their underwear, and let gangsta rap leak out of their headphones. I have a sense, in Europe, of a greater ease in living, but I don't have a sense of any great moral coherence there. And there is no doubt that one can be as lonely and alienated in Hamburg as in Minneapolis; of that I am quite sure (having lived in Germany for nearly a year). The graciousness of the antebellum South can certainly be found in Europe, as Hill suggests; but it is more or less optional, occurring more by chance than by design.

Where does that leave us, then? Are traditional societies completely a thing of the past, and are we condemned to variations on the theme of hustling and technological "progress"? One can point to Islam as an alternative, of course, but I think most Western readers would agree that if that's the remedy, we are probably better off with the disease. Many (or perhaps most) non-Western readers would see it differently, but that is a debate without end, and one I don't wish to get into at this point. As I suggested in the preface, it wouldn't hurt us to consider what is positive in those societies, although Americans are not given to that type of thinking. It would be nice, however, if there were some alternative to these two choices, a society without limits and a society with far too many of them.

One can talk in terms of individual solutions to the problem (which aren't really solutions), and social or geopolitical solutions. The first category is much easier to deal with. In a word, for those seeking something akin to the gemeinschaft society of the American South (sans slavery), all is not lost. There are pockets of traditional societies all over the world, although how long they can resist "the machine" is an open question. For would-be expatriates, it is also a matter of what you are willing to do without; the romantic fantasy of "going native" might hit a wall when, say, you discover that getting ink cartridges for your printer is a long and complicated process, and you can't just drive over to Office Depot. There are villages in Pakistan that do not allow the installation of satellite dishes—a decision I regard as true progress (I don't even own a TV)—but for some, that might prove to be a problem. Still, keep in mind that options within the United States, especially in the short term, are extremely limited; if you want a nonhustling life, you are definitely better off hitting the road. Before I talk about the internal (domestic) possibilities, then, let me say a few words about my experience as an ex-pat.

First off, the reader should be aware that I am no starry-eyed romantic when it comes to Mexico. I am fully aware of the data on homicide and kidnapping, the corruption and the drug wars, and the stats on poverty (half of the country is at or below the poverty line). I've traveled around Chiapas and Oaxaca, where barefoot kids tug at your shirtsleeves in the hope of getting you to part with a single peso. And although I don't see the place as falling apart, as I do the United States, I also don't see it getting any better. Despite its (misguided, in my view) attempt to emulate the United States, there is something archaic and primeval and eternal about Mexico; it just goes on and on. And it is this that I wanted in my life, for this is characteristic of traditional societies.

Crossing the border was like driving through a mirror: everything is immediately reversed. Instead of hostile, aggressive people I found gracious, relaxed ones. An hour into Mexico I stopped at a combination gas station-cafeteria for lunch and began kidding around with the teenagers behind the counter. In the United States, this is typically greeted with suspicion and/or a frozen kind of look (very well parodied by Tina Fey in her film *Mean Girls*). American youngsters are not a happy lot, by and large, and being humorous with adults is much too big a stretch for them. The Mexican youngsters, on the other hand, immediately began joking back, enjoying the banter immensely. What planet am I on? I thought to myself.

Mexico also is true to the stereotype of the mañana culture: why kill yourself when you can take your time? Instead of pressure, competition, and hustling, things are mostly left to take their course. For a gringo, this can be unsettling at first, not only because of endless delays, but also because nothing seems to work. If you want a bank transfer, or anything from an institution, it generally takes a few eons plus an act of Congress. Appliances and other techno-devices frequently break down; you have to rely on a network of friends and acquaintances to get them repaired. But things do eventually get done. I came up with a saying to capture the difference between north and south of the border: In the United States, everything works, but nothing works out; in Mexico, nothing works, but everything works out. For the most part, this is true.

Daily life in Mexico is not about drugs and crime, American news reports notwithstanding; it's about human interaction, which typically is polite and often quite gracious. As the time passed, I began increasingly to notice things that simply would never happen in the United States. Having lunch at a café in Mexico City with a (then) girlfriend, I was caught completely off-guard when an elderly woman came over to us and said, "God bless you both; I hope you will have a long and happy life." Or when another elderly woman stopped me on the street (I happened to be wearing a suit, for some reason) and spontaneously declared, "How handsome you are!" (How do you reply to *that*?) I was equally bowled over when my insurance agent took me under her wing, spending a year, off and on, fighting with bureaucracies to see to it that the university I had taught at for eighteen months paid me the pension that had accumulated in my account (it had nothing to do with her job as an insurance agent, and she wanted absolutely nothing in return).

Much of Mexican courtesy is so subtle you aren't even sure it's happening. I recall being in the gym I regularly go to, and there was a group of muchachos hanging out by some of the exercise equipment, just talking among themselves. I wanted to use those machines, so I had to sort of wend my way around the guys in order to do so. Very slowly, without saying anything, they drifted to the adjoining part of the gym to continue their conversation, thus enabling me to use the equipment without any inconvenience to myself. I can't imagine their American counterparts doing this; the attitude would be more on the order of, If it's inconvenient for you, too bad. How gracious these boys were, and it was all nonverbal.

(Unfortunately, the CDs they play at my gym are typically awful, a lot of American hip-hop, which they regard as cool. (I'm guessing they don't understand the lyrics; at least I hope they don't.) Occasionally I ask the guy at the desk if he could switch the disk, and he always does; but I hate to come across like a pushy gringo, so most of the time I wear a Walkman and drown the vulgar stuff out with something else.)

When things like this happen two to three times a week, you begin to notice a pattern after a few months, and you realize you are living in a different country. I could provide dozens of stories like these. I moved to Mexico because I believed that it still had elements of a traditional culture, and I was right. These are a people who know how to live, who have their priorities straight, and I'm grateful to be a guest in their country. My only regret, I tell people, is that I didn't make the move twenty years ago. There is a basic human decency here that simply doesn't exist in the United States. And the Southern grandmother is a real figure in this country; you can't just do whatever you want (though I do get a bit annoyed at teenagers putting their feet on the next row of seats in movie theaters).

If you are an American reading this, let me ask you: aren't you tired of it all? The endless pressure and anxiety, the awful atmosphere at work (that's if you can *get* work), the constant one-upsmanship that passes for friendship or social relations, the lack of community or of any meaningful connection with your neighbors. The "social capitalism" of Europe may solve one or two of these problems, perhaps, but not most of them. Traditional societies are sui generis.

But let's say you are going to remain in the United States, which is probably the case. In *The Twilight of American Culture* I talk about the "monastic option," of resisting the dominant culture and trying to do something meaningful with your life as opposed to living the mass dream. A hard slog, but I still believe it's worth it for those who want to do it. Recently I read about a café in Oakland, California—the Actual Café—that started a weekend no-laptop policy in February 2010. Customers were asked to leave their laptops at home and (horror of horrors!) talk to each other instead. The café opened in December 2009 with the intention of creating a community. "Instead," said Sal Bednarz, the owner, "it's just been a room full of laptops." He was disenchanted with cafés that consisted of little more than a row of computers. "When I walk into those places," he said, "I feel alienated . . . I don't feel like I want to spend time there. I don't think it's healthy to go out into a social place and pretend that you're by yourself." So he decided on the weekend experiment, taking the risk that it wouldn't lead to a mass exodus of customers. Amazingly enough, it worked out quite well.[19]

A small victory—one wishes the café would ban laptops altogether—but perhaps an important one, at least for those involved. Coffee shops, after all, used to be very different places before the advent of the cell phone and the personal computer. Customers came to read, perhaps write poetry, socialize, do homework, do artwork. The ambience was human; the Starbucks-type atmosphere is corporate and sterile. Curious as to how things turned out, I phoned the Actual Café in August 2010 and was told by the barista that it had proven to be a roaring

success: people love it, and business actually picked up on weekends as a result.

Here's another example: protecting your kids from the media.
Not an easy job, when they are constantly bombarded by television
and the Internet. But in 2000, a woman named Gloria DeGaetano
started something called the Parent Coaching Institute, to help
parents with what she felt was an extremely important challenge.
(I found out about it because she invited me to give a workshop
for the PCI two months before I left for Mexico.) The PCI has
been very successful, and Gloria herself has coauthored some
important books on the deleterious effects of American culture,
including *Parenting Well in a Media Age: Keeping Our Kids Human*
and *Stop Teaching Our Kids to Kill: A Call to Action Against TV,
Movie and Video Game Violence*.

I admire people such as Sal Bednarz and Gloria DeGaetano
more than I can say, and I wish them continued success. My
problem with these experiments is the larger context: I can't
help thinking that projects such as these are basically rear-
ranging the proverbial deck chairs on the *Titanic*. America is a
dying culture; it really has no future at all. As the ship sinks,
it's not clear what difference these experiments can ultimately
make, for they are but drops in the ocean. To see this, we have
to switch from the microlevel of individual experience to the
macrolevel of environmental and geopolitical change.

The Great Delusion, Steven Stoll calls it. In the early nineteenth century, he writes, growth took over the meaning of
progress. Economic growth has bestowed many positive benefits on millions of people, but the truth is that "it exists in a
bubble." Growth on the scale known to industrial societies during the past two hundred years is very exceptional. The loop
has been one of consumption and an expanding economy, but
"this loop exists in its own imaginary world." It finally is a
utopian agenda of salvation, a kind of eschatology. "Progress"
backfired; it proved to be an illusion. To believe that any society

can expand without limits is to ignore the relationship between economy and ecology. Ecosystems don't expand, he points out; there aren't infinite resources. As I indicated at the conclusion of chapter 2 (citing Bateson), there is a difference between the ethics of maxima and the ethics of optima; infinity is not part of the real world. Sooner or later we have to hit a wall, and that is finally happening.[20]

All of this, of course, is au courant: global warming, the Kyoto Protocol, the Copenhagen Conference, etc. The striking thing is that nothing is being done to address the issue that this path of endless economic expansion and technological progress has no future. For a whole variety of reasons, we—especially, the United States—continue to operate as if this were not true. Nor is this atypical of these types of situations. Drawing on Jared Diamond's study of collapse (and echoing Arnold Toynbee from decades before), Stoll points out that the ideology of growth cannot assimilate its own negative effects (or its shadow material, I would add; the alternative tradition). As civilizations collapse, there is a tendency to adhere to the very practices that are doing them in, and to values that no longer make sense. In short, the rule is that they prefer death to compromise, and we are seeing that today.[21]

Beyond the issue of ecology, there also is the issue of national decline, geopolitical decline. When I was writing about this in 2000 and 2006, the idea did not meet with easy acceptance, for obvious reasons. Now the notion of America on the way out is not all that radical; many scholars and political analysts are saying it. Steven Hill has given us good reasons for believing it, as we have seen; Mark Leonard, in *Why Europe Will Run the 21st Century*, frankly states, "America's centralized, militarized supremacy has become so overwhelming that it has defeated everything, including itself." A U.S. intelligence report released in 2008, "Global Trends 2025," predicts a steady decline in American dominance over the coming decades, with U.S. leadership eroding "at an accelerating pace" in "political, economic and arguably, cultural arenas." Looking at the planet today, nothing could be more obvious. It just ain't rocket science, as the saying goes; our time is up.[22]

And collapse could be a good thing, if not exactly fun to live through. The entire premise of America was a mistake from the beginning. A meaningful human society is not about endless hustling and technological progress; these can be part of the good life, but they are hardly equivalent to the good life, and the attempt to make them so has had some pretty untoward consequences. Sclerotic social formations need to step aside to make way for what is vibrant and flexible, although I think we can be sure that given the historical record, the American exit will not be a graceful one; it's not in our DNA. But even beyond that, the collapse could conceivably open the door to the alternative tradition discussed in this book, the world of Emerson and Thoreau and Mumford and Vance Packard and the South (without slavery). It's a long shot, to be sure, but let's consider it for a moment. An example of a political tendency (it's not really a political party, just yet) bearing this ideology is a fringe secession movement whose literature is, in fact, quite sophisticated. Thus the economist Thomas Naylor (professor emeritus at Duke University), in his manifesto *Secession: How Vermont and All the Other States Can Save Themselves from the Empire*, observes that both major political parties "want life in the United States to be bigger, faster, more complex, more commercial, more high-tech, more energy-dependent, more globally interdependent, more militaristic, and more regulated." To realize that vision, he says, both the Democrats and the GOP support an imperial war machine willing to sacrifice our children "to make the world safe for McDonald's, Wal-Mart, Fox News, gas-guzzling Hummers, Google, Bill Gates, and the rest of the *Forbes* 400 richest Americans." Their commitment is to "affluenza, technomania, e-mania, megalomania, robotism, globalization, and imperialism." In a word, this empire is not sustainable. It has no moral center, he tells us; it has lost its soul. Vermont needs to secede from this unholy Union because it

> still celebrates life rather than death. Its culture of the living derives its energy from the fact that it is small, rural, beautiful, democratic, nonviolent, noncommercial, egalitarian, humane, independent, and very radical. In Vermont the politics of human scale always trumps the politics of the left and the politics of the right.[23]

This is, of course, classic alternative tradition stuff, but with an important twist: Naylor has given up on (most of) the United States as a place where that tradition can be realized. As I have said repeatedly, the alternative tradition never had a chance here, especially after the Civil War. Naylor is talking about a "Southern" solution, a real geopolitical answer: this place will never change, so we (Vermonters) might as well circle the wagons and leave the rest of the country to its fate. If these clowns want "affluenza," let 'em have it. The only problem, as I see it, remains the one that has always dogged the alternative tradition: it has no real power. Back in the 1970s, Ernest Callenbach wrote a novel called *Ecotopia* that had the West Coast states (Southern California excepted, of course) seceding from the Union, made possible by claiming to have planted nuclear mines in New York and Washington, D.C., and threatening the U.S. government with them. That's power, no question about it. It is, however, as Callenbach was well aware, a highly unlikely scenario; but so is Thomas Naylor's. All Vermont has to do is declare its separation from the rest of the country and the marines will be in downtown Burlington in less than two hours. At the present time, then, this project doesn't have a hope in hell. But in thirty or forty years, it may not seem so far-fetched. The United States is getting weaker by the day. It is on a downhill slide both economically and politically, and as Naylor correctly states, it is morally bankrupt as well. At the "end of days" the center may not hold and breakaway movements might be able to act with impunity. Kirkpatrick Sale writes:

> If the edifice of industrial civilization does not eventually crumble as a result of a determined resistance within its very walls, it seems certain to crumble of its own accumulated excesses and instabilities within not more than a few decades, perhaps sooner, after which there may be space for alternative societies to rise.[24]

This may, in fact, be the only way that the alternative tradition might cease to be alternative. Not that the "Second Vermont Republic," as it likes to call itself, won't have problems of its own; of that we can be sure. But it's still a fascinating possibility, the more so if secession turns out to be contagious, and not just limited to Vermont.

One thing that might help at this point, at least conceptually, is looking at the past in a very different light. It's not easy for us; we are a culture that is endlessly tumbling into the future, erroneously believing that this is the path to salvation. Since all we finally managed to do was tumble ourselves into a cul-de-sac, perhaps now is the time for at least a few of us (it can't possibly be more than a few, as I have already said) to start thinking about what the past can do for us. Jackson Lears, in his review of Daniel Horowitz's biography of Vance Packard, talks about how folks such as Packard were always attacked for looking backward, for their supposed nostalgia. He goes on:

> The assault on nostalgia could come only from an intelligentsia drunk on disowning the past. Where else are

visions of the good society to come from, if not from our own memories that once life was different, and maybe better, than it is here and now?. . . In imagining more humane ways of life, why are recollections of the past held inferior to fantasies of the future? Perhaps because myths of progress continue to mesmerize intellectuals at all points on the political spectrum, from *The Nation* to the *National Review*.[25]

It's really not a question of political left or right, in other words, and I would add that it's obviously not something limited to intellectuals. "Progress" mesmerized all of us and still does, even while the ship is going down. In his review of John Diggins' *The Lost Soul of American Politics*, the historian Joseph Ellis maintains that what Diggins is really saying in this work is that "America has always been the land of [economic] liberalism and that our current plight as a people is both hopeless and deserved." A harsh assessment, but right on target. There was no wool pulled over our eyes; *we* did this, *we* brought about this result, and we did it from a very early date. *We* laughed at Thoreau, ignored Mumford, and vilified the South, refusing to grant that there was anything of value about that society. In a lecture he gave at NYU in 1961, Perry Miller argued that we are all implicated in the situation in which we find ourselves, "since we have all done our utmost, knowingly or inadvertently, to produce it." And all of that behavior continues to this day, as anybody reading these concluding words knows.[26]

And yet . . . and yet . . . I can't help thinking of T. S. Eliot's "vast, impersonal forces." When all is said and done, perhaps there really was no choice; perhaps America just did what it was supposed to do, and acted out what it was supposed to be, and the rest was history. Toward the end of *Moby-Dick*, Ahab says to his first mate, Starbuck,

What is it, what nameless, inscrutable, unearthly thing is it; what cozening, hidden lord and master, and cruel, remorseless emperor commands me; that against all natural lovings and longings, I so keep pushing and crowding, and jamming myself on all the time; recklessly making me ready to do what in my own proper, natural heart, I durst not so much as dare? . . . By heaven, man, we are turned round and round in this world, like yonder windlass, and Fate is the handspike.

Starbuck subsequently asks the captain,

Shall we keep chasing this murderous fish till he swamps the last man? Shall we be dragged by him to the bottom of the sea? Shall we be towed by him to the infernal world? Oh, oh,—Impiety and blasphemy to hunt him more!

And Ahab answers, "Ahab is for ever Ahab, man. This whole act's immutably decreed."[27]

ACKNOWLEDGMENTS

My greatest debt is to my former friend and colleague Ferenc Szasz, whom I met when I was doing a visiting professorship at the University of New Mexico during 1994–95. Frank was a terrific historian, with a great breadth of interests, and also a marvelous human being. He was generous, outgoing, and always available for a discussion of political and historical issues. In particular he provided me, on more than one occasion, with extensive bibliographies on American history, which proved to be extremely helpful in my research. Frank died very quickly, and unexpectedly, in 2010; I miss him very much.

I also wish to thank another friend and colleague, Nomi Prins, for both moral and logistical support. Some years ago, Nomi "defected"—gave up the hustling life for the life of service— providing inspiration to many as a result, myself included. We should all have folks like this in our camp.

Finally, I am grateful to my editor at Wiley, Eric Nelson, for his astute and in-depth criticism of the manuscript, which improved it enormously. And to my agent, Andrew Stuart, for making it possible for what is sure to be regarded as a very controversial book to see the light of day. In the America of 2011, this is not as common as one might think.

NOTES

Preface

1. Walter A. McDougall, *Freedom Just Around the Corner* (New York: HarperCollins, 2004), pp. xii and 32–35; David M. Potter, *People of Plenty* (1954; repr., Chicago: Phoenix Books, 1958), William Appleman Williams, *The Contours of American History* (1961; repr., Chicago: Quadrangle Books, 1966); and Leo Marx, *The Machine in the Garden* (1964; repr., New York: Oxford University Press, 2000), p. 38. Marx discusses the voyage of Captain Arthur Barlowe to Virginia in 1584, under the auspices of Sir Walter Raleigh. Barlowe's subsequent account of the journey emphasized the "incredible abundance" of the place, characterizing it as a land of plenty. (pp. 36–37 and 40)

2. According to Nomi Prins, *It Takes a Pillage* (Hoboken, N.J.: John Wiley & Sons, 2009), the figure rose to $13.3 trillion, but also see her "Bailout Reports," www.nomiprins.com/bailout.html, which at one point listed a figure of $19 trillion. Also relevant is Rick Wolff, "Whose Recovery? What Double Dip?," http://mrzine.monthlyreview.org/2010/wolff240810.html, 24 August 2010. On Summers see below, chap. 2, n.7.

"Demented ravings of the political right": not just. According to a recent poll, 55percent of Americans believe Mr. Obama is a socialist, which indicates how effective the political right has been in depicting an extremely pro-capitalist president as the opposite of what he is. As for right-wing movements such as the "Tea Party," the problem is that they fail to grasp the complexity of the situation, and that their political position contains a major contradiction. Thus they are motivated by a feeling that something is very wrong with the system (true enough), and

190

their anger is directed against "elites" whom they see as trying to tell ordinary Americans how to live. But their remedy is that the United States should return to a pure form of laissez-faire economics—no government at all, in this area, at least—while failing to understand that that system is run by elites (typically in a clandestine manner). See, for example, Jane Mayer, "Covert Operations," *The New Yorker*, 30 August 2010, p. 54, and Louise Story, "A Secret Banking Elite Rules Trading in Derivatives," *New York Times*, 12 December 2010.

3. Werner Sombart, *Why Is There No Socialism in the United States?*, trans. Patricia M. Hocking and C.T. Husbands (1906; repr., New York: International Arts & Sciences Press); Seymour Martin Lipset, *American Exceptionalism* (New York: W.W. Norton, 1997). On the absence of any real class mobility, see T.J. Jackson Lears, *No Place of Grace* (1981; repr., Chicago: University of Chicago Press, 1994), p. xviii; John Rapley, *Globalization and Inequality* (Boulder CO: Lynne Rienner Publishers, 2004), p. 20; and Joseph E. Stiglitz, *Freefall* (New York: W.W. Norton, 2010), p. 301n.14. I should add that I will also not be discussing utopian communities such as the Shakers, Mennonites, Amish, etc., since these groups have received extensive treatment elsewhere.

In addition to being delusional about how great their future might be, most Americans are delusional about how things are right now. Thomas Nagel writes: "The exceptional tolerance of Americans for substantial inequality appears to rest on their belief that rates of social mobility are unusually high in the United States and that anyone who works hard can get ahead in life. Yet this belief appears to rest on a misapprehension of the facts. [M]ost analysts have concluded that rates of economic mobility are no higher in the United States than in other advanced democratic nations and may actually be somewhat lower for poorer Americans." He adds that the whole scramble for possessions is self-defeating, "since the percentage of winners and losers never changes." See Thomas Nagel, "Who Is Happy and When?," *New York Review of Books*, December 23, 2010, pp. 46–48; Andrew Price, "Americans Are Horribly Misinformed About Who Has Money," www.good.is/post/americans-are-horribly-misinformed-about-who-has-money, September 28, 2010; and Robert Frank, *Luxury Fever* (New York: Free Press, 1999).

4. Lears, *No Place of Grace*, p. xx.

5. Julie Bykowicz, "Dixon Resigns," Baltimore Sun, January 7, 2010; Ben Nuckols, "Prosecutors Scold 'Unrepentant' Baltimore Mayor,"

Washington Post, February 2, 2010. There is by now a large literature on corporate profiteering in Iraq; see especially the film *Iraq for Sale* by Robert Greenwald (2006).

6. Jack Healy and Angela Macropoulos, "Wal-Mart Worker Dies in Apparent Shopping Stampede," *New York Times*, November 28, 2008. See also "Florida Woman Trampled by Shoppers," www.newsday.com, November 30, 2003.

7. On this point compare Vali Nasr, *Forces of Fortune* (New York: Free Press, 2009), with James Zogby, *Arab Voices* (New York: Palgrave Macmillan, 2010).

8. David E. Shi, *The Simple Life* (New York: Oxford University Press, 1985); Lears, *No Place of Grace*; Linda K. Kerber, "The Republican Ideology of the Revolutionary Generation," *American Quarterly*, 37 no. 4 (Fall 1985), 491; Drew McCoy, *The Elusive Republic* (Chapel Hill: University of North Carolina Press, 1980), pp. 236-39. On the cooptation of republicanism, see chapter 1, below. Martha Stewart's Web site, www.marthastewart.com, is typically filled with trendy references to sustainability, quiet time, family, and the beauty of simple things, all delivered via a multi-platform commercial-informational profit-generating empire. The corporate greening of America (Al Gore, Thomas Friedman) is well underway.

9. For example, see Thomas H. Naylor, *Secession: How Vermont and All the Other States Can Save Themselves from the Empire* (Port Townsend Wash: Feral House, 2008). Far from being a crank, the author is professor emeritus of economics at Duke University. I discuss this possibility at greater length in chapter 5.

10. See, for example, the scenarios limned by Professor Alfred W. McCoy (University of Wisconsin at Madison) in "The Decline and Fall of the American Empire," posted on www.tomdispatch.com/blog/175327 on December 5, 2010, and by Gary Shteyngart in *Super Sad True Love Story* (New York: Random House, 2010).

11. Patrick Cadell, quoted in Daniel Horowitz, *Jimmy Carter and the Energy Crisis of the 1970s* (Boston: Bedford/St. Martin's, 2005), p. 20; Winthrop quoted in Shi, *The Simple Life*, p. 13.

1. The Pursuit of Affluence

1. Walter A. McDougall, *Freedom Just Around the Corner* (New York: HarperCollins, 2004), pp. xvi, 5–7, and 15; Gordon S. Wood,

"Free to Be You and Me," *New York Times Book Review*, March 28, 2004, p. 7. There is a major debate among American historians as to exactly when capitalism took off on the American continent, some arguing for day one and others for only after the Revolutionary War. I am not particularly concerned with the semantics of all this; my focus is on the hustling mentality, which certainly can exist in a commercial but noncapitalistic context, and certainly did exist on the continent from the late sixteenth century. All capitalists are hustlers, in other words, but not all hustlers are, strictly speaking, capitalists. Thus Gordon Wood writes that New England farmers in the eighteenth century were often "sharp" and "avaricious," but that doesn't mean that there was a "determined pursuit of profit," which is characteristic of capitalism. For two good surveys of the debate see Paul A. Gilje, "The Rise of Capitalism in the Early Republic," *Journal of the Early Republic* 16, no. 2 (Summer 1996): 159–181, and Gordon S. Wood, "The Enemy Is Us: Democratic Capitalism in the Early Republic," ibid.: 293–308.

2. David E. Shi, *The Simple Life* (New York: Oxford University Press, 1985), pp. 3, 8, and 11–12; Richard L. Bushman, *From Puritan to Yankee* (New York: W.W. Norton, 1970), p. 35. Perry Miller notes that the radical individualism of the Puritan ethos was tethered, in the sense of being embedded in the notion of divine providence, but that eventually it slipped the tether and evolved into the maxim "The public be damned." In a word, this individualism was "developed at the expense of certain other elements that once were equally part of our tradition," but came to be celebrated as if it were the whole story. The truth, says Miller, is that it "once had sanctions which we have almost forgotten." See Perry Miller, "Individualism and the New England Tradition," in *The Responsibility of Mind in a Civilization of Machines*, ed. John Crowell and Stanford J. Searl, Jr. (Amherst: University of Massachusetts Press, 1979), pp. 32, 35–36, 38, and 43.

3. Joyce Appleby, *Capitalism and a New Social Order* (New York: New York University Press, 1984), p. 9.

4. Seymour Martin Lipset, *American Exceptionalism* (New York: W. W. Norton, 1997), p. 109; Richard D. Brown, *Modernization: The Transformation of American Life, 1600–1865* (1976; repr., Prospect Heights, Ill.: Waveland Press, 1988), pp. 9–11; William Appleman Williams, *The Contours of American History* (1961; repr., Chicago: Quadrangle Books, 1966), p. 44.

5. Daniel T. Rodgers, "Republicanism: the Career of a Concept," *Journal of American History* 79, no. 1 (June 1992), 13 and 37–38; Shi, *The Simple Life*, p. 70.

6. Gordon S. Wood, *The Creation of the American Republic, 1776–1787* (Chapel Hill: University of North Carolina Press, 1969), p. viii; Isaac Kramnick, "Republican Revisionism Revisited," *American Historical Review* 87, no. 3 (June 1982), 630, 657–658, and 661–662. I am using "liberalism" in the British economic sense of the term, not in the later American political sense.

7. On this and the following paragraph see Joyce Appleby, "The Social Origins of American Revolutionary Ideology," *Journal of American History* 64 (1978), 937, and *Capitalism and a New Social Order*, pp. 14–16 and 88–105; Rodgers, "Republicanism," p. 13; Kramnick, "Republican Revisionism Revisited," pp. 660 and 663; Louis Hartz, *The Liberal Tradition in America* (New York: Harcourt Brace, 1955), Richard Hofstadter, *The American Political Tradition and the Men Who Made It* (New York: Vintage Books, 1957), pp. v–xi and 3–17; and John Patrick Diggins, *The Lost Soul of American Politics* (New York: Basic Books, 1984), p. 5.

For a Victorian critique of laissez-faire capitalism, much in advance of its time, and based on the classical definition of virtue, see John Ruskin, *Unto This Last*, ed. Clive Wilmer (London: Penguin Books, 1985). Ruskin called this type of virtue "normal," but this was true only in terms of lip service in the England of 1860. The book nevertheless had a huge impact on the nation, eventually, and also worldwide. Gandhi wrote that it changed his life, and he translated it into Gujarati. See M.K. Gandhi, *Gandhi's Autobiography: The Story of My Experiments with Truth*, trans. Mahadev Desai (Washington, D.C.: Public Affairs Press, 1954), pp. 364–365.

8. Appleby, *Capitalism and a New Social Order*, pp. 14–16; Eric Foner, 1995 introduction,"The Idea of Free Labor in Nineteenth-Century America,"to *Free Soil, Free Labor, Free Men* (1970; repr., New York: Oxford University Press, 1995), p. xiii; Shi, *The Simple Life*, pp. 8, 14–16, and 19.

9. Bushman, *From Puritan to Yankee*, preface and pp. 58, 73, 76–77, 109, 232, and 237.

10. Ibid., pp. 278–280; Shi, *The Simple Life*, p. 27. For an excellent study of the conversion of religious ideals into capitalistic ones (shades of Max Weber) in eighteenth-century New England see James D. German,

"The Social Utility of Wicked Self-Love: Calvinism, Capitalism, and Public Policy in Revolutionary New England," *Journal of American History* 82, no. 3 (December 1995), 965–998.

11. Brown, *Modernization*, pp. 60, 90, 98, 101, 112, 130–131, and 136; Williams, *Contours*, pp. 115 and 117; Gilje, "The Rise of Capitalism in the Early Republic," p. 163. Samuel Adams and George Washington quoted in Shi, *The Simple Life*, pp. 66 and 68. For data on iron production see John F. Kasson, *Civilizing the Machine* (1976; repr., New York: Hill & Wang, 1999), p. 11. On the zeal for land acquisition and speculation as central to colonial society and beyond see Daniel M. Friedenberg, *Life, Liberty, and the Pursuit of Land* (Buffalo, N.Y.: Prometheus Books, 1992), and n. 13 below.

12. Rodgers, "Republicanism," pp. 27 and 36; Linda K. Kerber, "The Republican Ideology of the Revolutionary Generation," *American Quarterly* 37, no. 4 (Fall 1985), 491; Drew McCoy, *The Elusive Republic* (Chapel Hill: University of North Carolina Press, 1980), pp. 236–239; Lance Banning, "Jeffersonian Ideology Revisited: Liberal and Classical Ideas in the New American Republic," *William and Mary Quarterly* 43 (January 1986), 3–19.

13. Richard K. Matthews, "Liberalism, Civic Humanism, and the American Political Tradition: Understanding Genesis," *Journal of Politics* 49, no. 4 (November 1987), 1143; Diggins, *Lost Soul of American Politics*, passim.

The notion that the Founding Fathers were motivated by economics rather than idealism was first advanced by Charles Beard in *An Economic Interpretation of the Constitution of the United States*, published in 1913. Daniel Friedenberg's study (see above, n. 11) is something of an elaboration of this, showing that popular republican ideals were more often than not a cover for the pursuit of wealth via speculation in land. Figures such as Franklin, Washington, and Patrick Henry were, in fact, consummate hustlers, amassing enormous amounts of property during their lifetimes. Still, as Friedenberg admits, this was not necessarily a conflict of interest in their own minds: "There can be little question," he writes, "that the men who created the Constitution identified their class interest with the country's interest" (p. 324). Although the book suffers from a lack of discussion of the liberalism vs. republicanism debate of the 1970s and 1980s, it does provide a kind of "catalog of avarice" of colonial America that is sobering to contemplate.

A broader picture of these trends was provided by Marc Egnal and Joseph A. Ernst in "An Economic Interpretation of the American Revolution," William and Mary Quarterly, Third Series, 29, no. 1 (January 1972), 3–32. They argue that the flood of British goods into the colonies during 1745–75 created a crisis for colonial merchants, who were (as Caleb Crain parses it in "Tea and Antipathy," The New Yorker, 20/27 December 2010, p. 138) "the first to make their discontent political, because they were the first to see that the economic predicament could be eased if the colonies had the autonomy to . . . print paper money or trade with other nations." As in the case of slavery playing the role of a cover for the Northern desire for economic expansion (and expansion of its way of life), leading to the Civil War (see below, chap. 4), independence served as a cover for the desire for economic sovereignty, which was the goal of certain vested interests, in bringing on the American Revolution. Thus Egnal and Ernst write (pp. 3 and 24) that the colonial reaction to various British measures "was determined in large part by a growing concern for the economy and for economic sovereignty, a concern that only coincidentally reinforced the dictates of patriotic principle." "Hence, an understanding of the colonial merchants' long-term struggle for economic sovereignty is necessary to explain the nature of the Revolutionary movement in the commercial colonies and the leadership provided by the merchant class after Independence." It seems to be the same story on the American continent, over and over again, and this applies to the rank-and-file as well, whose focus was primarily on the acquisition of consumer goods. As Crain notes, patriotic boycotts of British goods didn't have much staying power. "The British never forced John Hancock to ship fine linen [from England] to Boston," he writes. "He just suspected that Americans wanted it in spite of themselves, however loudly they said they preferred independence. Even today, Americans don't want a revolution against their own consumerism." Plus ça change . . .

14. Gordon S. Wood, The Radicalism of the American Revolution (New York: Vintage, 1993), pp. 229–30, 250, 252, 255, 261, 305, 326–327, and 365–366. Rush and Adams quoted in Shi, The Simple Life, pp. 76, 81, and 90; and McDonald quoted in Matthews, "Liberalism," p. 1150.

15. The first quote is from Julian DelGaudio, review of Diggins, Lost Soul, in History Teacher 20, no. 1 (November 1986), 154; see also review by Joseph J. Ellis in William and Mary Quarterly, Third Series, 43, no.

1 (January 1986), 134. The second quote is from Diggins, *Lost Soul of American Politics*, p. 31.

16. Appleby, "Republicanism and Ideology," *American Quarterly* 37, no. 4 (Fall 1985), 472; Rodgers, "Republicanism," p. 30; Robert E. Shalhope, "In Search of the Elusive Republic," *Reviews in American History* 19, no. 4 (December 1991), 471.

17. Marvin Meyers, *The Jacksonian Persuasion* (New York: Vintage Books, 1960), pp. 45–46, 48, 50–51, 60, 99, and 123–127; Joyce Appleby, *The Relentless Revolution* (New York: W. W. Norton, 2010), pp. 179 and 197; Leo Damrosch, *Tocqueville's Discovery of America* (New York: Farrar, Straus & Giroux, 2010), pp. 22, 25, and 215–216.

18. Paul Buhle and Edward Rice-Maximin, "War without End," *Village Voice*, November 5, 1991, p. 5; William Fletcher Thompson Jr., review of Williams, *The Contours of American History,* in *Wisconsin Magazine of History* (Winter 1962–63), 139–140; Williams, *Contours*, pp. 115–116, 149, 189, and 223; Damrosch, *Tocqueville's Discovery of America*, pp. 74 and 79. Quote from Williams ("avarice and morality") in Greg Grandin, "Off Dead Center," *The Nation*, July 1, 2009. For the original text of the frontier thesis see Frederick Jackson Turner, "The Significance of the Frontier in American History," lecture to the American Historical Association, Chicago, 1893; reprinted in numerous anthologies and available at www.historians.org/pubs/archives/Turnerthesis.htm.

19. T. J. Jackson Lears, *No Place of Grace* (1981; repr., Chicago: University of Chicago Press, 1994).

20. Ibid., pp. 8 and 60; James M. McPherson, *Battle Cry of Freedom* (New York: Oxford University Press, 1988), pp. 6 and 14; Appleby, *Relentless Revolution*, p. 434; Morris Berman, *The Twilight of American Culture* (New York: W. W. Norton, 2000), pp. 115–117; Williams, *Contours*, pp. 331 and 353; David Shi, "The Triumph of the Therapeutic?," *American Quarterly* 36, no. 5 (Winter 1984), 711; Jackson Lears, *Rebirth of a Nation* (New York: HarperCollins, 2009), pp. 67 and 69. James' condemnations of hustling and Wall Street are particularly strong in *The Americans* (1877), in which Europe emerges, ironically enough, as the "New World."

21. Lears, *No Place of Grace*, pp. 49–52, and *Rebirth of a Nation*, pp. 7 and 68.

22. Williams, *Contours,* pp. 387–388 and 390; Shi, *The Simple Life*, pp. 155, 168, and 221; Lears, *No Place of Grace*, passim.

23. On this and the following see Shi, *The Simple Life*, pp. 189–193, and Lears, *No Place of Grace,* chap. 2 and p. 300. For an extended study of the failure of the craft ideal in America, see Eileen Boris, *Art and Labor* (Philadelphia: Temple University Press, 1986).

24. Daniel Horowitz, *The Anxieties of Affluence* (Amherst: University of Massachusetts Press, 2004), pp. 21–22. Lynd was a professor of sociology at Columbia University; "Middletown" was, in fact, Muncie, Indiana.

25. On this and the following paragraph see Donald L. Miller, *Lewis Mumford: A Life* (New York: Weidenfeld & Nicolson, 1989), pp. 300–302, and Shi, *The Simple Life*, pp. 230–232.

26. Morris Berman, *Dark Ages America* (New York: W. W. Norton, 2006), pp. 268–269.

27. Miller, *Mumford*, pp. 295–297.

28. Horowitz, *Anxieties of Affluence*, pp. 38–42.

29. Miller, *Mumford*, pp. 415–417. For the updated American version of this process see Nomi Prins, *It Takes a Pillage* (Hoboken, N.J.: John Wiley & Sons, 2009).

30. Giles Kemp and Edward Claflin, *Dale Carnegie: The Man Who Influenced Millons* (New York: St. Martin's Press, 1989); Barbara Ehrenreich, *Bright-Sided* (New York: Metropolitan Books, 2009), pp. 52–53. The comment regarding "false geniality" is from W. J. Cash, *The Mind of the South* (1941; repr., New York: Vintage Books, 1991), p. 419.

31. On this and the following see Shi, *The Simple Life,* pp. 233–247.

32. Berman, *Dark Ages America*, p. 270; Horowitz, *Anxieties of Affluence*, p. 23.

33. Horowitz, *Anxieties of Affluence*, pp. 2–4.

34. Robert E. Weir, review of Daniel Horowitz, *Vance Packard and American Social Criticism*, in *Journal of Social History* 29, no. 2 (Winter 1995), 449–451, and Horowitz, *Anxieties of Affluence*, pp. 128–130.

35. On this and the following see Horowitz, *Anxieties of Affluence*, pp. 15 and 110–20; Jackson Lears, "The Hidden Persuader," *New Republic* 211, no. 14 (October 3, 1994), 32–36; and Wilfred M. McClay, "The Loneliness of the Long-Distance Freelancer," *Reviews in American History* 23, no. 1 (1995), 123–128.

36. For example, see "Surprise: Americans Are Borrowing Again," posted on www.truthdig.com, March 7, 2010, or "Spending Habits: Back to Old Ways?," posted on www.cnnmoney.com, February 18,

2011. January 2010 saw an increase in consumer credit of 2.4 percent, or $5 billion; by the end of the year, consumer spending had risen 4.4 percent (see Jeannine Aversa, "Growth strengthened to 3.2 pct in Q4 of 2010," Washington Post, January 28, 2011). It is also interesting to note that the influence of Ayn Rand, and the sales of her novels, continue to be enormous. See Corey Robin, "Garbage and Gravitas," The Nation, June 7, 2010, pp. 21–27.

37. Shi, The Simple Life, summarizes some of this on pp. 251–262, but there is, of course, a very large literature on the subject that deals with these publications and events in exhaustive detail. For a mostly negative view of the period, in particular for England, see Jenny Diski, The Sixties (New York: Picador, 2009).

38. On this and the following paragraph see Shi, The Simple Life, pp. 262–270, and Horowitz, Anxieties of Affluence, pp. 203–205. For a lovely portrait of Gary Snyder see Dana Goodyear, "Zen Master," New Yorker, October 20, 2008, pp. 66–75.

39. Shi, The Simple Life, p. 265; Brown, Modernization, pp. 19–20, 187–188, 191, and 201.

40. Berman, Dark Ages America, pp. 133–134.

41. Shi, The Simple Life, p. 270; Daniel Horowitz, Jimmy Carter and the Energy Crisis of the 1970s (Boston: Bedford/St. Martin's, 2005), p. 140. On the solar panels see Dave Burdick, "White House Solar Panels," posted on www.huffingtonpost.com, January 27, 2009. There also is a documentary about the panels titled A Road Not Taken (www.roadnot-taken.info).

42. Berman, Dark Ages America, pp. 136–138; Horowitz, Jimmy Carter and the Energy Crisis, pp. 113–114.

43. Horowitz, Jimmy Carter and the Energy Crisis, pp. 11 and 159, and Anxieties of Affluence, pp. 210–211, 213–214, 220–221, and 224.

44. Horowitz, Jimmy Carter and the Energy Crisis, pp. 25 and 129.

45. Shi, The Simple Life, pp. 272–273; James B. Gilbert, review of Horowitz, Anxieties of Affluence, in Enterprise and Society 5, no. 4 (December 2004), 731.

46. Shi, The Simple Life, pp. 274–275; "American Consumerism," www.encyclopedia.com.

47. Lou Cannon, "In Reagan's Debt," New York Times, April 26, 2009; Andrew Bacevich, "Appetite for Destruction," American Conservative, September 8, 2008.

48. See above, n. 36. The notion promoted by James K. Galbraith in *The Predator State* (New York: Free Press, 2008), or Bruce Bartlett in *Impostor* (New York: Doubleday, 2006), that George W. Bush betrayed the Reagan revolution by dumping laissez-faire economics and limited government for the corporate welfare state, strikes me as misguided, the result of paying attention to what Reagan said and not to what he actually did (as noted in the previous paragraph). Mr. Clinton was certainly correct when he stated, in 1991, that the Reagan-Bush Sr. regime "exalted private gain over public obligation, [and] special interests over the common good," and that it was "a Gilded Age of greed and selfishness" (quoted by Paul Krugman in "Debunking the Reagan Myth," *New York Times*, January 21, 2008). In 2007, Krugman poopooed the notion of the Republicans trying to "reclaim the Reagan legacy," saying that the truth is that Reagan never left them ("Don't Cry for Reagan," *New York Times*, March 19, 2007). If Bush Jr. was different from Reagan, it was a difference of degree rather than kind.

2. The Reign of Wall Street

1. "American Consumerism," www.encyclopedia.com.

2. Janice Peck, *The Age of Oprah* (Boulder, Colo.: Paradigm, 2008). A good antidote to this type of foolishness is Barbara Ehrenreich's superb study *Bright-Sided* (New York: Metropolitan Books, 2009). Bill Maher does a wonderful job of skewering Oprah's "spirituality" in this video: http://www.huffingtonpost.com/2010/12/22/bill-maher-christmas-message_n_800216.html.

3. Ibid.; Paul Krugman, "All the President's Zombies," *New York Times*, August 24, 2009, and "Debunking the Reagan Myth," *New York Times*, January 21, 2008; William Greider, "The Gipper's Economy," *The Nation*, June 10, 2004; Mark Weisbrot, "Ronald Reagan's Legacy," http://www.commondreams.org, June 7, 2004; Benjamin M. Friedman, *Day of Reckoning* (New York: Random House, 1988).

4. David Harvey, *A Brief History of Neoliberalism* (Oxford, U.K.: Oxford University Press, 2005), pp. 3, 7, 10, 37, 47, 80–81, and 170.

5. Tim Reid, "Bush's Second Inauguration Will Be the Most Expensive in History," *Times* (London), December 16, 2004; Morris Berman, *Dark Ages America* (New York: W. W. Norton, 2006), pp. 14 and 18–21; Daniel Horowitz, *Anxieties of Affluence* (Amherst: University

of Massachusetts Press, 2004), pp. 250–251; Jill Lepore, "I.O.U.," *New Yorker*, April 13, 2009, p. 34; Robert Scheer, "Foreclosure Fiasco," http:// www.truthdig.com, June 24, 2009; and John Rapley, *Globalization and Inequality* (Boulder, Colo.: Lynne Rienner, 2004), p. 73. The information regarding one thousand corporate executives is from a study undertaken by *Fortune* magazine (see issue of August 11, 2002) and cited (along with the data on Qwest) by Nomi Prins in *Other People's Money* (New York: New Press, 2004), p. 1.

6. Tim Reid, "Bush's Second Inauguration"; Joe Miller, "Comparing Inauguration Costs," http://www.FactCheck.org, January 21, 2009; "Bush and Gore Do New York," http://www.cbsnews.com, October 20, 2000; Andrew Bacevich, "Appetite for Destruction," *American Conservative*, September 8, 2008. On James Galbraith and the "predator state" see above, chap. 1, n. 48.

7. Paul Krugman, "Debunking the Reagan Myth" and "All the President's Zombies"; Joe Miller, "Comparing Inauguration Costs"; Jeff Madrick, "They Didn't Regulate Enough and Still Don't," *New York Review of Books*, November 5, 2009, pp. 54–57; Joseph Stiglitz, *Freefall* (New York: W. W. Norton, 2010), pp. 36-37; Andy Kroll, "The Greatest Swindle Ever Sold," *The Nation*, May 26, 2009. On the figure of $19 trillion that the government gave to Wall Street, see above, preface, n. 2. On Lawrence Summers and kickbacks: Mark Ames, "Is Larry Summers Taking Kickbacks from the Banks He's Bailing Out?," www.truthdig .com, May 30, 2009; Matt Taibbi, "Obama's Top Economic Adviser Is Greedy and Highly Compromised," www.alternet.org, April 10, 2009; Philip Rucker, "Summers Raked in Speaking Fees from Wall Street," www.washingtonpost.com, April 3, 2009; Jeff Zeleny, "Financial Industry Paid Millions to Obama Aide," *New York Times*, April 3, 2009. For an analysis of how destructive Summers was for the U.S. economy, see Robert Scheer, "So Long, Summers," www.truthdig.com, September 21, 2010. Scheer also notes that during the time when Summers was adviser to Obama the Democratic candidate, he received nearly $8 million in consulting and lecture fees from Wall Street firms.

The complete integration of the Obama administration with the ideology of hustling and "progress" emerged quite clearly in the 2011 State of the Union Address, in which the president ignored the actual plight of the American people and declared: "We are poised for progress. . . . the stock market has come roaring back. Corporate profits are up." The day after the speech, Robert Scheer pointed out that

Mr. Obama "embraced clean air and a faster Internet while ignoring the depth of our economic pain and the Wall Street scoundrels who were responsible." At no point, says Scheer, did he "blame the actions of the Wall Street hustlers to whom [he] is now sucking up." Thus less than three weeks before the SOTU Address Obama appointed William Daley, the Midwest chairman of JPMorgan Chase, as his new chief of staff, and (four days before the Address) GE CEO Jeffrey Immelt (a pioneer in the securitization of mortgage debt and of the exportation of jobs abroad) as the head of his new job creation panel, the Council on Jobs and Competitiveness. See Robert Scheer, "Hogwash, Mr. President," www.truthdig.com, January 26, 2011.

That the Democratic Party is essentially about hustling, and that it (correctly) views the American people as being committed to hustling first and foremost, can be seen in these words of advice from Al From, founder of the Democratic Leadership Council: "In a general election, the candidate with the most hopeful message is going to win it. Most people in the U.S. want to be rich, they want to get ahead, and that's why an opportunity-oriented message works." (So much for "vision.") Quoted in Sheldon Wolin, *Democracy Incorporated* (Princeton: Princeton University Press, 2008), p. 202.

8. Julianna Goldman and Ian Katz, "Obama Doesn't 'Begrudge' Bonus for Blankfein, Dimon," www.bloomberg.com, February 10, 2010; Taibbi, "Obama's Top Economic Adviser." See also Stiglitz, *Freefall*, p. 42, on officials in the financial industry being appointed to frame the rules for their own industry.

9. Matt Taibbi, "The Great American Bubble Machine," http://www.rollingstone.com, July 13, 2009; Chris Hedges, "Wall Street Will Be Back for More," http://www.truthdig.com, January 10, 2010. See also "The Quiet Coup" by a former chief economist at the International Monetary Fund, Simon Johnson, in the May 2009 issue of the *Atlantic Monthly*. As Chris Lehmann notes in "The Great Squid Hunt," *The Nation*, December 27, 2010, pp. 45-48, there were some errors in the Taibbi article, such as overestimating the power of GS to drive markets, or mischaracterizing CDOs (collateralized debt obligations) as derivative deals—errors which Taibbi later addressed in *Griftopia* (New York: Spiegel & Grau, 2010)—but "the brunt of his argument about Goldman's particular outsize role in the housing debacle has been proven correct, and has gained remarkable traction in our emerging and impressionistic understanding of the past decade of Wall Street

larceny." In addition, writes Lehmann, Taibbi's accusation that GS had engaged in securities fraud was derided by financial journalists until the SEC (Securities and Exchange Commission) subsequently charged GS with precisely that.

10. Nomi Prins, *It Takes a Pillage* (Hoboken, N.J.: John Wiley & Sons, 2009), chap. 4; John D. McKinnon and Susanne Craig, "Goldman Is Bruised, Defiant in Senate," Michael M. Phillips, "Senators Seek, Fail to Get an Apology," *Wall Street Journal*, April 28, 2010, p. A5.

11. Stiglitz, *Freefall*, pp. 6, 36, 41, 279, and 282, and John Cassidy, "What Good Is Wall Street?," *New Yorker*, November 29, 2010, pp. 49–57.

12. George Walden, *God Won't Save America: Psychosis of a Nation* (London: Gibson Square, 2006), pp. 9–10.

13. Benjamin R. Barber, "A Revolution in Spirit," *The Nation*, January 22, 2009; Steven Hill, "The Missing Element of Obama's Economic Plan," http://www.opendemocracy.net, January 27, 2009, and *Europe's Promise* (Berkeley: University of California Press, 2010). On consumer spending see above, chap. 1 n.36.

14. James Surowiecki, "Inconspicuous Consumption," *New Yorker*, October 12, 2009, p. 44; Peter S. Goodman, "Millions of Unemployed Face Years without Jobs," *New York Times*, February 21, 2010; Ehrenreich, *Bright-Sided*, p. 7; and Stiglitz, *Freefall*, p. 64. Official data on unemployment are unreliable, and typically manipulated by the government to make things look better than they actually are. For example, individuals collecting unemployment insurance for a few months are officially unemployed, but once that support dries up they are no longer among the statistics of the unemployed even though they are still out of work. In addition, the millions of Americans who are underemployed, who work only a few hours per week, are included in the ranks of the employed. Between 2006 and 2009, 20 percent of American workers were laid off; 50 million live in real poverty, and many more in a category called "near poverty." See Chris Hedges, *Empire of Illusion* (New York: Nation Books, 2009), pp. 168 and 182. According to Joseph Stiglitz, true unemployment reached 17.5 percent in October 2009—this from data provided by the Bureau of Labor Statistics. The figure was roughly the same a year later. In addition, many of the unemployed chose to go on disability rather than collect unemployment insurance, to the tune of $106 billion in 2008 (4 percent of the government budget). This further conceals the actual

rate of unemployment (Stiglitz, *Freefall*, pp. 18, 65, and 305, n.18; Jeff Madrick, "How Can the Economy Recover?," *New York Review of Books*, November 23, 2010, p. 74).

15. Andrew Oxford, "The Land of the Unfree," *Le Monde diplomatique*, English edition, September 6, 2009; Cathie Madsen, "Crime Rates around the World," http://www.nationmaster.com, December 2006; Jill Lepore, "Rap Sheet," *New Yorker*, November 9, 2009, pp. 79–83.

16. Jeremy Rifkin, *The European Dream* (New York: Tarcher/ Penguin, 2004), pp. 31–32; Lepore, "Rap Sheet."

17. On this and the next paragraph see Morris Berman, "Ik Is Us: The Every-Man-for-Himself Society," in *A Question of Values* (Charleston, S.C.: CreateSpace, 2010), pp. 65–68.

18. "In Plain Sight, a Woman Dies Unassisted on Hospital Floor," http://blogs.wsj.com, July 1, 2008 (*Wall Street Journal*).

19. Douglas LaBier, "Empathy: Could It Be What You're Missing?," *Washington Post*, December 25, 2007; Amanda Robb, "A Little Empathy, Please," http://www.oprah.com, January 1, 2006. Cf. the recent survey reported on by Erik Hayden, "Today's College Students Lacking in Empathy," http://www.miller-mccune.com/culture/todays-college-students-lacking-in-empathy-16642, May 31, 2010.

20. Jacqueline Olds and Richard S. Schwartz, *The Lonely American* (Boston: Beacon Press, 2009), pp. 2 and 79; Thomas Lewis et al., *A General Theory of Love* (New York: Random House, 2000), pp. 76, 80, 209, 211, and 225.

21. Dick Meyer, *Why We Hate Us* (New York: Three Rivers Press, 2008), pp. 9, 23, 26–27, 43–44, 52, 67–69, 77, 117, and 121.

22. Zygmunt Bauman, *Consuming Life* (Cambridge, U.K.: Polity Press, 2007), p. 50; Meyer, *Why We Hate Us*, p. 67; Ehrenreich, *Bright-Sided*, pp. 3–4; Louis Menand, "Head Case," *New Yorker*, March 1, 2010, p. 68.

23. On this and the following see Chris Hedges, "America Is in Need of a Moral Bailout," http://www.truthdig.com, March 23, 2009.

24. To take just one example: Paul Stiles, *Is the American Dream Killing You?* (New York: HarperCollins, 2005).

25. Richard A. Easterlin, *Growth Triumphant* (Ann Arbor: University of Michigan Press, 1996), pp. 136–139; John Rapley, *Globalization and Inequality* (Boulder, Colo.: Lynne Rienner, 2004), p. 164; Derek Bok, *The Politics of Happiness* (Princeton, N.J.: Princeton University Press, 2010); and Elizabeth Kohlbert, "Everybody Have Fun," *New Yorker*, March 22, 2010, pp. 72–74.

26. Easterlin, *Growth Triumphant*, pp. 140–142, 144, and 153; Robert H. Frank, *Falling Behind* (Berkeley: University of California Press, 2007); Daniel Gross, "Thy Neighbor's Stash," *New York Times Book Review,* August 5, 2007, p. 15. For a tragicomic send-up of the consumerist treadmill see the film *The Joneses* (2009), directed by Derrick Borte.

27. Tony Judt, "What Is Living and What Is Dead in Social Democracy," *New York Review of Books*, December 17, 2009, p. 86.

28. Dmitri Orlov, *Reinventing Collapse* (New York: New Society Publishers, 2008).

29. Gregory Bateson, "The Cybernetics of 'Self': A Theory of Alcoholism," in *Steps to an Ecology of Mind* (London: Paladin, 1973), pp. 280–308. On optimization vs. maximization see "Bali: The Value System of a Steady State," pp. 80–100 of the same volume. I discuss Bateson's work in *The Reenchantment of the World* (Ithaca, N.Y.: Cornell University Press, 1981), chaps. 7 and 8, and in *A Question of Values*, pp. 215–222 ("The Parable of the Frogs").

30. Cf. Robert H. Frank, "The Invisible Hand, Trumped by Darwin?," *New York Times*, July 12, 2009; Richard A. Posner, *A Failure of Capitalism* (Cambridge, Mass.: Harvard University Press, 2009); John Cassidy, "Rational Irrationality," *New Yorker*, October 5, 2009, pp. 30–35; Thomas Frank, "The 'Market' Isn't So Wise After All," http://www.huffingtonpost.com, December 31, 2008; and Stiglitz, *Freefall*, pp. 249–256. For a powerful indictment of the "economics is rational" school of thought, but from a right-wing point of view, see Paul J. Cella III, "The Financial Crisis and the Scientific Mindset," *New Atlantis* 26 (Fall 2009–Winter 2010), pp. 30–38.

31. Nader quoted in Chris Hedges, "Nader Was Right: Liberals Are Going Nowhere with Obama," http://www.truthdig.com, August 10, 2009. "Progressive" is being used here in the sense of positive social or political change, not a commitment to technological or material "progress."

32. Rapley, *Globalization and Inequality*, pp. 8 and 164–165.

33. Chris Hedges, "The American Empire Is Bankrupt," www.truthdig.com, June 14, 2009.

3. The Illusion of Progress

1. Leo Marx, *The Machine in the Garden* (1964; repr., New York: Oxford University Press, 2000), pp. 24, 149, and 215; James M.

McPherson, *Battle Cry of Freedom* (New York: Oxford University Press, 1988), pp. 11 and 15; John F. Kasson, *Civilizing the Machine* (1976; repr., New York: Hill & Wang, 1999), pp. 183–184; Joyce Appleby, *The Relentless Revolution* (New York: W. W. Norton, 2010), p. 307.

2. Morris Berman, *Dark Ages America* (New York: W. W. Norton, 2006), pp. 252 and 254.

3. Albert Borgmann, *Technology and the Character of Contemporary Life* (Chicago: University of Chicago Press, 1984), pp. 112–113.

4. Zygmunt Bauman, *Consuming Life* (Cambridge, U.K.: Polity Press, 2007), p. 145.

5. Jean Le Rond D'Alembert, *Preliminary Discourse to the Encyclopedia of Diderot*, trans. Richard N. Schwab (Indianapolis: Bobbs-Merrill, 1963); translator's introduction, pp. xii, xxviii, xlv, and xlviii, and Diderot's *Prospectus*, included in the text, pp. 124–125, 131–132, and 137–139; Paul Hazard, *European Thought in the Eighteenth Century*, trans. J. Lewis May (1946; repr., Cleveland: Meridian Books, 1963), pp. 210–211; Appleby, *Relentless Revolution,* p. 144; Keith Michael Baker, "Condorcet," in Paul Edwards, ed., *The Encyclopedia of Philosophy*, vol. 2 (New York: Macmillan, 1967), p. 184, and Crane Brinton, "Enlightenment," in the same volume, p. 521.

6. Marx, *Machine in the Garden*, pp. 152–155, 163, 180–188, 191–198, 206, 208, and 234; Kasson, *Civilizing the Machine,* pp. xiv, 8, 41, 117, and 173–178; Eric Foner, *Free Soil, Free Labor, Free Men* (1970; repr., New York: Oxford University Press, 1995), p. 39; David E. Nye, *American Technological Sublime* (Cambridge, Mass.: MIT Press, 1994), pp. xix and 120–122.

On Whitman's adoration of the machine, cf. the following remarks by Octavio Paz: "There comes a moment . . . when the industrial object finally turns into a presence with an aesthetic value: when it becomes useless. It is then transformed into a symbol or an emblem. The locomotive that Whitman sings of is a machine that has stopped running and no longer propels trainloads of passengers or freight: it is a motionless monument to speed." See Octavio Paz, "Use and Contemplation," trans. Helen Lane, in *In Praise of Hands* (Greenwich, Conn.: New York Graphic Society, 1974), p. 19; commissioned by the World Crafts Council.

7. On this and the following paragraph see Marx, *Machine in the Garden*, p. 225; Nye, *American Technological Sublime*, p. 43; and Perry Miller, "The Responsibility of Mind in a Civilization of Machines," in

John Crowell and Stanford J. Searl, Jr., eds., *The Responsibility of Mind in a Civilization of Machines* (Amherst: University of Massachusetts Press, 1979), pp. 198–199, 202, and 206. Thoreau quoted in Steven Stoll, *The Great Delusion* (New York: Hill & Wang, 2008), p. 103.

8. Nye, *American Technological Sublime*, pp. xiii–xiv, xx, 1, 36, 40, 85, and 240; Regina Lee Blaszezyk, review of Nye, *Isis* 87, no. 2 (June 1996), 379.

9. Nye, *American Technological Sublime*, p. 282. See also the 1982 film *The Atomic Café*, directed by Jayne Loader and Kevin Rafferty.

10. On this and the following paragraph see Carl L. Becker, *The Heavenly City of the Eighteenth-Century Philosophers* (New Haven, Conn.: Yale University Press, 1932), and John Gray, *Black Mass* (New York: Farrar, Straus & Giroux, 2007), pp. 1–2, 25, 74, 187–189, 204, 210, and passim. (I have, however, elaborated a bit on their conclusions.) Some years after Becker, Eric Voegelin would make a career out of arguing that modern politics was ancient Gnosticism in secular dress. His *Collected Works* runs to thirty-four volumes.

11. Marx, *Machine in the Garden*, pp. 247–248 and 384; Kasson, *Civilizing the Machine,* pp. 118, 130, and 135. Thoreau quoted in Miller, "The Responsibility of Mind in a Civilization of Machines," p. 205.

12. William Appleman Williams, *The Contours of American History* (1961, repr., Chicago: Quadrangle Books, 1966), pp. 272–274; Marx, *Machine in the Garden*, pp. 27 and 318; Kasson, *Civilizing the Machine*, p. 49; Henry G. Fairbanks, "Hawthorne and the Machine Age," *American Literature* 28, no. 2 (May 1956), 155–163. Text of "The Celestial Railroad" may be found at http://www.online-literature.com/poe/127/.

13. David E. Nye, *America as Second Creation* (Cambridge, Mass.: MIT Press, 2003), pp. 262 and 282; David Shi, "The Triumph of the Therapeutic," *American Quarterly* 36, no. 5 (Winter 1984), 709; Jackson Lears, *Rebirth of a Nation* (New York: HarperCollins, 2009), p. 274; Henry Adams, *The Education of Henry Adams* (Mineola, N.Y.: Dover, 2002).

14. Marx, *Machine in the Garden*, pp. 218–219; Miller, "The Responsibility of Mind in a Civilization of Machines," p. 202. Cf. the words inscribed above the entry gates to the Chicago World's Fair, 1933: "Science Explores, Technology Executes, Man Conforms." This remains the dominant ideology; very few Americans, then or now, would see this, in Dantean fashion, as a possible motto for the entry into hell.

15. Lewis Mumford, "An Appraisal of Lewis Mumford's 'Technics and Civilization' (1934)," *Daedalus* 88, no. 3 (Summer 1959), 527 and 536.

16. Donald L. Miller, *Lewis Mumford: A Life* (New York: Weidenfeld & Nicolson, 1989), p. 531.

17. Ibid., pp. 163–166 and 326–329.

18. Ibid., pp. 533 and 540–541.

19. The literature on Weber is, of course, quite vast; the interested reader might start with Julien Freund, *The Sociology of Max Weber*, trans. Mary Ilford (Harmondsworth, U.K.: Penguin Books, 1972).

20. Charles P. Loomis, "Tönnies," in Paul Edwards, ed., *The Encyclopedia of Philosophy*, vol. 8 (New York: Macmillan, 1967), pp. 149–150; Clifford Wilcox, *Robert Redfield and the Development of American Anthropology* (Lanham, Md.: Lexington Books, 2006), pp. 19, 53, and 57; Robert Redfield, *The Primitive World and Its Transformations* (1953; repr., Harmondsworth, U.K.: Penguin Books, 1968), p. 13. By the early 1950s Redfield modified the dichotomy, arguing that the two orders were dialectically linked, and also that the technical order would eventually give rise to a new moral order; but this latter-day attempt at optimism was finally not very convincing. Ultimately he really did see the technical order as inevitably wiping out the moral one, and regarded this as tragic. See Wilcox, *Redfield*, pp. 6, 125–127, and 184.

21. Wilcox, *Redfield*, pp. 98–99; Redfield, *Primitive World,* pp. 30–35.

22. Thomas Hylland Eriksen, *Tyranny of the Moment* (London: Pluto Press, 2001), p. 30. The second list is taken from the work of Manuel Castells.

23. Redfield, *Primitive World*, p. 139; Bauman, *Consuming Life*, p. 145 (italics in original); Adam Gopnik, "Take a Card," *New Yorker*, March 17, 2008.

24. Carroll Pursell, "The Rise and Fall of the Appropriate Technology Movement in the United States, 1965–1985," *Technology and Culture* 34, no. 3 (July 1993), 629–637, and Kelvin Willoughby, *Technology Choice* (Boulder, Colo.: Westview Press, 1990).

25. Pursell, "Rise and Fall of the Appropriate Technology Movement."

26. McLuhan quoted in Nicholas Carr, *The Shallows: What the Internet Is Doing to Our Brains* (New York: W. W. Norton, 2010), pp. 3–4.

27. Borgmann (see above, n. 3) is undoubtedly the most sophisticated critic of the lot, in particular with his concept of the "device paradigm." As I have dealt with this at length elsewhere, however, I shall not discuss his work beyond the remarks made at the beginning of this chapter. See Berman, *Dark Ages America*, pp. 67–77.

28. Langdon Winner, *Autonomous Technology* (Cambridge, Mass.: MIT Press, 1977), p. 326, *The Whale and the Reactor* (Chicago: University of Chicago Press, 1986), p. 54, and "How Technology Reweaves the Fabric of Society," *Chronicle of Higher Education*, August 4, 1993, pp. B1–B3.

29. On this and the following paragraph see Neil Postman, *Technopoly* (New York: Vintage Books, 1993), pp. 22–29, 45, 48, and 50. A more recent version of this argument may be found in Patrick J. Deneen, "Technology, Culture, and Virtue," *New Atlantis*, no. 21 (Summer 2008), in which the author distinguishes between "technologies of tradition" and "technologies of rupture."

30. Postman, *Technopoly*, pp. xii, 50–52, and 182. Literature on the life, work, and significance of Frederick Taylor is quite extensive; he had a very large influence on American life, being lionized by Louis Brandeis, among other notable figures. Taylor was, however, a fraud who fudged his data to promote his vision and himself. See Robert Kanigel, *The One Best Way* (New York: Viking Press, 1997); Jill Lepore, "Not So Fast," *New Yorker*, October 12, 2009, pp. 114–122; David F. Noble, *America by Design* (Oxford, U.K.: Oxford University Press, 1979), pp. 82, 264, 268–277, 281, 283, and 290; and Appleby, *Relentless Revolution*, p. 258. Quote from Taylor cited in Carr, *The Shallows*, p. 150.

31. The full text of the Unabomber manifesto can be downloaded from www.washingtonpost.com/wp-srv/national/longterm/Unabomber/manifesto.text.htm.

32. Kirkpatrick Sale, "Is There Method in His Madness?," *The Nation*, September 25, 1995, pp. 305–311. The bit about how technology operates as a whole can be found in paragraph 128 of the manifesto.

33. See www.crm114.com/algore/quiz.html.

34. The line from the *New Yorker* about the Unabomber in all of us is paraphrased by Sale in "Is There Method in His Madness?," p. 311.

35. Ibid. There is also a biography of Kaczynski by Alston Chase, *Harvard and the Unabomber* (New York: W. W. Norton, 2003), but its arguments are rather dubious. See Todd Gitlin, "A Dangerous Mind," "Book World" section, *Washington Post*, March 2, 2003.

36. Eriksen, *Tyranny*, pp. vii, 4, and 143; Mark Bauerlein, *The Dumbest Generation: How the Digital Age Stupefies Young Americans and Jeopardizes Our Future* (New York: Tarcher, 2009).

37. Robert Kraut et al., "Internet Paradox: A Social Technology That Reduces Social Involvement and Psychological Well-Being?,"

American Psychologist 53, no. 9 (September 1998): 1016–1031. Quote from Michael Kinsley in Christine Rosen, "Virtual Friendship and the New Narcissism," *New Atlantis*, no. 17 (Summer 2007). This article is also useful for information on the negative effects of virtual socializing. For an excellent portrayal of how the combination of hustling and ideology leads to the obliteration of real friendships while creating five hundred million virtual ones (i.e., Facebook), see the 2010 film *The Social Network*, directed by David Fincher.

38. Erik Hayden, "Today's College Students Lacking in Empathy," www.miller-mccune.com/culture/todays-college-students-lacking-in-empathy-16642, May 31, 2010; Carr, *The Shallows*, pp. 220–221.

39. Paul J. Cella III, "The Financial Crisis and the Scientific Mindset," *New Atlantis* 26 (Fall 2009–Winter 2010).

40. Christine Rosen, "The Myth of Multitasking," *New Atlantis*, no. 20 (Spring 2008); Walter Kirn, "The Autumn of the Multitaskers," *Atlantic Monthly*, November 2007.

41. Kirn, "Autumn of the Multitaskers," and Christine Rosen, "People of the Screen," *New Atlantis*, no. 22 (Fall 2008).

42. Carr, *The Shallows*, pp. 77 and 90–91.

43. Ibid., pp. 73, 114–115, 136, 138, 140–141, and 196.

44. Ibid., pp. 86–87; Wolf in the *New Yorker*, letters to the editor, January 28, 2008, p. 5; Rosen, "People of the Screen."

45. Carr, *The Shallows*, pp. 150–151, 156–157, 165–166, 172–173, and 196.

46. Dick Meyer, *Why We Hate Us* (New York: Three Rivers Press, 2008), pp. 225–227.

47. Christine Rosen, "Our Cell Phones, Ourselves," *New Atlantis*, no. 6 (Summer 2004).

48. Carr, The Shallows, p. 222; Rosen, "Myth of Multitasking"; William Deresiewicz, "The End of Solitude," "Chronicle Review" section *Chronicle of Higher Education*, January 30, 2009. For more recent discussions of the destructive aspects of the Internet, see Adam Gopnik, "The Information," *New Yorker*, February 14/21, 2011, pp. 124-130; Evgeny Morozov, *The Net Delusion* (New York: Public Affairs, 2011); and Sherry Turkle, *Alone Together* (New York: Basic Books, 2011).

49. Jörg Müller, *The Changing City* (Arrau, Switz.: Sauerländer AG, 1976; English text by Atheneum, 1977).

50. Octavio Paz, *The Labyrinth of Solitude*, trans. Lysander Kemp et al. (1950; repr., New York: Grove Press, 1985), p. 24; Appleby, *Relentless Revolution*, p. 26.

4. The Rebuke of History

1. I am, of course, using the word "liberal" here in the political rather than the economic sense. Other texts in the "freedom" genre in addition to McPherson's include David W. Blight, *Race and Reunion* (Cambridge, Mass.: Harvard University Press, 2001), and Eric Foner, *Reconstruction: America's Unfinished Revolution, 1863–1877* (New York: Harper & Row, 1988). David Feller calls this version of the war "nearly canonical"; see his review essay "Libertarians in the Attic, or a Tale of Two Narratives," *Reviews in American History* 32, no. 2 (June 2004), 184–195. An important exchange on the subject between John Ashworth and Marc Egnal was posted on the H-CivWar list serve (H-CIVWAR@H-NET.MSU.EDU) on May 28, 2010. While Ashworth correctly claims that slavery as a cause of war means slavery in its political and economic dimensions, and not just as a moral question, Egnal argues (also correctly) that "idealism or moral concerns . . . characterize the prevailing outlook" among historians today.

2. Quoted in Thomas J. Pressly, *Americans Interpret Their Civil War* (New York: Free Press, 1962), p. 10.

3. Eric Foner, *Free Soil, Free Labor, Free Men* (1970; repr., New York: Oxford University Press, 1995), p. 310. Foner does state, however, on p. 9, that the Republicans believed that "two profoundly different and antagonistic civilizations . . . had developed within the nation." See also pp. 67–71.

4. Pressly, *Americans Interpret Their Civil War*, pp. 94–95 and 238–243; Charles A. Beard and Mary R. Beard, *The Rise of American Civilization* (1933; repr., New York: Macmillan, 1956).

5. See Ashworth as cited above, n. 1; and James M. McPherson, *Battle Cry of Freedom* (New York: Oxford University Press, 1988), pp. 310–311. In *Social Origins of Dictatorship and Democracy* (Boston: Beacon Press, 1966), Barrington Moore argues that moral issues arose from economic differences and that there was no antagonism between the two factors. I am grateful to Professor G. Frederick Thompson for bringing Moore's discussion of the Civil War to my attention.

6. McPherson, *Battle Cry*, pp. vii, 186, 311–312, and 508–509; Eli Ginzberg and Alfred S. Eichner, *The Troublesome Presence* (New York: Mentor Books, 1966), pp. 112 and 117; Moore, *Social Origins*, p. 134; Foner, *Free Soil, Free Labor, Free Men*, p. 309; and Ashworth as cited above, n. 1. In 1863 the government sponsored the settlement of 453 black colonists on an island near Haiti, but starvation and smallpox

ended the experiment, and 368 survivors were brought back the following year. In addition to Lincoln's desire that American blacks leave the country, Eric Foner notes his early opposition to their having political rights; his defense (as an attorney) of a Southerner trying to repossess a slave family that had fled to Illinois; and a remark he once made that blacks were responsible for the Civil War by the mere fact of living in America. See Eric Foner, *The Fiery Trial* (New York: W. W. Norton, 2010).

7. McPherson, *Battle Cry*, p. 497. Northern ditty quoted in Walter L. Hixson, *The Myth of American Diplomacy* (New Haven, Conn.: Yale University Press, 2008), p. 77.

8. Quoted in Ginzberg and Eichner, *Troublesome Presence*, pp. 111 and 119.

9. On this and the following paragraph see Foner, *Free Soil, Free Labor, Free Men*, pp. 310–313 and 316, and Raimondo Luraghi, "The Civil War and the Modernization of American Society: Social Structure and Industrial Revolution in the Old South Before and During the War," *Civil War History* 18 (September 1972), 241. The "stew pot" metaphor is John Ashworth's (see above, n. 1), not Foner's.

10. Moore, *Social Origins*, pp. 124–125, 136, and 140–141, and Luraghi, "The Civil War," p. 242. Moore describes the conflict as being between two types of capitalistic civilizations, not between a capitalistic one and a neo-feudal one. The argument over the exact nature of the slave economy has been ongoing, and I shall say more about it below (see n. 41).

11. McPherson, *Battle Cry*, pp. 40, 91, and 95. McPherson doesn't specifically say so, but I am assuming that his figures for urban populations and vocational engagement are for the year 1860.

12. Gabor S. Borritt, *Lincoln and the Economics of the American Dream* (Memphis: Memphis State University Press, 1978); (italics mine). See also the review by Steven S. Berizzi on Amazon.com, December 26, 2000, and that of Allan Peskin in *The History Teacher* 12, no. 4 (August 1979), 609. As president, Lincoln raised the import duties on manufactured goods (i.e., tariffs) to 50 percent, prompting the Cambridge University economist Ha-Joon Chang to remark recently that although Lincoln has been celebrated as the Great Emancipator, he "might equally be labeled the great protector—of American manufacturing." See John Cassidy, "Enter the Dragon," *New Yorker*, December 12, 2010, p. 98.

13. Eric Foner, "The Idea of Free Labor in Nineteenth-Century America," 1995 introduction to *Free Soil, Free Labor, Free Men*, pp. ix, xx, xxiv–xxvi; and 1970 text pp. 11, 14, 20, 23, 26, and 30–31; McPherson, *Battle Cry*, pp. 28–29.   Steinbeck quoted in Ronald Wright, *What Is America?* (Cambridge, Mass.: Da Capo Press, 2008), p. 105.

14. Foner, *Free Soil, Free Labor, Free Men*, pp. xxvi, xxxvi, xxxviii, 29, 32, and 66. Data on wealth distribution and lack of actual social mobility cited in Leo Damrosch, *Tocqueville's Discovery of America* (New York: Farrar, Straus & Giroux, 2010), pp. 26–27; his source is Edward Pessen, "The Egalitarian Myth and the American Social Reality: Wealth, Mobility and Equality in the 'Era of the Common Man,'" *American Historical Review* 76 (1971), 989–1034. On the lack of social mobility in more recent times see the references cited in the preface (to my work), n. 3.

15. Foner, *Free Soil, Free Labor, Free Men*, pp. 50–51 and 67–68. Olmsted quoted in David E. Shi, *The Simple Life* (New York: Oxford University Press, 1985), p. 224.

16. Foner, *Free Soil, Free Labor, Free Men*, pp. 52–54 and 72; the phrase "scorched soul" is mine, not Foner's. On Southern civilian deaths see Jackson Lears, *Rebirth of a Nation* (New York: HarperCollins, 2009), p. 15. Lears calls it "state terrorism" and notes that Lincoln had General Order 100, which was designed to restrict the killing of civilians, but which also said that these restrictions could be ignored in cases of "military necessity." Lincoln on destroying the South quoted in McPherson, *Battle Cry*, p. 558. Thaddeus Stevens quoted in Moore, *Social Origins*, pp. 143–144. For the example of Japan, see my essay "Rope-a-Dope: The Chump Factor in U.S. Foreign Policy," in *A Question of Values* (Charleston, S.C.: CreateSpace, 2010), pp. 20–26.

17. McPherson, *Battle Cry*, pp. 818–819 and 826–827.

18. McPherson, *Battle Cry*, p. 241; Pressley, *Americans Interpret Their Civil War*, pp. 183, 202–203, and 208.

19. McPherson, *Battle Cry*, pp. 8, 41, 46, and 310; Moore, *Social Origins*, pp. 137 and 139; Williamjames Hull Hoffer, *The Caning of Charles Sumner* (Baltimore: Johns Hopkins University Press, 2010), p. 47. In reply to a query I posted on the H-CivWar list serve (see above, n. 1) regarding the "clash of civilizations" thesis, Professor Adam Arenson also argued for the importance of the West and Manifest Destiny as heating up the slavery conflict. See his *The Great Heart of the Republic* (Cambridge, Mass.: Harvard University Press, 2011).

20. Foner, *Free Soil, Free Labor, Free Men*, pp. 27–28 and 55–58; James Oakes, "From Republicanism to Liberalism: Ideological Change and the Crisis of the Old South," *American Quarterly* 37, no. 4 (Fall 1985), 571; Moore, *Social Origins*, pp. 127–141; and Eugene D. Genovese, *The Political Economy of Slavery* (New York: Pantheon Books, 1965). See also McPherson's review of the latter in *Journal of Social History* 1, no. 3 (Spring 1968), 280–285.

21. Michael O'Brien, "The Nineteenth-Century American South," *Historical Journal* 24, no. 3 (September 1981), 761 and 763; Jonathan M. Wiener, *Social Origins of the New South* (Baton Rouge: Louisiana State University Press, 1978).

22. Genovese, *Political Economy of Slavery*; O'Brien, "Nineteenth-Century American South," p. 758; Pressly, *Americans Interpret Their Civil War*, p. 282; Frank Lawrence Owsley, "The Irrepressible Conflict," in Twelve Southerners, *I'll Take My Stand* (1930; repr., Baton Rouge: Louisiana State University Press, 1977), p. 91; and Richard D. Brown, *Modernization: The Transformation of American Life, 1600–1865* (1976; repr., Prospect Heights, Ill.: Waveland Press, 1988), pp. 142–148, 171–172, 178, and 183–186. The North, of course, was hierarchical as well, but the ideology embodied in "free soil, free labor," etc. was one of social mobility—theoretically, anyone could climb the ladder of success. The Southern version of hierarchy was much more fixed—that is, neo-feudal and traditional. (More on this below.)

23. Luraghi, "The Civil War," pp. 233–234 and 242.

24. The discussion that follows is taken from James M. McPherson, "Antebellum Southern Exceptionalism: A New Look at an Old Question," *Civil War History* 29 (September 1983), 230–244.

25. C. Vann Woodward, "The Search for Southern Identity" and "The Irony of Southern History," pp. 3–25 and 167–191, respectively, of *The Burden of Southern History* (New York: Vintage Books, 1960).

26. McPherson, "Antebellum Southern Exceptionalism," pp. 243–244, and *Battle Cry*, pp. 860–861. Joyce Appleby makes a similar point in *The Relentless Revolution* (New York: W. W. Norton, 2010), p. 93 and passim.

27. W. J. Cash, *The Mind of the South* (1941; repr., New York: Vintage Books, 1991), pp. xlvii–xlix, 40–41, 69–70, 75, and 382, and pp. ix and xvii–xx from the introduction by Bertram Wyatt-Brown ("The Mind of W. J. Cash"). On the uniqueness of the South see also John Shelton Reed, *The Enduring South: Subcultural Persistence in Mass Society* (Chapel Hill: University of North Carolina Press, 1975).

28. Cash, *Mind of the South*, pp. 46, 51, and 96; Michael O'Brien, *Conjectures of Order* (Chapel Hill: University of North Carolina Press, 2004).

29. Cash, *Mind of the South*, pp. 43, 60, and 82–83; Bertram Wyatt-Brown, *Southern Honor* (1982; repr., New York: Oxford University Press, 2007), pp. 366 and 368; Eric Foner, "Restless Confederates," *The Nation*, August 2/9, 2010, p. 39. W. E. B. DuBois quoted in Elizabeth Fox-Genovese and Eugene D. Genovese, *Fruits of Merchant Capital* (Oxford, U.K.: Oxford University Press, 1983), p. 90. Tocqueville quoted in Damrosch, *Tocqueville's Discovery of America*, p. 219. Russia abolished slavery in 1723, Spain in 1811, Mexico in 1829, Great Britain in 1833, Sweden in 1847, France in 1848, Argentina in 1853, Holland in 1863, etc.

30. Cash, *Mind of the South*, pp. 61 and 105; Damrosch, *Tocqueville's Discovery of America*, p. 168.

31. Louis Menand, "Dispossession," *New Yorker*, October 2, 2006, p. 92; Cash, *Mind of the South*, p. 137.

32. Wyatt-Brown, *Southern Honor*, pp. xxii–xxiii, xxxviii, 5, and 493. On biblical sanction of slavery see Exodus 21:2 and 7, Leviticus 25:44, Ephesians 6:5, Luke 12:47, Colossians 3:22, and several other references.

33. Ibid., pp. 19–21.

34. Twelve Southerners, *I'll Take My Stand*; Shi, *The Simple Life*, pp. 223–226; Willard B. Gatewood Jr., "The Agrarians from the Perspective of Fifty Years: An Essay Review," *Florida Historical Quarterly* 61, no. 3 (January 1983), 314–317; Paul V. Murphy, "Agrarians," *Tennessee Encyclopedia of History and Culture*, online at http://tennessee-encyclopedia.net/imagegallery.php?EntryID=A008, and *The Rebuke of History* (Chapel Hill: University of North Carolina Press, 2001), pp. 2 and 64–66; Daniel Joseph Singal, review of *A Band of Prophets*, ed. William C. Havard and Walter Sullivan, *Journal of Southern History* 48, no. 4 (November 1982), 597. Reference to Robert Penn Warren in Virginia Rock, "The Twelve Southerners: Biographical Essays," in *I'll Take My Stand*, p. 369. Sheldon Hackney, a Southern historian, has held various academic posts, including provost of Princeton University, president of the University of Pennsylvania, and chairman of the National Endowment for the Humanities.

35. *I'll Take My Stand*, 1977 introduction to the book by Louis D. Rubin Jr., pp. xiv–xv and xxii, and 1962 introduction pp. xxx–xxxi. Amazon reviewer is Michael A. Brooks, June 27, 2002.

36. John Crowe Ransom, "Reconstructed but Unregenerate," in *I'll Take My Stand*, pp. 3, 5, and 8–10; Andrew Nelson Lytle, "The Hind Tit," pp. 206 and 231–232 of the same volume. Thornton Wilder quoted in Woodward, "The Search for Southern Identity," p. 24. Chris Rock quoted in Gary Greenberg, "The War on Unhappiness," *Harper's Magazine*, September 2010, p. 30.

Americans not only seem to approach everything with an agenda, but they also seem to have their "radar" constantly out for the agenda of others. I remember trying to start a book discussion group with colleagues of mine at a major northeastern university in 1970 soon after I was hired, and how the entire evening of our first meeting they kept circling each other like cats, trying to figure out "what was happening." They were apparently baffled by the fact that I was serious: the goal was to read books and discuss them, nothing more. (Surely you jest!) Needless to say, there was no second meeting. "Social life" in America.

37. Lyle H. Lanier, "A Critique of the Philosophy of Progress," in *I'll Take My Stand*, pp. 123, 148–149, and 151; Stark Young, "Not in Memoriam, but in Defense," p. 350 of the same volume; Owsley, "The Irrepressible Conflict," p. 67.

38. Allen Tate, "Remarks on the Southern Religion," in *I'll Take My Stand*, p. 155 n.; Murphy, *Rebuke of History*, pp. 2, 6–8, 148–149, and 159–160.

39. Benjamin Schwartz, "Another World," *Atlantic Monthly*, October 2005, p. 112.

40. John Herbert Roper, "Marxing Through Georgia: Eugene Genovese and Radical Historiography for the Region," *Georgia Historical Quarterly* 80, no. 1 (Spring 1996), 83; James M. McPherson, review of *The Political Economy of Slavery* in *Journal of Social History* 1, no. 3 (Spring 1968), 280 and 282–283; and Genovese, *Political Economy of Slavery*, passim. See also below, n. 41.

41. "The Janus Face of Merchant Capital," in Elizabeth Fox-Genovese and Eugene D. Genovese, *Fruits of Merchant Capital* (Oxford, U.K.: Oxford University Press, 1983), pp. 3–25; Eugene D. Genovese, *The World the Slaveholders Made* (New York: Pantheon Books, 1969) and *The Slaveholders' Dilemma* (Columbia: University of South Carolina Press, 1992), Michael O'Brien, "Conservative Thought in the Old South," *Comparative Studies in Society and History* 34, no. 3 (July 1992), 568–569; Manisha Sinha, "Eugene D. Genovese: The Mind of a Marxist Conservative," *Radical History Review*, no. 88 (Winter 2004), 6–7; James

Livingston, "'Marxism' and the Politics of History: Reflections on the Work of Eugene D. Genovese," *Radical History Review*, no. 88 (Winter 2004), 36; Peter Kolchin, "Eugene D. Genovese: Historian of Slavery," *Radical History Review*, no. 88 (Winter 2004), 57; and Murphy, *Rebuke of History*, p. 257.

The topic of the exact nature of the slave economy, and whether it was a profitable, ongoing capitalist enterprise, has a huge bibliography attached to it, and it is not something that I feel the need to discuss in the text beyond what is already there, inasmuch as it would consume many pages and to my mind finally not get us too far past Genovese's modified analysis (though a number of historians would disagree). Let me use this space, then, to give the interested reader an overview of the crucial arguments and texts.

Basically, as Mark M. Smith observes (in *Debating Slavery* [Cambridge, U.K.: Cambridge University Press, 1998], pp. 12–13), there are two schools of thought. The first aims to show that the Old South was noncapitalistic, unprofitable, and inefficient. It holds that the Southern slaveholders constituted an "acommercial" class and had an aversion to making money for its own sake. The absence of free wage labor meant that capitalism couldn't flourish in the South, and therefore the planters were like feudal lords. The second school claims that free wage labor is not the litmus test of capitalism; that it was the way the slaveholders organized their workforce, and their involvement in the market economy, that defined them as capitalists; and that at the end of the day, slavery was profitable for the slaveholders and the Southern economy alike.

The argument that slaveholding was burdensome, and an obstacle to economic progress, was originally advanced by Ulrich B. Phillips (a student of Frederick Jackson Turner) in 1918 (see Phillips' *American Negro Slavery* [Gloucester, Mass.: Peter Smith, 1928], and also his *Life and Labor in the Old South* [1929; repr., Boston: Little, Brown, 1963]). With the aid of plantation records, including journals and diaries, Phillips made a good case for slavery being an economic dead end by 1860, unable to compete with free wage labor. Genovese rehabilitated Phillips's work in the 1960s and expanded on it (see "Race and Class in Southern History: An Appraisal of the Work of Ulrich Bonnell Phillips," *Agricultural History* 41 [October 1967], 345–358); C. Vann Woodward was also a great admirer of Phillips' work.

The first major assault on Phillips' argument was by Kenneth M. Stampp in *The Peculiar Institution* (1956; repr., New York: Vintage Books, 1989), which argued that slavery was not only profitable for the planter class but also that it was a key factor in the economic growth of the antebellum South. This was soon followed by Douglass C. North, *The Economic Growth of the United States, 1790–1860* (Englewood Cliffs, N.J.: Prentice-Hall, 1961), which claimed that cotton was the crucial factor in the expansion of the entire U.S. economy (although he did say that this process was deleterious to the South per se). In addition, Alfred H. Conrad and John R. Mayer, in "The Economics of Slavery in the Ante Bellum South," *Journal of Political Economy* 65 (April 1958), 95–130, were the first to apply the computer to the question and to claim that their calculations demonstrated that slavery was indeed profitable. But as would happen with Fogel and Engerman (see below), this "cliometric" (econometric-historical) approach got challenged, in this case by Noel G. Butlin (*Ante-bellum Slavery—Critique of a Debate* [Canberra: Australian National University Press, 1971]), who found much of their work incorrect or misleading. In any case, the effect of these works was to put Phillips and the noncapitalist school in abeyance for a while. In the post-Stampp period, so to speak, there were numerous studies that, according to Mark Thornton, served to empirically confirm the view that slavery was profitable. (On this and the above discussion see Mark Thornton, "Slavery, Profitability, and the Market Process," *Review of Austrian Economics* 7, no. 2 [1994], 24–25.)

Also following Stampp et al. came the first wave of Genovese's work, and (as noted) the rehabilitation of the Phillips thesis. For example, Phillips wrote that slaveholding was bad for the Southern economy because planters reinvested their profits in slaves instead of in industry. Genovese agreed with this, adding that the planters were willing to tolerate industrialization on only a small scale. (This in 1965; note that Fred Bateman and Thomas Weiss, in *A Deplorable Scarcity* [Chapel Hill: University of North Carolina Press, 1981], showed that only 6 percent of the planters were willing to invest in industry in 1860, indicative of an aversion to capitalist risk-taking.) There is by now a general agreement that Genovese's original formulation was overstated—which is why he later moved to the "hybrid" argument mentioned in the text—but his claim that slavery impeded the long-term economic development of the South (based on Harold

D. Woodman, "The Profitability of Slavery: A Historical Perennial," *Journal of Southern History* 29 [1963], 303–325) still stands. (See Sinha, "Eugene D. Genovese," p. 5, who thus weighs in against Fogel and Engerman and the notion that slavery was a progressive capitalist institution.) Genovese's focus (à la Antonio Gramsci, from whom he derives much, in particular the notion of the cultural "hegemony" of the ruling class) is on the importance of worldviews or mental frameworks in influencing the economic situation. Thus the "hybrid" thesis includes the notion that the planters may have wanted to make money, but that they were basically "in but not of" the capitalist system, and hence only *appeared* to be modern. If they had an acquisitive spirit or commercial orientation, it was difficult for them to act on it because Southern society was the antithesis of capitalism in spirit and direction. Paternalism, rather than bourgeois acquisitiveness, was the standard of human relations in the South, which was an aristocratic society. Thus the real goal was not profit as much as social status. But even as early as 1968, Genovese displayed a lot of flexibility. In "Marxian Interpretations of the Slave South," in Barton J. Bernstein, ed., *Towards a New Past: Dissenting Essays in American History* (New York: Pantheon Books, 1968), pp. 90–126, he wrote that "a strong dose of capitalism" did exist in the South but that "the argument turns on the proportions and their significance." Shades of gray, in short (Smith, pp. 13, 17, 23, and 91–92).

To skip ahead for a moment, before I pick up the thread of the procapitalist school with Fogel and Engerman, one of the best defenders of the Genovese argument is Douglas R. Egerton in "Markets without a Market Revolution: Southern Planters and Capitalism," *Journal of the Early Republic* 16, no. 2 (Summer 1996), 207–221. Egerton says that Genovese's point is that slave labor produced a nonmarket *society* that was fundamentally different from the society of the capitalist North. He writes, "Those who would argue that the South was merely the North with whips and chains, should ponder the ways in which dominant southern social relations both kept a capitalist mentality at bay and hindered the growth of precisely those market mechanisms necessary for a well-rounded capitalist economy. More than simply an economic investment, slave labor provided the foundation for a premodern society that grew increasingly distinct from that of the northern Atlantic world as it continued to mature throughout the antebellum period." The key ingredient in the Northern economy was the existence of a free labor force, exactly what was lacking in the South. He makes the point already mentioned in the text: capitalism involves more than commerce or a desire for profit, for if it didn't, it would go back millennia. This means that one cannot draw any conclusions from the wealth of a few Southern planters: "the question of whether slavery was profitable for some," he notes, "has little to do with whether it was a capitalist enterprise." "Industrialists there were in the South," he concludes, "but the laboring force that flocked toward factory towns in New England . . . was nowhere to be found."

And so, on to Robert W. Fogel and Stanley L. Engerman, *Time on the Cross* (2 vols.; Boston: Little, Brown, 1974). It was, as Thornton notes (p. 25), the pinnacle of the "cliometric" revolution, and made quite a splash when it first appeared. It was greeted with uncritical acclaim, as it trumpeted not only a complete revision of the history of slavery but also a "scientific," computer-based revision that would put all other historical methodologies into the dustbin of historiography. The *New Yorker*, the *New York Times*, the *Wall Street Journal*—all of them gushed like they had never gushed before. The authors made the rounds of the TV talk shows and became celebrities, of sorts. Apparently everyone who could read, not just historians and economists, was gaga over *Time on the Cross*.

The argument was that slavery in the antebellum South was part of the larger capitalist economy and was in general pretty successful— profitable, in a word. The book depicts slavery as a rational business enterprise, with plantations organized like Northern factories. The authors claimed that the interests of master and slave often converged and that blacks received more income as slaves than they would have as free farmers (Thomas L. Haskell, "The True and Tragical History of 'Time on the Cross,'" *New York Review of Books*, October 2, 1975). Indeed, according to Fogel and Engerman, slavery was 35 percent more efficient than Northern family farming. Slaves were "hardworking, highly motivated, and more efficient than their white counterparts" (Thornton, p. 25). Stated briefly, the slaveowners managed to imbue their slaves with the values of the Protestant work ethic. Fogel and Engerman calculated how efficiently they worked, and measured the profitability of Southern agriculture; they were not interested in the world- view of the planter class. For the two authors, the absence of free wage labor was not important; more to the point was that the investment in slaves was profitable. Thus most slaveholders could expect a return of 10 pecent on agricultural enterprises, which was about the same rate of return that nine of the most successful New England textile firms were realizing during 1844–1853. In addition, Fogel and Engerman claimed that the South was richer than Germany and France in per capita income by nineteenth-century standards. The whole thing was thus worth the planters' while (Smith, pp. 24–25, 67, and 70; Norman R. Yetman, "The Rise and Fall of *Time on the Cross*," *Reviews in American History* 4, no. 2 [June 1976], 195).

But then the critiques started coming in, and they weren't pretty. It's doubtful that any history book ever had such a precipitous fall from grace. A symposium on the book at the University of Rochester, October 24–26, 1974, literally hacked it to pieces, and the major assailants were cliometricians who attacked the thing on its own turf and in its own terms. Every major figure in the field was there: Genovese, Stampp, Woodward, David Brion Davis, and so on. As Thomas Haskell says, the book, "judged by its own premises, proved to be too severely flawed to sustain any sort of profound controversy." Richard Sutch of the University of California at Berkeley, for example, exposed statistical blunders of a completely elementary nature. It turned out that Fogel and Engerman made estimates without any basis for them. Their second volume, supposedly providing the statistical evidence for the arguments of the first volume, did no such thing. The book was a colossal failure of documentation (Haskell, "True and Tragical History"; Sutch's essay is included in Paul A. David et al., *Reckoning with Slavery* [New York: Oxford University Press, 1975], as is Gavin Wright's [below]).

According to Gavin Wright, the real cause of the prosperity of the Southern economy, and its alleged efficiency, lay in the consumer demand for cotton, not in the virtues of slave labor cited by Fogel and Engerman. This made for a shaky foundation for prosperity, which (he claimed) would have collapsed with or without the Civil War. In *The Political Economy of the Cotton South* (New York: W. W. Norton, 1978), Wright further showed that the cotton economy did not generate enough investment capital in the long run to make capitalist "takeoff" possible. This was clearly a major support for the Genovese argument.

Other errors: the claim that "the houses of slaves compared well with the housing of free workers in the antebellum era"; that most plantation overseers were black slaves; that the masters managed to protect the integrity of the slave family; that Southern agriculture was 35 percent more efficient than the family farms of the North, etc. All of these claims were shown to be full of holes, including the central argument that slaves were more efficient workers than free men. (Haskell, "True and Tragical History"). As Lawrence Stone put it in *The Past and the Present Revisited* (London: Routledge & Kegan Paul, 1987), p. 31, the results of *Time on the Cross* were false or meaningless, and their statistical manipulations defective. In general, the consensus was that the data had been misrepresented to bolster a priori conclusions. (See especially David et al., *Reckoning with Slavery*, and Herbert G. Gutman, *Slavery and the Numbers Game* [Urbana: University of Illinois Press, 1975].)

Consider, for example, the argument that the South was richer than France and Germany in terms of per capita income. The first problem with this is that it is completely at odds with the observations of contemporary observers who traveled through the South in the antebellum period and noted how backward the place was economically. The second problem is that per capita income is not a reliable indicator of economic growth. In fact, as Robert L. Ransom showed in *Conflict and Compromise* (New York: Cambridge University Press, 1989), the Fogel and Engerman figures for income distribution are skewed. Large plantations were prosperous, smaller ones not so much. In effect, there were two Souths, one that experienced growth and one that did not. Average per capita income figures fail to make this distinction and thus are completely misleading (Smith, pp. 83–86).

But then there is good economic history and bad economic history, and if Fogel and Engerman offered an excellent example of the latter, they did manage to stimulate a fair amount of the former in their wake. James Oakes, in *The Ruling Race* (New York: Alfred A. Knopf, 1982), argued for the expansionist and acquisitive tendencies of the planter class. Insisting that capitalism cannot be equated solely with free wage labor, he claimed that planters were indeed capitalists; that paternalism had nearly disappeared prior to the Civil War; and that the commercial tendencies of slavery encouraged a tilt toward materialism and capitalism. Central to this discussion is the fact that Oakes focused on small and middling slaveholders—those who owned fewer than twenty slaves—while Genovese had focused on the larger, more aristocratic ones. Hence Oakes was able to differentiate the slaveowning class and to show that the lesser ones, especially those who went west for commercial gain, were clearly capitalistic. In *Slavery and Freedom* (New York: Alfred A. Knopf, 1990), however, Oakes saw modern and pre-modern forces existing side by side in the Old South, to the point that the relationship between slavery and capitalism had become ambiguous for him. As with Genovese, he too has felt the pull toward a more middling position (Smith, pp. 26–27 and 29).

There have been other responsible pro-capitalist studies: Shearer Davis Bowman, *Masters and Lords* (New York: Oxford University Press, 1993), for example, or Ralph V. Anderson and Robert E. Gallman, "Slaves as Fixed Capital: Slave Labor and Southern Economic Development," *Journal of American History* 64 (1977), 24–26. What we can say in general is that in microeconomic terms—the large plantation, for example—Genovese was wrong: the system was profitable. But in macroeconomic terms—the Southern economy as a whole—he was right: slavery was a drag on the economy of the region. As he himself said (see above), it turns on the "doses" of capitalism, their proportions and their significance. Both Oakes and Karl Marx spoke of the grafting of capitalism onto slavery, the emergence of capitalist characteristics that "may occur *sporadically*" but don't necessarily dominate the society. This is why, finally, neither school won the argument: both capitalist and noncapitalist impulses existed in the Old South. If Genovese won, it was by a hair (Smith, pp. 92–94).

42. Eugene D. Genovese, *The Southern Tradition* (Cambridge, Mass.: Harvard University Press, 1994), p. xi.

43. David L. Chappell, review of *The Southern Tradition*, in *Arkansas Historical Quarterly* 55, no. 1 (Spring 1996), 111; Livingston, "'Marxism' and the Politics of History," p. 36.

44. Genovese, *The Southern Tradition*, pp. xi, 2–4, 38, and 102–103; Murphy, *Rebuke of History*, p. 259.

45. Elizabeth Fox-Genovese and Eugene D. Genovese, *The Mind of the Master Class* (New York: Cambridge University Press, 2005), Schwartz, "Another World," p. 113; Mark A. Noll, "A Moral Case for the Social Relations of Slavery," *Modern Intellectual History* 4, no. 1 (2007), 195–196; George M. Frederickson, "They'll Take Their Stand," *New York Review of Books*, May 25, 2006; Murphy, *Rebuke of History*, p. 258.

46. Smith, *Debating Slavery*, p. 3. Drew Gilpin Faust essentially reiterated and updated Potter's comment in 1987, pointing out that the enormous increase in factual knowledge regarding the Old South

over the previous twenty years had not led to any consensus. "The choice between alternative interpretations of a body of data," he wrote, "is often a theoretical rather than an empirical problem." (Quoted in Smith, p. 89) The shift among historians to a more global context was pointed out to me by Joseph Yannielli. See, for example, Sven Beckert, "Emancipation and Empire: Reconstructing the Worldwide Web of Cotton Production in the Age of the American Civil War," *American Historical Review*, 109, no. 5 (December 2004), 1405–1438.

47. Hixson, *Myth of American Diplomacy*, pp. 6–7, 13–15, 23, and 65; Morris Berman, *Locating the Enemy: Myth vs. Reality in U.S. Foreign Policy* (Cedar City, Utah: Southern Utah University, 2007), repr. in *A Question of Values* (Charleston, S.C.: CreateSpace, 2010), pp. 34–59. On the etymology of the word "savage," Charles Mills writes that it "derives from the Latin *silva*, "wood," so that the savage is the wild man of the wood, *silvaticus, homo sylvestris*, the man into whose being wildness, wilderness, has so deeply penetrated that the door to civilization, to the political, is barred." He goes on to say that this is a classic example of creating an identity through opposition (Hegel's notion of "negative identity"; see below), i.e. "the characterization of oneself by reference to what one is not." Civilization, then, is us; savagery, them. As for the enemy as *untermenschen*, Mills refers to the My Lai massacre of 1968 (not, as I document in *Dark Ages America*, an isolated incident in the Vietnam war) as a good illustration of this, Lt. William Calley having told the military psychiatrists who subsequently examined him that "he did not feel as if he were killing humans but rather that they were animals with whom one could not speak or reason." In general, he adds, "American troops committing atrocities [in Vietnam] simply appealed to the well-established moral principle of the M.G.R.—the 'mere gook rule'." See Charles W. Mills, *The Racial Contract* (Ithaca NY: Cornell University Press, 1997), pp. 42-43, 101, and 157.

48. Hixson, *Myth of American Diplomacy*, pp. 7, 11, and 58–59; Berman, *Locating the Enemy*.

49. Quoted in Hixson, *Myth of American Diplomacy*, p. 59.

50. Ibid., p. 78.

51. Quoted by Rubin in the 1962 introduction to *I'll Take My Stand*, p. xxvi.

52. On this and the following see Woodward, "The Irony of Southern History," pp. 167–191. This essay was possibly revised in the late 1950s for inclusion into *The Burden of Southern History* (see above, n. 25) (italics at the bottom of p. 157 mine).

5. The Future of the Past

1. This phrase is actually that of David Harlan, describing Bercovitch's analysis of American culture. See David Harlan, "A People Blinded from Birth: American History According to Sacvan Bercovitch," *Journal of American History* 78, no. 3 (December 1991), 949–971.

2. See chapter 1, n. 10.

3. I provided a good bit of the data on this in previous work, since which books with titles such as *American Idiot, The Dumbest Generation,* and *Just How Stupid Are We?* have rolled off the press. See also the following article in *Newsweek* from 2010: http://www.newsweek.com/photo/2010/08/24/dumb-things-americans-believe.html. Perry Miller characterized his countrymen as massively indifferent to the technological and political context in which they lived, embedded in a "mental fog," hostile to the life of the mind, and as being little more than children: "Virtually all reports on the general behavior of Americans add up, so far, to a pattern of further and further regression into the womb of irresponsibility. There is everywhere documented a refusal to accept what I would hopefully term adult status." This was in 1961; it's not difficult to guess what he would have thought of us in 2011. See "Liberty and Conformity," pp. 187 and 189, and "The Responsibility of Mind in a Civilization of Machines," pp. 207–208 and 211, in John Crowell and Stanford J. Searl, Jr., *The Responsibility of Mind in a Civilization of Machines* (Amherst: University of Massachusetts Press, 1979).

4. Harlan, "A People Blinded from Birth," p. 954; Morris Berman, "Locating the Enemy: Myth vs. Reality in U.S. Foreign Policy," in *A Question of Values* (Charleston, S.C.: CreateSpace, 2010), pp. 41–42; Sacvan Bercovitch, *The Puritan Origins of the American Self* (New Haven, Conn.: Yale University Press, 1975), and *The American Jeremiad* (Madison: University of Wisconsin Press, 1978).

5. Bercovitch, *American Jeremiad*, p. 176, and "Investigations of an Americanist," *Journal of American History* 78, no. 3 (December 1991), 974 and 977; Harlan, "A People Blinded from Birth," pp. 962–963.

6. Hixson, *Myth of American Diplomacy*, pp. 58–59; Leo Damrosch, *Tocqueville's Discovery of America* (New York: Farrar, Straus & Giroux, 2010), p. 213; John C. McCarthy, review of Pierre Manent, *Tocqueville and the Nature of Democracy*, in *Review of Metaphysics* 51, no. 4 (June 1998), 947. For more on American unconscious programming see my

essay "conspiracy vs. Conspiracy in American History" in *A Question of Values* (Charleston, S.C.: CreateSpace, 2010), pp. 8–19.

7. Ronald Wright, *What Is America?* (Cambridge, Mass.: Da Capo Press, 2008), pp. 9 and 15.

8. Ibid., p. 223.

9. For example, the *Toledo Blade* published an exposé in October 2003 (for which it was subsequently awarded a Pulitzer Prize) that revealed that the My Lai massacre of 1968 was hardly unique. See my *Dark Ages America* (New York: W. W. Norton, 2006), p. 123, for further details.

10. On this and the following see Dave Cohen, "The Meaning of Gettysburg," http://peakwatch.typepad.com/decline_of_the_empire, September 1, 2010, and Dick Meyer, *Why We Hate Us* (New York: Three Rivers Press, 2008), pp. 17, 19, 52, and 194–195. Bradford quoted in Paul V. Murphy, *The Rebuke of History* (Chapel Hill: University of North Carolina Press, 2001), p. 233.

11. Erick Brunet, "Eminem: El misántropo diletante," *d'noche* (monthly supplement to *El Universal*) 1, no. 11 (2010), 10. Eminem is perhaps not the best example to take; the work of his protégé 50 Cent is arguably much worse overall. Mathers is quite brilliant; he writes about class issues and personal salvation, and authored what is probably the best-selling antiwar single since Bob Dylan, namely "Mosh." The problem is that his quality as a musician doesn't make much difference for what I am talking about, and given his talent, "Drips" is even more incriminating. The real issue is the response, as Dick Meyer points out. Apparently young women don't mind being called "bitches," or hearing about how they function for men as a kind of sexual garbage. Mathers' talent aside, we have arrived at a cultural nadir, where such stuff is not merely acceptable but actually lionized.

12. Steven Hill, *Europe's Promise* (Berkeley: University of California Press, 2010). For a similar argument see Thomas Geoghegan, *Were You Born on the Wrong Continent?* (New York: New Press, 2010).

13. Hill, *Europe's Promise,* pp. xii–xiv, 1–2, 19–20, and 102.

14. Ibid., pp. 101, 292–293, and 296.

15. Ibid., pp. 365–366.

16. Ibid., pp. 22, 33–37, and 47.

17. Ibid., pp. 125–129 and 132.

18. Ibid., pp. 130–131.

19. Carolyn Jones, "Café Owner Asks Patrons to Log off, Talk," *San Francisco Chronicle*, February 6, 2010, p. A-1; Shilanda Woolridge, "Actual Café in Golden Gate Goes Laptop Free on the Weekends," http://oaklandnorth.net/2010/02/06/actual-cafe-in-golden-gate-goes-laptop-free-on-the-weekends, February 6, 2010.

20. Steven Stoll, *The Great Delusion* (New York: Hill & Wang, 2008), pp. 5–6 and 21.

21. Ibid., pp. 151–152; Jared Diamond, *Collapse: How Societies Choose to Fail or Succeed* (New York: Viking Adult, 2004).

22. Morris Berman, *The Twilight of American Culture* (New York: W. W. Norton, 2000) and *Dark Ages America* (New York: W. W. Norton, 2006); Mark Leonard, *Why Europe Will Run the 21st Century* (New York: PublicAffairs, 2006), from the product description; Joby Warrick and Walter Pincus, "Reduced Dominance Is Predicted for U.S.," *Washington Post*, suburban edition, September 10, 2008, p. A2.

23. Thomas H. Naylor, Secession: How Vermont and All the Other States Can Save Themselves from the Empire (Port Townsend, Wash.: Feral House, 2008), pp. 28, 32, and 113–114. Also note that the Vermont state senate once voted to impeach George W. Bush, and in January 2011 introduced legislation for a constitutional amendment to revoke the notion of corporations as persons. See Christopher Ketcham, "Vermont Weighs Constitutional Amendment to Ban Corporate Personhood," www.truthdig.com, January 24, 2011.

24. Kirkpatrick Sale, *Rebels Against the Future* (Reading, Mass.: Addison-Wesley, 1995), pp. 261–279. In an interesting article entitled "A Postindustrial Prelude to Postcolonialism" (*Critical Inquiry*, 22, no. 3 [Spring 1996], pp. 466-85), Patrick Brantlinger quotes André Gorz as saying, "those who propose a fundamentally different society can no longer be condemned in the name of realism. On the contrary, realism now consists of acknowledging that 'industrialism' has reached a stage where it can go no further, blocked by obstacles of its own making." Brantlinger goes on to say that the idea of an alternative path, "the nonindustrial, nonviolent, decentralized, democratic, communitarian, and economically and ecologically sustainable path…may turn out to be the only rational blueprint for survival." This doesn't mean it will actually come to pass, but it might have some chance under conditions of major geopolitical disintegration.

25. Jackson Lears, "The Hidden Persuader," *New Republic*, October 3, 1994, pp. 32–36.

26. Joseph J. Ellis, review of John Patrick Diggins, *The Lost Soul of American Politics*, in *William and Mary Quarterly,* Third Series: 43, no. 1 (January 1986), 134; Perry Miller, "The Responsibility of Mind in a Civilization of Machines," p. 211. Miller was talking about the response to technology, but obviously his assessment extends to wider contexts.

27. Herman Melville, *Moby-Dick* (1851; repr., New York: Penguin Books, 2009), pp. 592 and 611.

INDEX